For
a tr   !

Thanks For
your help!

Joe
Bawlands
Nov 2022

THE
ALASKA COMPANION
A STORYTELLER'S JOURNEY

The maps in this book are not to be used for navigation.

2018 Edition

Coastal Publishing
PO Box 110, Vinalhaven, Maine, 04863

Maps by Joe Upton

Photographs by Joe Upton unless noted with the following abbreviations:
BCARS - British Columbia Archives and Records Service.
BCRM- British Columbia Royal Museum.
CRMM - Columbia River Maritime Museum, Astoria, Oregon
MOHAI - Museum of History and Industry, Seattle.
SFM - San Francisco Maritime Museum.
THS - Tongass Historical Society, Ketchikan, Alaska.
UAF - University of Alaska, Fairbanks
UW - University of Washington Special Collections.
WAT - Whatcom County (WA) Museum of History and Art

ISBN 978-0-9914215-1-0

Printed in Canada

THE
ALASKA COMPANION
A STORYTELLER'S JOURNEY

BY JOE UPTON

COASTAL PUBLISHING
VINALHAVEN ISLAND
MAINE

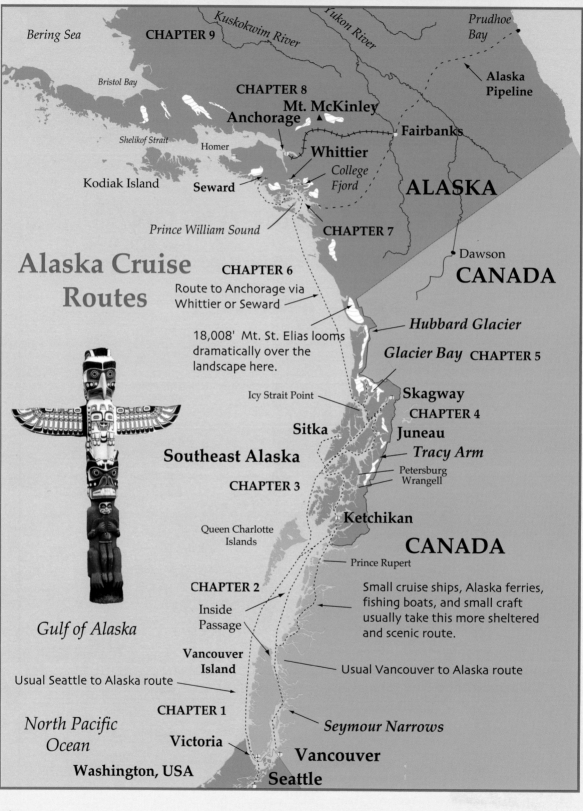

Bering Sea

CHAPTER 9

Kuskokwim River

Yukon River

Prudhoe
Bay

Bristol Bay

CHAPTER 8

Mt. McKinley

Anchorage

▲

**Alaska
Pipeline**

Fairbanks

Shelikof Strait

Homer

Whittier

Kodiak Island

Seward

*College
Fjord*

ALASKA

Prince William Sound

CHAPTER 7

Alaska Cruise
Routes

CHAPTER 6

Route to Anchorage via
Whittier or Seward

18,008' Mt. St. Elias looms
dramatically over the
landscape here.

Dawson

CANADA

Hubbard Glacier

Glacier Bay **CHAPTER 5**

Icy Strait Point

Skagway

CHAPTER 4

Sitka

Juneau

Tracy Arm

Southeast Alaska

Petersburg
Wrangell

CHAPTER 3

*Queen Charlotte
Islands*

Ketchikan

CANADA

Prince Rupert

Small cruise ships, Alaska ferries,
fishing boats, and small craft
usually take this more sheltered
and scenic route.

CHAPTER 2

Inside
Passage

Gulf of Alaska

**Vancouver
Island**

Usual Vancouver to Alaska route

Usual Seattle to Alaska route

CHAPTER 1

*North Pacific
Ocean*

Victoria

Seymour Narrows

Washington, USA

Vancouver

Seattle

CONTENTS

Wilderness Adventurer approaching Dawes Glacier in Endicott Arm, southwest of Mile 900. Occasionally when Tracy Arm is ice choked, large cruise vessels will use this arm as an alternate place to view glaciers.

When I was a green kid of 18, I had a powerful experience: my first Alaska job - on a fish buying boat working for a native cannery on a remote island. Mickey Hansen, the grizzled Norwegian mate, with fifty seasons "up North" took me under his wing. Taught me the tricks of salmon fishing: how to tell the valuable red salmon from similar looking but much less valuable dog salmon. How to pick our way into an uncharted, rocky harbor.

And more than that: he taught me the lore and legends of **The North**. That kindly old man had a story about each harbor we passed or channel we transited, and instilled in me a passion for The North that continues to this day.

For me, that long ago summer of 1965 was ALASKA in capital letters. There were totems at the dock, eagles in the trees. All I wanted to do afterwards was to go up there to fish commercially in my own boat.

Eventually I did, building a tiny waterfront cabin near a small and roadless fishing settlement. Our store floated on logs, and was also a bar. The bartender was the fish buyer. You could sell your fish for bar credit: whiskey and water, whiskey and coke, or whiskey and Tang. And they saved the ice for the fish.

In the spring we fished the windy outside coast. In the summer, we worked nearby Sumner Strait. In the fall we traveled north to the natural wind tunnel called Lynn Canal, for the 10-dollar-a-fish chum salmon. And in the long, kerosene lantern-lit winters, there was time for visiting.

The stories came out. The experiences of my friends and neighbors, an oral history of the coast. I was an amateur photographer, and a writer. "Write a book," my friends said, "Tell our story." One book became another.

When I first started fishing, cruise ships were few and small. Then more ships began traveling the coast, and I designed a series of illustrated maps to better share with these new visitors the drama and beauty of The North.

For me the books and maps are a way to share with you a sense of the mystery and the power of this remarkable and glorious state.

So come, take this journey through this land that remains much as it was when the first explorers came through.

Mickey and me, Southeast Alaska, 1965

Glacier Bay National Park

USING OUR MAP

Reid Inlet

Reid Glacier

1892

Adams

VIDEO LINKS
SEE BELOW

Tide Inlet

rical ice limits

1860

1010

Glacier, calving up to 15 big bergs an hour, ery popular with early cruise ships, before shattered by the 1898 earthquake etreated rapidly up its fjord.

Charpentier Inlet

Geikie Inlet

Glacier Bay

MAJOR CRUISE ROUTES

Muir and his dog almost fell into a asse on this glacier.

Park Headquarters

Glacier Bay

← 1 inch is 9 miles →

In 1794, the ice was so thick in Icy Strait that Capt. Vancouver could barely get through with his ships.

MILEMARKER NUMBERS
(SEATTLE IS MILE ZERO)

Many commcercial salmon fishing vessels work these waters.

1794

1770

Brady Glacier

ouse r comes to the cean

Dundas Bay

1005

VIDEO PAGE AT ALASKACRUISEHANDBOOK.COM

VIDEOS ARE NUMBERED ACCORDING TO THEIR NUMBERED MAP LOCATION

The Alaska Story Project Video Page

HOW IT WORKS

The Alaska Cruise Handbook and Alaska Cruise Companion both use maps with a 'Seattle as Mile Zero' route numbering system. The newest edition -2012- of The Alaska Cruise Handbook has video icons on the map to make it easier to identify where the videos were taken or are about, but these videos are all identfied by milemarker number for the convenience of users of all editions. This is an ongoing project, with videos added regularly, so keep checking back. Also see Making the Videos

INTRODUCTION

MILE 30 - Leaving Seattle

MILE 195E - Desolation Sound is Not So Bad

MILE 205 - Vancouver Departures & Seymour Narrows

MILE 208 - A Young Man Goes North

MILE 695 - How Stormy Got His Name

MILE 720W - Spring at Noyes Island

MILE 730 - The Bush Pilot's Tale

MILE 742 - Building a Home in The North

PLANNING YOUR ALASKA TRIP

Top: your author and wife, Mary Lou, in Reid Inlet, Glacier Bay. Kayaks launched from small ship *Wilderness Explorer*, operated by Un-Cruise. Below: hiker, rain forest, Chichagof Island.

"Whenever a bunch of fellows would get together, someone would start to talking about going up north...

Things were pretty much settled to the south of us. We didn't seem to be ready for steady jobs. It was only natural we'd start talking about The North. We'd bought out the Russians. We'd built canneries up there. The fellows who hadn't been up was hankering to go. The rest of us was hankering to go back.

- Mont Hawthorne in "The Trail Led North"

Headed "Up North?" Whether you go by ship, bus, plane, car, or dog sled, an Alaska trip is one of your best travel experiences. If you are considering a cruise, here are some things to consider.

First come **itineraries**; there are several choices:

Seattle to Seattle round trip: Generally the most affordable cruises, these typically make two or three port calls, plus part of a day at either Glacier Bay, Hubbard Glacier, or Tracy Arm. While these are often billed as 'Inside Passage' cruises, their route usually is up the west or outside coast of Vancouver Island and rejoining the Inside Passage again in Alaska. At least one ship, the *Norwegian Pearl*, often travels up the outside coast on the way north, and inside waters on the way south.

Vancouver to Vancouver round trip: Until about 1996, this was about the only itinerary available. Like Seattle sailings, it offered usually three ports and glacier viewing. Modestly priced in that you didn't have to fly back from Alaska as you would with a one way cruise, and also offering the advantage of traveling both northbound and southbound up the traditional and very scenic Inside Passage, east of Vancouver Island

Vancouver to Seward or Whittier: Pioneered by Princess Cruises in 1996, and often called some variation of 'Voyage of the Glaciers,' most lines operating large cruise ships in Alaska offer some variation of this. Basically these are one way cruises either to or from Alaska, offering an additional part of a day of glacier viewing, usually at College Fjord in Prince William Sound or Hubbard Glacier near Yakutat. A particular advantage of these cruises are that they afford you an opportunity to explore interior as well as coastal Alaska. The most popular add-on itinerary is to spend a day or two in both Fairbanks and Anchorage, take one of the wonderful vista dome style railroad cars on the Alaska Railroad between those towns, combined with a one or two day stopover in the Denali or McKinley National Park area. Many families will start with a Seattle or Vancouver round trip cruise, find that it whets their appetite for more, and then follow up in later years with a one way cruise to or from Alaska combined with a week or so exploring Alaska's great interior.

Top: early morning light on the *Volendam* in Queen Charlotte Sound, British Columbia.
Below: be sure to spend time exploring your ship; most have hidden little nooks, like this one on the *Carnival Legend*.

The big ships come in all flavors, but easily the most colorful are those of Norwegian Cruise Line, like the *Norwegian Pearl* here.

Opposite - on a glacier near Skagway.

Below: The *Aurora Explorer* and the *Uchuck III* carry passengers as they deliver freight to remote logging camps and fish farms.

Which ship? There's a lot of choice here; presently some 25 large and a dozen or so smaller ships operate on the Alaska run. Today's big Alaska cruise ships are essentially floating resorts with multiple restaurants, extensive shopping, elegant theaters, a wide variety of art, and many public spaces. Free dining (most drinks extra) is usually offered in the large formal dining rooms as well as in a large buffet area on the upper decks. The most recent trend is to charge a fee in the smaller, themed, restaurants, typically $15 - $20 a person, a modest price for the excellent food and service you will usually receive. Take some time to check out the restaurant choices aboard your ship.

A very valuable feature for ships operating in Alaska is an eating or viewing area that stretches the full width of the front of the ship on an upper deck. You may find eating buffet style with a 180 degree view preferable to the traditional dining rooms, with full service and presentation, but usually little view.

Travel tips

It's only formal if you want it to be. Don't feel like you have to bring suits and dresses unless that is your style. Alaska is a very casual place, and even if you travel by cruise ship there are always other places to eat than the main dining room on formal night.

Bring binoculars. There's a lot to see, so consider an investment in a good pair.

Your camera. Most visitors just bring their cell phone, which actually yield surprisingly good photos. However, if you have the interest and can swing it, consider getting a camera with a zoom lens that lets you get closer to eagles, glaciers, etc.

Bring fleece and rain-gear. Southeast Alaska especially is a rainy place. But generally the rain is of the light misting variety, so if you have a good rain jacket, you won't be bothered too much. Don't worry about rain-pants unless you're determined to hike, rain or not. Many excursions from ships offer free rain-gear to use. Make sure you have at least one good warm fleece that you can layer under a jacket. Even in mid summer it can get mighty chilly around glaciers.

Look for Native crafts. There's a **lot** of stuff... for sale in gift shops. I find that the mementos that have the most meaning to me are ones that created by one of Alaska's many native craftspeople. Almost every town that you visit will have excellent crafts if you take the time to seek them out.

On the ships: eat where there's a view. I can't emphasize this enough, especially on ships that have a forward eating area on an upper deck. Especially on your first night out of Vancouver, Whittier, or Seward, you'll be missing some truly spectacular scenery if you don't.

On the ships: always look for whales. Although most ships have naturalists with a beeper who can be called to the bridge if there is a whale sighting, there are a lot of competing activities on board, and the whales may or may not be announced. Know what to look for: a puff of what looks like smoke, easily seen from a distance. It is a whale exhaling. If you know what to look for, you'll see a lot more whales.

THE
SMALL SHIP EXPERIENCE

Top: *Wilderness Adventurer* launches kayaks in Misty Fiords. Below: small doesn't mean spartan - most small ships don't forget the important things!

Usually carrying 100 passengers or less, small ships offer a very different experience. The focus is much less on entertainment–floor shows, casino gambling, etc. and more on the history, wildlife, and culture of the passing landscape. Many small ships have daily presentations by one or more naturalists, and have a more flexible schedule allowing them to linger, say when a pod of orcas was sighted, than the larger ships which often have tighter schedules.

The atmosphere on board is apt to be very informal, with perhaps a cocktail hour discussion of the day's activities, and ship's staff often joining passengers for meals.

One of the biggest advantages of small ship cruising is simply that they go where the big ships can't, stopping at off the beaten track towns like Petersburg and Wrangell, or poking into exquisite little coves.

In recent years most small ships operating in Alaska carry kayaks and/or Zodiacs, sturdy inflatable boats which are often launched at sites of particular interest like bird rookeries and sea lion haul outs.

Prices are usually significantly higher than for similar accommodations aboard the big cruise ships.

The major companies offering small ship Alaska cruises are Un-Cruise and Lindblad Expeditions, both with Seattle offices, Alaska Dream Cruises in Sitka, and Discovery Voyages in Whittier.

A Wilderness Adventurer Cruise:

Day 1: Ketchikan to Misty Fjords; orientation.
Day 2: Explore Misty by kayak & hike to lake & swim!
Day 3: Move to Short Bay, kayak, snorkel, & jump into a creekful of salmon with our masks & snorkels: **WOW!**
Day 4: Anan Creek to watch bears, of which there was no shortage - in the trees, grabbing fish out of the water, then over to Canoe Pass for a delightful long afternoon paddle, wrapped it up with walk at Steamboat Bay.
Day 5: Thomas Bay for a choice of challenging hikes - an hour back to a lake to kayak around small icebergs, or a very steep one up to a spectacular view of the bay.
Day 6: **Wow**: ashore to hike up to the top of Baird Glacier and wander among crevasses. Awesome!
Day 7: They saved the best for last - steamed way up Endicott Arm and launched the kayaks in the ice near the face of Dawes Glacier. Hot chocolate with rum waiting for us when we returned!

THE INSIDE PASSAGE

Top: Small craft in the winding channels near Yuculta Rapids, east of Seymour Narrows.
Below: north of Vancouver Island, the traditional Inside Passage winds through the mountain heart of British Columbia.

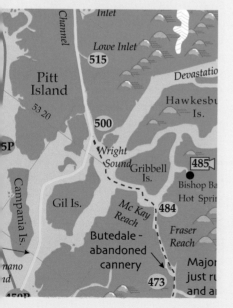

When the Pleistocene glaciers scoured out the fjords and channels of the northwest coast thirty or forty thousand years ago, they created protected waters and a boater's paradise.

Behind the eight large islands between Cape Flattery, WA, and Cape Spencer, AK, is a roughly northwest-southeast route that has become known as the Inside Passage. Stretching for a thousand miles between Seattle and Skagway, Alaska, it allows small and large craft alike to travel in protection and comfort.

The Inside Passage was explored, charted, and mostly named in the 1790s by a British Navy captain, George Vancouver, who came seeking the legendary Northwest Passage. This channel was supposed to connect the Atlantic and Pacific somewhere around the latitude of the US-Canada border.

In many places vessels have a choice of routes. Generally speaking, the smaller vessels seek the most protected routes through the often narrower and most twisting channels. For the purposes of this book, the Inside Passage means the traditional route laid out for medium and small craft in the *Hansen Handbook*, now out of print, but before electronic aids to navigation, the essential navigational aid for mariners headed up or down the Inside Passage.

In few waterways in the world does the tide so influence mariners as much as it does along the northwest coast. From the tipsy sailor who exits a tavern, only to discover that now the ramp down to his boat is a steep 45 degrees, to the skipper of a 6,000 horsepower tug who steers to the side of Johnstone Strait when the current is against him, the mariner here must always consider the tide.

In the Kvichak River of western Alaska, propellers of anchored boats spin, turned by the tidal current. In Sergius Narrows, near Sitka, the big Coast Guard navigational buoys disappear underwater, pulled down by the current when the tide is running hard.

In some constricted passages, the tide rushes with a force like rapids in a river. In numerous places like Seymour Narrows, and Yuculta Rapids in southern British Columbia, safe passage for vessels even as large as big cruise ships is only possible around the times of slack water, the top or bottom of the tide.

Tides are caused by the moon's gravity (and to a lesser degree the sun and other planets) pulling the Earth's oceans into bulges that try to follow the moon as it orbits the earth. And because the moon takes one day and about 50 minutes to orbit the Earth, each tide is about 50 minutes later than the previous day. Tidal ranges are about 10 feet in Seattle and up to 30 feet in western Alaska.

Top: salmon gillnetters in Bristol Bay, where sometimes 25 feet of water rushes into the rivers after a big low tide. Many the newcomer who has anchored in a creek here at high tide, only to discover a few hours later that they are sitting on the mud! Below: tide chart for the Bristol Bay area shows a typical tide cycle. The difference between low and high tide on this particular day is 21 feet! Such large tides create very strong currents.

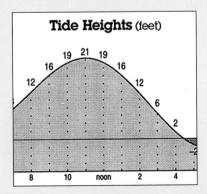

Tide Heights (feet)

16 19 21 19

12   16

12

6

2

8   10   noon   2   4

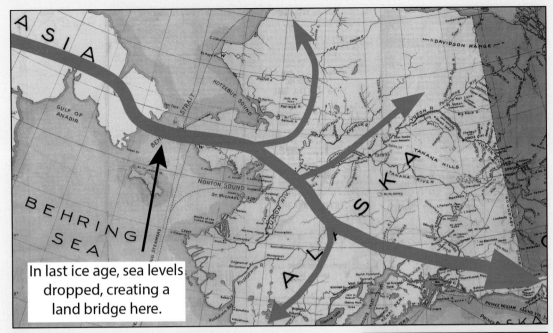

In last ice age, sea levels dropped, creating a land bridge here.

During the last ice age, thirty or forty thousand years ago, vast amounts of water was frozen in the giant glacial sheet that covered much of North America. This had the effect of lowering the level of the oceans so much so that a land bridge between Siberia and Alaska was created across much of the shallower parts of the northern Bering Sea, and southern Arctic Ocean and Chukchi Sea.

And across this bridge, probably following the migrations of caribou and other game, came hunting parties of Siberian natives. Crossing into the New World that was North America, they eventually separated into streams that became major ethnic groupings.

These were journeys that took many thousands of years. The migration split into first two and then many streams of new settlers. The biggest division was between the bands that streamed east into the great interior of Alaska and those that traveled south and east along the coasts of what is now Alaska, British Columbia, and Washington State.

The interior stream moved first east and then eventually south as well to become the many tribes and bands that settled what is now the interior of the United States and Canada.

The coast streams just followed the coast wherever it led, using what were to become their traditional skin boats or umiaks - of walrus, sea lion, and seal hides, stretched over a frame of whalebone or driftwood - to cross bays and straits to colonize the islands as well.

Many tribes never developed a written language, so what we now call totems were created not to worship, but to tell an important story or bit of history of a people that had no other way to record it.
Opposite page: members of the Sitka Tribe in ceremonial regalia, circa 1910. Isabel Miller Museum.

17

For the coastal tribes that lived along the Washington, British Columbia, and Southeast Alaska coasts, warmed by the Japanese current offshore, the sea and the forest provided. There is an old expression in the Northwest: "When the tide is out, the table is set." In reality, the sea provided much more than shellfish to be harvested from the beaches.

There was halibut, crab, seals, and candlefish - small herring-like fish that were so oily that they could actually be dried and lit like a candle. But most of all there was salmon, that ran in large numbers each summer and fall up almost every river, creek, and down to almost the smallest stream or trickle. These were the perfect fish to sustain the coastal tribes: easy to catch, and easy to preserve for when they weren't available fresh by drying or smoking, both of which created a product that would last a long time with no ice or refrigeration.

Most tribes had permanent village sites consisting of large multi-family lodges set on a protected cove with a place to haul up the canoes in front. But many also went to 'summer camp,' or temporary village sites on a stream or river or bay where there was a particularly strong salmon run, where the tribe could catch and dry or smoke the fish against the long winter ahead.

Top: Sitka natives, circa 1900. Dancing, especially with masks, hats or other regalia, also became an important part of native culture. The dances in which the participants often wore costumes with symbolic meaning, were another way to express history or cultural events in a tribe that had no written history. Isabel Miller Museum.

And so the coastal tribes developed this sophisticated and wealthy (by the standards of the times) culture.

There was little or no agriculture as we understand it, because of the bounty of the sea and the forest. As well as providing shelter, the mighty cedar tree provided material for clothing and woven baskets as well as firewood. Additionally there were three or four different varieties of berries, and the occasional deer that wandered close enough to be speared.

Communities were established throughout the coast - there were once ten substantial S'kallam villages just in the 35 miles between Sequim and Port Townsend on the Strait of Juan de Fuca, the border between the US and western British Columbia. Tribes spread and built villages on the protected harbors of the Washington ocean coast, the west coast of Vancouver Island, and on islands and coves all the way up the Alaska coast, out to the Aleutians, and all the way up and east along the Alaskan Arctic coast.

In general the tribes got along with another, although disputes leading to battles and the taking of slaves was not unheard of.

Traveling up and down the coast in their long canoes carved from cedar logs, a substantial trade was carried on between villages of different tribes and nations.

Top: Alert Bay house fronts, circa 1890..

Tlingit tribal dancer, Juneau, 2010.

So who was it who brought the first case of measles or mumps or gonorrhea to the Northwest Coast? Was it a gunner with Captain Vancouver, a sail-maker with Captain Cook, a mate with the Russian explorer Vitus Bering?

It mattered little. For as soon as the sails of British, Spanish, Russians, and Americans arrived off the coast beginning in the 1740s, a series of diseases began spreading up and down the coast no less virulent than the plagues that swept Europe in the dark and middle ages.

As the whites began to set up sawmills and canneries, attracting natives from the remotest villages to participate in the cash economy, these villagers, now infected with diseases for which they had no immunity, would travel back to their remote homes and infect all them as well.

David Bower, who operated a whaling station and trading post in remote Point Barrow, north of the Arctic Circle in Alaska in the 1890s, remembered an American whaler dropping off a native sick with measles while a big dance ceremony was taking place with some 200 Eskimos from villages all over northern interior Alaska. The dance ended and the participants headed home. Soon trappers reported coming across bodies of Eskimo travelers: of the 200 Eskimos that came to dance and were exposed to measles, almost every single person was dead within a week.

Top: Vancouver's ships in Desolation Sound, 1792. John Horton painting.
Bottom: old and new totems at Sitka National Historical Park, 2012.

"THERE WAS NOT A SOUL HERE TODAY. THE
LARGE TOTEM THAT I TOOK A PHOTO OF A YEAR
OR TWO AGO IS NOW LYING ON THE GROUND AND
THE HOH HOH TOTEM THAT I PHOTOGRAPHED LAST
YEAR HAS NOW ONE WING. SO IT GOES UNTIL AT
LAST THEY ROT."

- BETH HILL, UPCOAST SUMMERS

Typically totems, even made of rot resistant cedar, only last 60-80 years out in the wet climate of the Pacific Northwest. These two are preserved inside at the University of British Columbia at Vancouver. Opposite: deteriorating totem, Kah Shakes Village, Ketchikan, Alaska.

Their wealth allowed them to create stunning works of art, in particular masks, generally used in ceremonial dances, and totem poles, used to record history in cultures without a written language.

But when the first sails of the European explorers appeared off the Northwest Coast starting in the 1750s, a curtain was about to be drawn on a powerful native culture that had endured for centuries.

By the 1890s or so, native culture was essentially collapsing, and spectacular works of art which had previously symbolized their greatness were rapidly disappearing into the forest as whole villages were first decimated by disease and then abandoned.

Very fortunately, collectors from the great museums of Europe and the East Coast were aware of the situation and came to the Northwest Coast to buy and salvage what they could. In the 1920s and 30s and 40s, boaters here would come upon evidence of a disintegrating culture - whole villages abandoned with the big lodges standing empty, being reclaimed by the forest. Today native guides live at the old sites to protect them and share with visitors the history of their powerful culture that once ruled the coast, but was swept aside by disease.

Today, native culture is more prosperous, thanks to fishing, logging, and government programs. Many tribes have their own museums, and the legacy masks and other art is slowly being returned to their rightful owners. Today coastal natives, called First Nations in Canada, live in modest communities called reserves among the coastal islands. As in Alaska, their economy is a combination of state provided social services, and income from logging, commercial fishing, and in Alaska, income from tribal investments.

Top: abandoned lodge, Village Island, BC, BCARS G-07265.
Right: Tlingit Hoona dancers, Icy Strait Point, Alaska.
Opposite top: Tlingit masks, Alaska Native Arts Center, Port Chilkoot, AK.
Opposite bottom: Yup'ik style mask from author's collectio.n.

GEORGE HUNT AND
THE COLLECTORS

When the collectors came from the great museums of New York and Europe, they found a truly remarkable man to help them: George Hunt. His dad was the manager of the Hudson Bay Trading Post in a big native village; he grew up surrounded by Kwakiutl culture, married the daughter of an influential chief, had an intimate knowledge of native traditions, and was a trusted member of the Kwakiutl community. He was able to lead the collectors deep into the island wilderness to the most remote villages, to collect the stunning pieces of art that are all that remain from that era. Much fine art simply disappeared into the forest as village after village was abandoned, destroyed by the twin scourges of disease and alcoholism.

Fortunately by the late 20th century, the fortunes of many of the once impoverished and dying tribes have improved, some of the great art that was saved is being repatriated to small museums operated by the tribes, particularly in British Columbia.

Top: the Native settlement of Church House, British Columbia, around 1972. Sadly, today the village is abandoned and little remains.
Below: Native guide at the tribal owned Mt. Roberts Tramway in Juneau.
Opposite: marcher at the 2010 Native Festival in Juneau.

By the second half of the 20th century, the fortunes of many of the coastal tribes had stabilized and begun to improve. Social programs administered by the US and Canadian governments, rising prices for timber and fish - much of native income came from fishing and logging on native land, all contributed to better living conditions.

For the tribes in Alaska, a huge event was the settlement of the Alaska Native land claims, triggered by the discovery of oil on the shores of the Arctic Ocean in far northern Alaska. In exchange for relinquishing native claims to vast tracts of land all over the state, the various tribes received substantial deeded plats of land around their ancestral homes, and a substantial cash payment.

These Alaska tribes formed corporations to manage these substantial funds, and today tribal members income comes from a combination of fishing and woods work, and dividends from the tribal investments. In the Juneau area, for example, the Goldbelt Corporation, representing many of the natives of Southeast Alaska, built and operates the very popular tramway the runs from downtown Juneau to the top of Mt. Roberts.

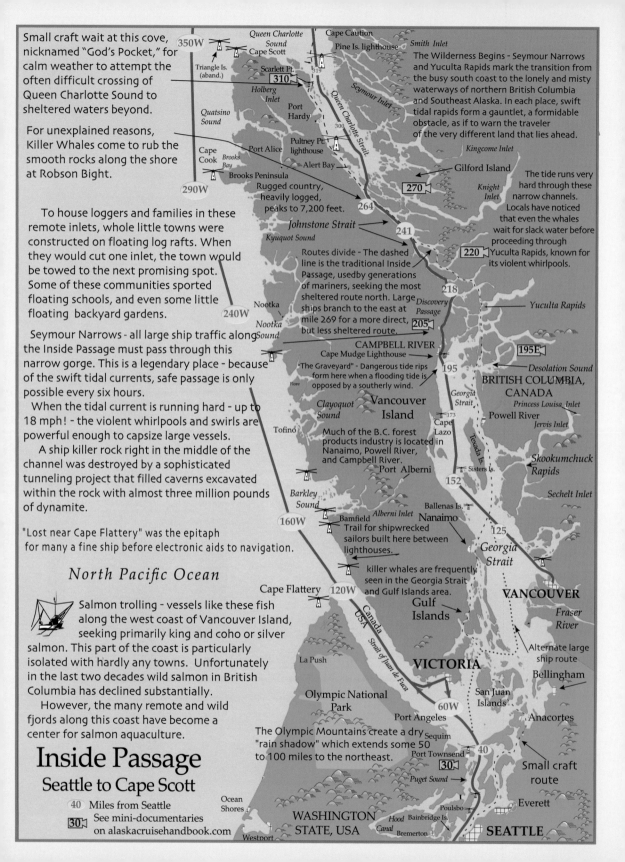

Small craft wait at this cove, nicknamed "God's Pocket," for calm weather to attempt the often difficult crossing of Queen Charlotte Sound to sheltered waters beyond.

For unexplained reasons, Killer Whales come to rub the smooth rocks along the shore at Robson Bight.

To house loggers and families in these remote inlets, whole little towns were constructed on floating log rafts. When they would cut one inlet, the town would be towed to the next promising spot. Some of these communities sported floating schools, and even some little floating backyard gardens.

Seymour Narrows - all large ship traffic along the Inside Passage must pass through this narrow gorge. This is a legendary place - because of the swift tidal currents, safe passage is only possible every six hours.

When the tidal current is running hard - up to 18 mph! - the violent whirlpools and swirls are powerful enough to capsize large vessels.

A ship killer rock right in the middle of the channel was destroyed by a sophisticated tunneling project that filled caverns excavated within the rock with almost three million pounds of dynamite.

"Lost near Cape Flattery" was the epitaph for many a fine ship before electronic aids to navigation.

North Pacific Ocean

Salmon trolling - vessels like these fish along the west coast of Vancouver Island, seeking primarily king and coho or silver salmon. This part of the coast is particularly isolated with hardly any towns. Unfortunately in the last two decades wild salmon in British Columbia has declined substantially.

However, the many remote and wild fjords along this coast have become a center for salmon aquaculture.

Inside Passage
Seattle to Cape Scott

40   Miles from Seattle

30   See mini-documentaries on alaskacruisehandbook.com

The Wilderness Begins - Seymour Narrows and Yuculta Rapids mark the transition from the busy south coast to the lonely and misty waterways of northern British Columbia and Southeast Alaska. In each space, swift tidal rapids form a gauntlet, a formidable obstacle, as if to warn the traveler of the very different land that lies ahead.

The tide runs very hard through these narrow channels. Locals have noticed that even the whales wait for slack water before proceeding through Yuculta Rapids, known for its violent whirlpools.

Routes divide - The dashed line is the traditional Inside Passage, used by generations of mariners, seeking the most sheltered route north. Large ships branch to the east at mile 269 for a more direct, but less sheltered route.

"The Graveyard" - Dangerous tide rips form here when a flooding tide is opposed by a southerly wind.

Much of the B.C. forest products industry is located in Nanaimo, Powell River, and Campbell River.

Trail for shipwrecked sailors built here between lighthouses.

killer whales are frequently seen in the Georgia Strait and Gulf Islands area.

The Olympic Mountains create a dry "rain shadow" which extends some 50 to 100 miles to the northeast.

Map labels

Queen Charlotte Sound
Cape Scott
Cape Caution
Smith Inlet
Pine Is. lighthouse
Triangle Is. (aband.)
Scarlett Pt.
350W
310
319
Holberg Inlet
Quatsino Sound
Port Hardy
Seymour Inlet
Queen Charlotte Strait
300
Cape Cook
Brooks Bay
Port Alice
Pultney Pt. lighthouse
Alert Bay
Kingcome Inlet
Gilford Island
270
Knight Inlet
Brooks Peninsula
Rugged country, heavily logged, peaks to 7,200 feet.
264
290W
Johnstone Strait
241
Kyuquot Sound
220
240W
Nootka
Nootka Sound
Discovery Passage
218
Yuculta Rapids
205
CAMPBELL RIVER
Cape Mudge Lighthouse
195
195E
Flore
Desolation Sound
BRITISH COLUMBIA, CANADA
Clayoquot Sound
Vancouver Island
Georgia Strait
Princess Louisa Inlet
Powell River
Cape Lazo
Tofino
173
Jervis Inlet
Texada Is.
Skookumchuck Rapids
Port Alberni
Sisters Is.
152
Sechelt Inlet
Barkley Sound
160W
Ballenas Is.
Bamfield
Alberni Inlet
Nanaimo
125
Georgia Strait
Cape Flattery
120W
Gulf Islands
VANCOUVER
Fraser River
La Push
Canada / USA
Strait of Juan de Fuca
VICTORIA
Alternate large ship route
Bellingham
Olympic National Park
San Juan Islands
Anacortes
Port Angeles
Sequim
60W
Port Townsend
Small craft route
40
30
Puget Sound
Ocean Shores
Everett
Poulsbo
WASHINGTON STATE, USA
Hood Canal
Bainbridge Is.
Bremerton
SEATTLE
Westport

CHAPTER 1-THE SOUTH END:
SEATTLE, MILE ZERO TO
CAPE SCOTT, MILE 350W

This is stunning country; the drama of the mountains and the sea is everywhere; when the sun comes out suddenly after a long dreary week, the sight of Rainier looming over Seattle and Puget Sound is literally spectacular enough to stop you in your tracks.

These are big, big mountains, 6,000 footers on the west and all the way up to 14,000 foot plus on the east. Their tops are snow covered year round, and the range on the east, the North Cascades, is high enough to scrape much of the water out of the clouds as they head across the state. This is part of the Ring of Fire – some of the earth's great plates that form the crust meet along the ridge of the North Cascades. If you fly in or out, look as your plane gets up over the mountains and if it's clear you'll see a chain of volcanoes: Rainier, Adams, St. Helens, and Hood, stretching out of sight to the south.

And the fire is still present: after two months of throat clearing, Mt. St. Helens blew the top 1,300 feet of mountain and a cubic mile of ash into the atmosphere in May of 1980.

Much of the east side of the Sound, the Seattle - Tacoma - Everett corridor is fast paced, growing rapidly with all the attendant problems: congestion, traffic, pollution and noise.

But across the sound is very different. The old Puget Sound of cedar bungalows, forests sloping to the water's edge, driftwood fires, soaring eagles, and native settlements lingers here.

Top: yacht in Puget Sound with 14,00' Mt. Rainier looming behind.
Above: winter scene in West Port Madison, one of the sleepy bedroom communities on Bainbridge Island, a 35 minute ferry ride and a world away from the busy crowded streets and highways of the east side of Puget Sound.

FINDING THE STRAIT

Early morning, April 29, 1792 - Captain George Vancouver, searching for the elusive Strait of Anian (the supposed entrance to the legendary Northwest Passage - ice free between the Pacific and Atlantic) is startled to see another vessel, the first they have seen beside their consort, in almost eight months.

It was an American trader, Robert Gray. He told Vancouver the Strait lay just to the NE. A little later Vancouver entered what is now the Strait of Juan de Fuca. 10 miles wide and 500 feet deep, leading east between high snowy mountains, Vancouver thought he had found the elusive passage.

At that time, Philadelphia and Boston had cobblestone streets and daily newspapers, but the known world ended just west of the Mississippi River, and another 13 years would pass before Meriwether Lewis and William Clark were to reveal the vastness and beauty of the American West.

A week after entering the Strait, Vancouver and his two ships - exploring and charting - continually following the shore to be sure they didn't miss any channel that might lead to

the Atlantic, turned and entered the waterway that he named for one of his lieutenants, Peter Puget. They were all stunned by the beauty of the land that they had found.

For three long summers, he and his two ships and their four smaller rowing and sailing boats worked their way up the Inside Passage. In that complex maze of winding waterways with violent tidal currents, he lost just one man to shellfish poisoning before returning to England via Cape Horn. It was a remarkable achievement.

Top; Land Ho by Canadian artist John Horton.
Left: a section of the chart that Vancouver created. This is Puget Sound (Seattle is the dot that I put in) on the bottom and San Juan Islands on top - compare to the lower right part of the map on the previous spread.

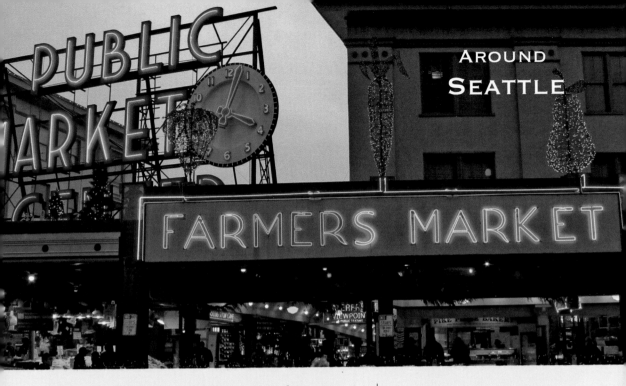

Seattle's first settlers trudged ashore in the pouring rain in November of 1851. The families had braved the rigors of the Oregon Trail, had a stormy trip up the coast by boat. "And for this?" they might have said, as they found out what they had traveled all that way for: a half finished cabin on the edge of the gloomy forest with scowling natives as a welcoming committee.

But less than a month later a small schooner dropped anchor in front of the settlers and offered them $1000 for a load of fir pilings from the forest behind the settlement, and the industry that was to drive the region far into the 20th century, logging and saw-milling, was born.

A century later, the Boeing Aircraft Company was the biggest game in town as it prepared to usher in the jet age with the plane management bet the future of the company on: the 707.

Twenty- five years after that, a new industry that would truly transform the region and the world was beginning just east of Seattle: computer software and the amazing rise of Microsoft.

Today Seattle has a broad based economy where Boeing and Microsoft are still the employment leaders, and a very outdoor oriented population. A climate that allows either skiing or sailing on almost any day from Thanksgiving to Easter and a dress code where bluejeans and a clean shirt will get you in almost anywhere, has made Seattle and the Northwest very popular with young professionals.

THINGS TO DO:

- **Explore the waterfront** - the Alaska Way area is a great place to walk around - restaurants, a great aquarium, shops, even a new Ferris wheel.

- **Take a ferry** - boats leave from the waterfront for Bainbridge Island, (35 min, nice shops and restaurants) and Victoria, B.C.

- **Take the train** - Amtrak to either Vancouver or Portland - both are super pleasant destinations and the ride is particularly scenic.

- **Go to Pike Place Market.** Just two blocks above the waterfront, it is jam packed with food and craft shops plus the famous flying fish.

- **Visit Pioneer Square**, the Underground Tour, and the Gold Rush Museum - all are a short walk from the waterfront.

- Got more time? Consider a **loop trip** around the Olympic Peninsula, or across the North Cascades Highway eastbound and back via Stevens Pass.

THE MIGHTY EMPIRE
OF THE WOODS

When the timber barons came to Puget Sound, it was not just the trees that awed them–they were used to big doug firs on the California and Oregon coasts, but it was the harbors! Because on those bold coasts the ships could only get in to load lumber in the best of conditions because there were hardly any harbors worthy of the word.

In places there was wonderful timber but no harbors at all–ships had to run a cable from their mast to the dock while they lay at an exposed mooring, and tediously receive lumber by cable, steam up in their boilers, ready to leave immediately if the weather deteriorated.

But in Puget Sound it was the combination of good harbors and protected waters next to great stands of trees that created the vast timber economy that was to dominate the region for its first hundred years. Port Blakely, Port Madison, Port Gamble, Port Ludlow, and other sheltered sleepy coves became the destination of ships from all over the world as big mills and little towns sprang up to harvest the great trees and load them aboard ships.

Top: a happy skipper with his deck-load of fine Puget Sound Douglas Fir. Above: A tug tows a big square rigger across the Columbia River bar. Almost every harbor on the West coast north of San Francisco was guarded by a dangerous to cross bar. SFMNHP J5.28163n

Opposite page: schooners, small steamer, and 5 square full rigged ships loading lumber, Port Blakely, 1900. SFMM

LEAVING SEATTLE

Seattle itineraries depart from the waterfront, site of all the action in the 1897-98 Yukon gold rush, when it was crowded with men seeking passage north to make their fortune and merchants trying to make their fortune selling supplies...

Have a look at the steeply sloped waterfront north of the city. In really wet winters, these hillsides get super saturated and the homes occasionally slide to the bottom.

A few miles north of the Edmonds ferry terminal on the east at **Mile 19,** Port Susan, and Everett harbor open to the right or east of your ship. Over the bluff here is The Boeing Aircraft Companies big plant, home to the amazingly venerable 747, 777, and now the new "Dreamliner," the fuel efficient carbon fiber 787.

Small craft headed to Alaska like to stay in the narrowest waters, and unless the tides and the weather forecast are both perfect, usually branch off here, taking a scenic, but more winding route up among the San Juan Islands and then on into Canada. A favorite stop for these boats is La Conner, a very picturesque small town located along the shores of the Swinomish Slough. This area is all very fertile bottomland, part of the Skagit River delta. Hundreds of acres are planted in flowers, and a popular event each spring is the Tulip Festival.

At **Mile 39**, the **Point Wilson Lighthouse,** your ship and the landscape make a major change. Point Wilson is the intersection between the sheltered waters of Puget Sound and the much wider and windier waters of the Strait of Juan de Fuca. There is a lot of tide here; look for rips close to the point, as well as sea

lions and seals having a supper on the salmon which are swept by the tide close to the point.

The landscape changes dramatically at Point Wilson. Narrow Puget Sound opens up to the wide Strait of Juan de Fuca. Most large cruise ships leaving Seattle for Alaska will turn to the west here, staying to the right or north side of the traffic lanes as they parallel the Washington coast, along the US-Canada border.

On the bluff to the west at **Mile 38** is **Port Townsend,** a decidedly Victorian town with a wonderfully eclectic flavor. Realtors had really gotten excited in the 1880s when for a time it looked as if The Northern Pacific Railroad would select PT (as it is known locally) as its western terminal. But after a geography check, the NPRR wisely chose Tacoma instead. So while Seattle and Tacoma boomed, Port Townsend grew at a much slower pace, with Victorian style houses perched on the steep hills around town with commanding views of the intersection of Puget Sound and Juan de Fuca Strait.

If you look closely, just north of town, and south of the lighthouse at Point Wilson, you'll see what looks a bit like a New England college campus. This is **Fort Worden**, one of three major US Army facilities situated on the three points overlooking the entrance to Puget Sound. The fields of fire from their hidden cannon formed a killing zone to prevent enemy ships from entering Puget Sound. Today the cannons are gone but the forts are available for rent and are busy with many functions year round from soccer tournaments to sea kayaking.

THE SAN JUAN ISLANDS

Straddling the US - Canada border is a sprawling archipelago - the Gulf Islands in Canada and the San Juans in the US.

"A place in the San Juans" was the ultimate for North-westerners – a little waterfront bungalow somewhere among the large and small islands of this sleepy group just 50 miles north of Seattle, but a world away. With four major islands served by ferries out of Anacortes, and dozens of smaller ones, they are a major destination for vacationers.

Washington State has a number of very popular parks among these islands. Some, often just an acre or two of land with a bit of beachfront, are specifically for kayakers or other small craft. Others are mini-marinas with every-thing but a store.

In recent years the price for all land has shot up, and a bit of a two tier society has developed with teachers and other workers finding it very hard to find affordable places to buy. It is also a place where the pace of life in the winter slows way down, especially on the small-er islands. There are a number of summer camps here where generations of Northwest families have sent their children.

Top: "Waterfront fixer upper" Wouldn't it be a dream to find a place like this for a modest price? Ac-tually it is one of the cabins at Camp Four Winds, a boys and girls camp that has changed little over the years. Above: Seal and classic sailboats, West Sound, Orcas Island.

VICTORIA

Top: Empress Hotel.
Above: Chief Maquinna, tribal leader when the Europeans first arrived.
Opposite page: Parliament building with statue of Queen Victoria.

While Vancouver—just 75 miles to the NW—is a totally cosmopolitan modern city with a heavy sprinkling of Asian immigrants, Victoria seems a bit more like a taste of Olde England. The British fondness for gardens is especially evident in the many private and public gardens and plantings that line its streets.

Originally settled when a Hudson's Bay Company trading post was established here in 1843, this city and Vancouver Island became a crown colony in 1849. Ten years later another colony was established on the mainland to support the many prospectors that had arrived with the 1858 Fraser River gold strike. Eventually the two colonies merged to form what is today British Columbia and Victoria became its administrative capital, while Vancouver became the industrial center.

Victoria is a good place to shop for First Nations (coastal native) art and craft souvenirs. Additionally many shops specialize in goods from England that would be hard to find elsewhere on your cruise.

What to see: Fortunately, many of Victoria's attractions are centered around the harbor:

The Royal British Columbia Museum is one of the best small museums you'll ever encounter. If you want to see Northwest Native culture up close, this will be probably your best opportunity. While the tribes in British Columbia are distinct from those along the areas of Coastal Alaska that you will be traveling through, their art such as totem poles share many of the same themes.

The Empress Hotel was part of a series of large and very notable resorts built by the Canadian Pacific Railway. Make a point of visiting the restored lobby, where afternoon tea is a major local event.

Across the harbor are the seaplane docks and the booking and boarding area for **whale watching tours**. This area is particularly suited for seeing orcas or killer whales.

12 miles from downtown are **Butchart Gardens**, which has become one of the most visited sites in the province. What is now a stunning 50 acre showpiece had rather humble beginnings. In 1904 Jennnie Butchart, whose husband operated a cement plant near the site, got tired of staring at the ugly scar in the land that his limestone quarrying operations left. She brought in a few plants to spruce up the area and one thing led to another!

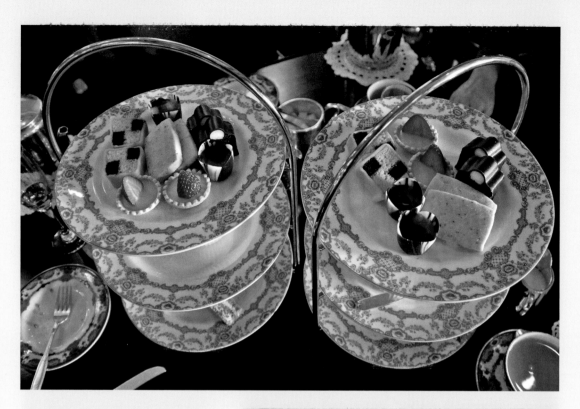

Top: dessert tray at afternoon tea at The Empress Hotel.

Bottom: sign on truck - actually Victoria is a great place to get out and go whale watching - there is a resident pod of orcas usually nearby and there are fast boats that leave from the harbor downtown. Even if there are no orcas that day, just cruising in and out of the harbor in the boat is pretty exciting just by itself!

Right: in the Bengal Lounge (part of The Empress.)

In Butchart Gardens

Top: the west coast of Vancovuver Island and Washington were basically one big meatgrinder for any ship that happened ashore when a sea was running..
Below: the crew of this schooner were lucky - they came ashore in calm weather. PSMHS 2727-3 b

About six hours after your ship leaves Seattle, you'll be at the place that sailors truly dreaded, before the advent of electronic aids to navigation. For decades, "Lost off Cape Flattery without a trace" was the epitaph for too many ships. This was the entrance to the Strait of Juan de Fuca, an area of strong currents, and frequent fogs. Captain Cook, exploring the coast, never found this ten mile wide entrance, wisely staying out of the fog near the coast.

The consequences of a navigational error were severe; the coasts of northwest Washington and Vancouver Island were fringed with reefs, isolated spires, and rocks. The surf was almost always heavy and any ship caught in its grip would be quickly destroyed.

Tugboat skippers knew how sailing masters felt about the entrance to the strait, and in those days before good radio communications, would patrol the entrance, hoping to pick up a big square rigger, anxious about the weather and looking for a tow up the strait to its final destination.

So many ships were lost along the British Columbia shore north of Cape Flattery that a trail was constructed along the very rugged shore of Vancouver Island, north of the entrance to the Strait. At intervals cabins were built, stocked with food and firewood and a telephone to the nearest lighthouse.

The straits also marks the place where the coast road ends, on both sides, cut off by the rugged geography. From here to the north on the Vancouver Island side, there are a few small towns, but only reached by long and twisting roads heavily used by log trucks.

THE WILD WEST COAST
OF VANCOUVER ISLAND

The overnight passage from Seattle takes you to a very different land. Gone are the waterfront homes, a road that follows the shore, lights at night, buildings or other signs of man seen by day.

The west coast of Vancouver island is very rugged, open to the full force of the storms that drive in off the North Pacific and almost completely isolated from the busy east coast. For most of the 20th century, the economy here was almost totally resource driven: salmon, herring, halibut, and timber. You were either producing them, processing them, or supporting the folks who did.

If someone had told a West Coast logger or fishermen in the boom years of the 1950s that a new economy would come to the coast, based on whale watching, kayaking, eco-tours, and vacationers, chances are he might have fallen over backwards laughing in disbelief. Back then the life was so rough, so rugged, so remote from anything not connected immediately to the business at hand–logging and fishing–that a change of that dimension seemed totally out of the question.

Yet this is exactly what happened. The salmon stocks that the West Coast fishermen depended on slumped badly in the 1970s and 1980s, due to a combination of mismanagement–overfishing–and damage done to salmon habitat. At the same time a growing awareness by the native tribes and commercial fishermen of the ecological damage of certain logging practices led to logging restrictions.

Fortunately the new economy, based on eco-tourism, surfers, kayakers, whale watchers, fish farming and Vancouverites looking for second homes came along just when the old was disappearing

Top: hiker exploring remote Vancouver Island beach.
Above: surfers on Long Beach, near Tofino. Wet suits even in summer here!

41

ON THE KYUQUOT RUN:
ABOARD THE UCHUCK III

She's an old minesweeper, but they put in new timbers every year to keep her strong. *The Uchuck III* serves the remote logging camps, fish farms, and fish lodges in Esperanza, Tahsis, and other remote Vancouver Island inlets. As roads slowly came to the coast, the ship added seats and a comfortable cabin so passengers could experience that remote coast as well.

Top: The *Uchuck III* leaves Gold River, way up at the head of Muchalat Inlet with a load of freight.
Above: at Kyuquot, skiffs take passengers to their evening's lodgings.
Left: Captain Spencer Larson at the controls.

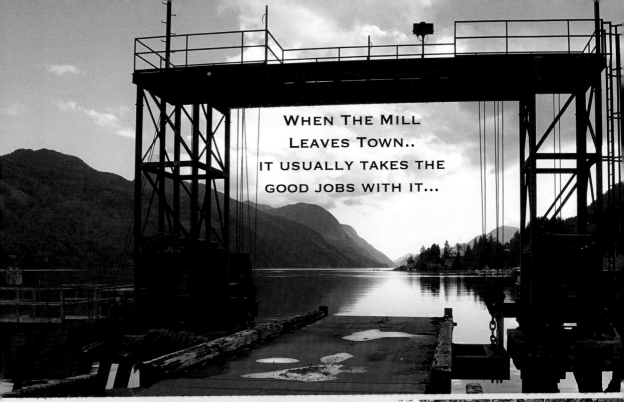

WHEN THE MILL LEAVES TOWN.. IT USUALLY TAKES THE GOOD JOBS WITH IT...

Life was good in Tahis and its 2500 residents when the big lumber mill was running. The inlet was full of logs waiting to be milled, the dock full of loading ships.

Then market conditions changed said the mill owners. The equipment was dismantled, loaded on barges, towed down the inlet and away.

The population collapsed to 700, the year round economy became, like that of many Vancouver Island villages, a seasonal one, serving sportsfishermen and vacationers

The loaders at the Tahis Mill were legendary. Ships bound for Asia would make their last stop way up the remote inlet that led to the town. They knew that they could depend on the crews to stack and lash securely enough for a passage across the stormy North Pacific.

Today trees grow up on the acres of ashphalt that used to hold lumber waiting for export, and a huge shackle in the leaves waits for ships that may never wind up the inlet again.

43

VANCOUVER

Top: one of many gorgeous buildings diowntown.
Above: Chinatown sign
Right: decorated bear, Canada Place.
Opposite right Inside Granville Island Market.

Like most Northwest coast cities, forest products played a huge part in Vancouver's history, with big square riggers waiting to take lumber to Asian, Australian, and Pacific ports as soon as it could be milled. It still continues today. When you cross the Fraser River entering the city, look down and most likely you'll see BC's premier product, logs, (some say marijuana is the province's biggest export...) traveling by barge or raft to a sawmill or a waiting ship.

With one of the best harbors on the coast and good road and rail connections, it quickly developed into Canada's premier west coast port as well. With a dramatic mountain and waterfront setting, the city became one of the favorite spots in the British Empire within a few decades of being founded, as evidenced by the many large and elegant Victorian era homes.

In more modern times, concerns about what would happen in Hong Kong after the mainland Chinese took over in 1997 led to the arrival of large numbers of Chinese immigrants, many of whom brought substantial personal wealth with them. The result is a noticeably multi-ethnic city with the second biggest Chinatown in North America.

Around town: Many of the sights are easily accessible from where your ship docks. Within walking or short taxi distance is much of the city core with almost unlimited shopping and dining. There is also a subway/elevated rail system called the Skytrain which makes getting around fairly simple.

Top: with the Lion's Gate Bridge ahead, a ship is ready to begin her trip up to Alaska.
Above: Thunderbird totem at Stanley Park.

A few blocks east of Canada Place is **Gastown**, where the city was first settled, and today is an eclectic neighborhood of old warehouses made into restaurants, artist's lofts, condos, and all manner of shops.

Chinatown is a few more blocks to the south (consider a taxi) and its size reflects Vancouver's popularity with Asians. This is the real thing! If you don't read Chinese, make sure your menu has English as well. With the waters of Georgia Strait and the North Pacific close at hand, many restaurants feature live tanks from which patrons may select their meal.

Visitors and Vancouverites alike are indeed fortunate that its founders set aside the 1,000 or so acres that today is **Stanley Park**. It features restaurants, a zoo, the ubiquitous totems, but most of all a stunning waterfront setting right next to downtown. A popular walk leads through the park to a dramatic overlook at Lion's Gate.

Take the foot ferry to **Granville Island** on False Creek. Granville Island is a combination of a farmer's and craftsman's market, with restaurants. These foot ferries or Aquabusses, are also just a good inexpensive way to see town from the water!

Within walking distance west of Granville Island is the **Vancouver Maritime Museum**, whose showpiece exhibit is the brave little steamer *St. Roche*, which spent much of her epic two year Vancouver to Newfoundland Northwest Passage transit frozen into the Arctic ice.

Fly to Victoria - float-planes operate almost hourly from the docks right next to Canada Place, where many ships leave from. The 30 minute flight gives you a spectacular view of the Gulf Islands and lands right in downtown Victoria. **Explore the Gulf Islands** by ferry and car. Take a few days; there are many islands and ferries: Saltspring Island is my favorite.

Top: salmon trolling vessel on display at Granville Island, a bustling venue with many craft, produce, jewelry and other shops plus numerous restaurants.

Left Steam clock in Gastown, just five blocks east of Canada Place.

Chapter 2 - The Wilderness Begins:
Vancouver, mile 95
to Alaska Border, mile 575

"Tracing shining ways through fiord and sound, past forests and waterfalls, islands and mountains and far azure headlands, it seems as if surely we must at length reach the very paradise of the poets, the abode of the blessed."
- John Muir, Travels in Alaska

Look to the right a few miles after you pass under Lion's Gate Bridge, leaving Vancouver, to the Point Atkinson Lighthouse. If you want to get a clear sense of what much of the coast of British Columbia and Alaska is like, look beyond the lighthouse.

This is **Howe Sound**, the first of the many deep and winding inlets that penetrate far into the interior. For example, there is no road around the head of the inlet—the land is too rough, you have to take a ferry across instead.

And it was here that the first explorers, like British Captain George Vancouver, who explored and named much of the B.C. and Southeast Alaska coasts, had their troubles. At the time, the British were under the impression that there was a passage somewhere across or through North America from the Pacific to the Atlantic—the "Northwest Passage"—and his job was to see if it

Top: troller passing **Sara Pt, Mile 195E**, just north of where the coast road ends, cut off by steep mountains.
Above: Point Atkinson Lighthouse.

WATCH OUR DOCUMENTARY
"**Mile 205**: Leaving Vancouver & Seymour Narrows" at:
alaskacruisehandbook.com

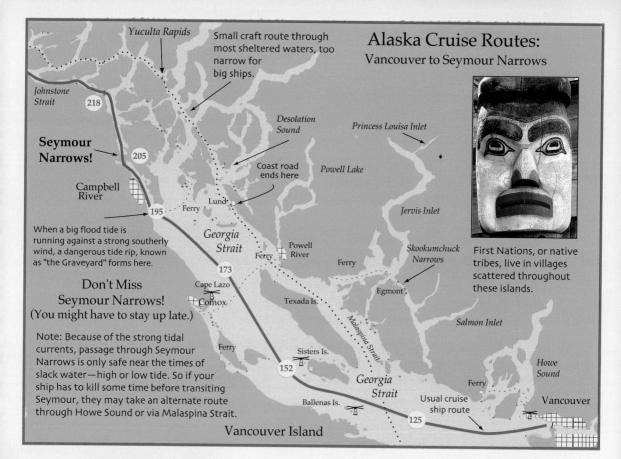

Yuculta Rapids

Small craft route through
most sheltered waters, too
narrow for
big ships.

Alaska Cruise Routes:
Vancouver to Seymour Narrows

Johnstone
Strait

218

Desolation
Sound

Princess Louisa Inlet

**Seymour
Narrows!**

205

Coast road
ends here

Powell Lake

First Nations, or native
tribes, live in villages
scattered throughout
these islands.

Campbell
River

195

Lund

Ferry

*Georgia
Strait*

Jervis Inlet

When a big flood tide is
running against a strong southerly
wind, a dangerous tide rip, known
as "the Graveyard" forms here.

Powell
River

Ferry

Skookumchuck
Narrows

173

Ferry

Don't Miss
Seymour Narrows!
(You might have to stay up late.)

Cape Lazo

Comox

Texada Is.

Egmont

Note: Because of the strong tidal
currents, passage through Seymour
Narrows is only safe near the times of
slack water—high or low tide. So if your
ship has to kill some time before transiting
Seymour, they may take an alternate route
through Howe Sound or via Malaspina Strait.

Ferry

Salmon Inlet

Sisters Is.

152

*Georgia
Strait*

Howe
Sound

Ferry

Ballenas Is.

Usual cruise
ship route

125

Vancouver

Vancouver Island

existed. This meant that each promising inlet or channel
had to be explored to make sure it wasn't the legendary
channel.

Leaving Vancouver, you enter **Georgia Strait**, sort of
an inland sea that is the home to much of the population
and industry of lower British Columbia.

It also has a climate that is often noticeably drier from
that just a hundred or so miles to the north - the rain
shadow effect of the mountains of Vancouver Island. The
coast to the east here is nicknamed The Sunshine Coast.

Looking for a great place to retire? **The Gulf Islands**,
directly across Georgia Straits, with dozens of islands
large and small, served by several ferries, would truly be
a great choice. They are particularly popular with boaters, and noticeably less crowded than the American San
Juan Islands, just across the border to the south. Many
Canadians have second homes here, a short ferry ride
away from Victoria or Vancouver.

Things to look for:

• **Log and chip barges**: British Columbia is a legendary
producer of forest products. Wood chips are moved in
big high-sided barges so full they seem almost submerged.

Above: not a bad berth: cottage
on Mayne Is. in the Canadian Gulf
Islands.

• **Log booms**: The rectangular rafts of logs towed slowly behind tugs are hard to see at night, because frequently they are marked only by dim and flickering kerosene lamps.

• **Alaska-bound tugs and barges** from Puget Sound, stacked high with container vans with large items, such as boats, strapped on top.

• **The big mills**: Most noticeable is Powell River, east of **Mile 173,** one of the largest in the world.

Vancouver Cruise Ship Departures: look to the north, or to the right of your ship's course with the last of the daylight. If it is at all clear, you should be able to see the dramatic mountains in the **Desolation Sound** area, west of about **Mile 180** on your map.

Captain Vancouver was here on a particularly wet June in 1792, described it as 'gloomy and forlorn.' OK, in reality he had a bit of a melancholy disposition to start with and he was finding what would be a three year search for the Northwest Passage a bit... tedious.

But this is easily the most misnamed place on the entire coast: it is totally spectacular. And the best part is: there are no roads—the steepness of the mountains ends the BC coast road a few miles south—and it is almost all a protected marine park!

And this: the salt water is warm enough for great swimming and oysters grow wild on the shores—for boaters it doesn't get much better than that. The reason is that the tidal currents from the south, coming in Juan de Fuca Strait and the north, coming in from Johnstone Strait meet here. The effect is that you have the normal high and low tides here, but the water doesn't move very far and just gets warmer and warmer. Plus the effect of

Top: kayaker in standing wave in the tide rip at **Skookumchuck Narrows,** east of **Mile 152** where the current runs almost 15 mph.

Above: the traditional flat log raft is used in sheltered waters.

Above lower: the big paper mill at **Powell River, east of Mile 173,** was the largest in the world when it was first built. A dam was built nearby to supply all the power.

When the living is good: summer in Desolation Sound, where the salt water reaches almost 75 degrees at times!

WATCH OUR DOCUMENTARY
"Mile 195E: Desolation Sound is Not So Bad." at alaskacruisehandbook. com

the high mountains seems to throw the heat back at the water sometimes. We were here the last week of June in 2004, and it was so warm that we would go up to the flying bridge of our chartered boat in the early evening to have our gin and tonics in the shade! Only when the sun went over the mountain did it get cool enough to cook!

Fortunately it is a long ways from the major Puget Sound yachting centers. But it is definitely a Mecca for boaters, for whom a trip to Desolation is something to yarn about all winter!

In the early 1970s several remote old farms in this area became counter culture homesteads for Americans seeking a quieter lifestyle away from the worry of getting drafted into the army and sent to Vietnam. I was exploring this area with my girlfriend in a small sailboat in the summer of August of 1971, and anchored in remote Galley Bay. Among the old apple trees rising up from the shore were what appeared like yurts and geodesic domes. We were sitting enjoying a glass of wine when there was a commotion in the water off our stern and **there was this exquisite young woman, swimming nude, and wondering if we could spare any cigarettes!**

52

Top: **Laura Cove** on the last day of September 2016. In July or August it would be almost wall to wall boats anchored with their sterns tied to trees on shore.

Left: our drone catches filmmaker Dan kayaking quietly west through the islands toward Prideaux Haven.

Above: Toba Wilderness Lodge, just north of Desolation Sound.

The Gauntlet: Yuculta Rapids Area

It's almost as if nature set a barrier across the route north, right in the spot where civilization ends and the wilderness begins. As if to say, 'Watch Out, what lies ahead is very different from what lies behind. Be careful.'

Devil's Hole Whirlpool

Dent Rapids

To Alaska

Guillard Passage

Arran Rapids

To Seattle

212 E

Yuculta Rapids

Several cubic miles of water must pass through these narrow passes with each tide change, creating violent eddies and whirlpools. Safe passage is only possible at slack water, and careless mariners have lost their lives here.

Top: drone photograph taken from about 400' above the dock at Big Bay, B.C. Guillard Passage is the main tidal rapids on the small craft route north.

I was aboard a 75 passenger cruise ship here, the *Spirit of Endeavor,* when the Captain made the poor choice of attempting passage while the current was still running at strength. A strong eddy lay the boat over enough that all the glasses and bottles slid off the bar, and one of the big liferaft cannisters broke loose, inflated and drifted away in the tide. Fortunately no one was injured. 58' seiners have been capsized here by tide rips.

Right: getting ready to retreive the Phantom 4 drone near Shoal Bay, BC. Our chartered boat was moving around a little too much to land it on the piece of plywood at lower left, so I told filmmaker Dan Kowalski to get ready to grab the drone out of the air.. and be careful with his fingers and the spinning propellors! We filmed all the way in and in the video you can definitely see a bit of anxiety in Dan's face, but it went fine!

"I was tied up to a log raft, up in Teak-erne Arm, you know where it is, about 10 miles south of Yucultas, waiting for the tide. There was a Canadian salmon troller laying there, and the owner was out on the logs, so we visited for a bit. I was asking him about good places to duck in out of the weather if it got bad, and he knew some that I'd never heard of.

Then there was a sound from his boat, like a woman crying out, and he excused himself and walked back along the logs and disappeared into his boat. A long while passed with more crying, and then it got quiet and he came out again, wiping his hands on a rag. It looked like blood, so I asked him if everything was alright.

'Ah,' he said, 'that was the baby coming out.' He shrugged. 'A little girl. They're both fine.'"

- A salmon fisherman

MILE 205:
MIGHTY SEYMOUR NARROWS

Oosterdam in **Seymour Narrows, Mile 205,** just about to pass over the exact spot where **Ripple Rock** was blasted out of the middle of the channel. Several cubic miles of water must pass through this channel every few hours as the tide rushes in and out, creating very swift currents. Safe passage through the Narrows is only possible near the times of high or low tide. On Saturday nights when north and southbound cruise ships must all transit the Narrows within a fairly short period, it can get a bit anxious for the Captains and British Columbia pilots!

"Hey, kid, wake up, ya gotta see this..!"

It was June, 1965, I was a kid of 18, just left Seattle on my first Alaska fishing boat job, and the 70-year old mate woke me. I stumbled up into the wheelhouse, amazed at what I was seeing: great, slowly turning whirlpools, through which the skipper struggled, turning the wheel back and forth, trying to find a safe way between them.

"It used to be worse, before they blasted Ripple Rock!" The mate told me, explaining that along the waterfront, **Seymour Narrows, mile 205,** was a legendary place. A ship killer rock had lurked, right in the middle of the channel, creating whirlpools large enough to suck down good sized boats. Safe passage was only possible at slack water, near the times of low and high tide. For big ships, this was the only sheltered route north, and as they got bigger, "Old Rip" became more and more of a hazard.

First they tried drilling from a barge anchored with

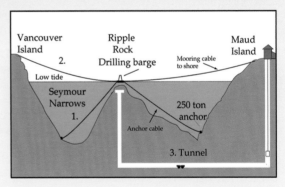

Vancouver Island

Ripple Rock

Maud Island

2.

Drilling barge

Mooring cable to shore

Low tide

Seymour Narrows 1.

250 ton anchor

Anchor cable

3. Tunnel

four 250 ton anchors! Didn't work—the violent current meant that the drill bits kept breaking off.

Finally a huge drilling project was undertaken—over 3200′ of tunnels and vertical shafts—reaching up into the interior of the rock. This was before the sophisticated sort of surveying equipment that we take for granted today was available, and drillers would explore with small diameter drills—until they broke through to the water. Then they'd plug the hole and use the information to create a 3D map of where they were.

Finally tugs pushed barge loads of dynamite—2.8 million pounds to load into the cave they had excavated, and on April 7, 1958: Adios Ripple Rock!

Top: goodbye Ripple Rock - 2.8 million pounds of DuPont Nitramex dynamite erupts in Seymour Narrows to convert Ripple Rock, lurking just below the surface, to Ripple Shoal, almost 40 feet below the water. Above left: the ill fated drilling attempt. The current moved the barge around too much to drill, despite cables to the shore and 250 ton anchors! Plus the capsize of a work skiff threw workers into the swirling current where they drowned. After that tragedy, the immense tunneling project was begun.

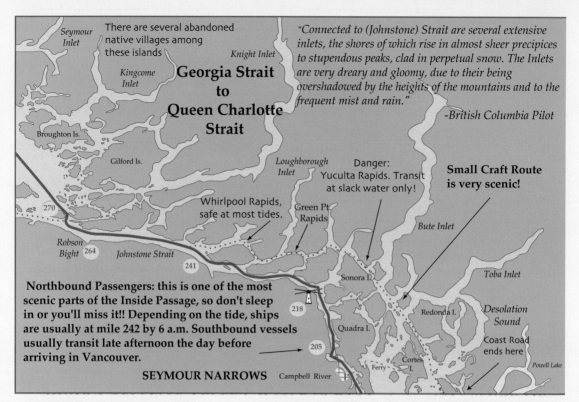

Seymour Inlet

There are several abandoned native villages among these islands

Knight Inlet

Kingcome Inlet

Georgia Strait to Queen Charlotte Strait

"Connected to (Johnstone) Strait are several extensive inlets, the shores of which rise in almost sheer precipices to stupendous peaks, clad in perpetual snow. The Inlets are very dreary and gloomy, due to their being overshadowed by the heights of the mountains and to the frequent mist and rain."

-British Columbia Pilot

Broughton Is.

Gilford Is.

Loughborough Inlet

Danger: Yuculta Rapids. Transit at slack water only!

Small Craft Route is very scenic!

270

Whirlpool Rapids, safe at most tides.

Green Pt. Rapids

Bute Inlet

Robson Bight 264

Johnstone Strait

241

Sonora I.

Toba Inlet

Northbound Passengers: this is one of the most scenic parts of the Inside Passage, so don't sleep in or you'll miss it!! Depending on the tide, ships are usually at mile 242 by 6 a.m. Southbound vessels usually transit late afternoon the day before arriving in Vancouver.

218

Redonda I.

Desolation Sound

Quadra I.

205

Coast Road ends here

SEYMOUR NARROWS

Campbell River

Ferry

Cortes I.

Powell Lake

Most large ships take the route marked by the blue line through this area. Smaller ships—say up to 225'—usually take the more winding and scenic route further east via Yuculta Rapids.

Bottom: along the small craft route east of Quadra Island.

— Passenger Tip: —

Vancouver departing passengers: the area between Seymour Narrows, Mile 205 and Pine Island, Mile 319, is very scenic. If you sleep in, you'll miss it.

WATCH OUR DOCUMENTARY

"Mile 212E:"Watch Out in Yuculta Rapids" at alaskacruisehandbook.com

---

MAJOR LANDSCAPE CHANGES

Seymour marks a huge transition in your trip. Literally it is as if there were an invisible line that ran from just south of Seymour to just south of Yuculta Rapids. To the south is civilization—towns, roads, lights on the shore at night, a warmer climate.

But the land to the north is very different—wilder, lonelier, cloudier, and chillier. This is the wild north coast where vast areas are sort of de facto wilderness, with here and there a logging camp, native village, or sportfishing resort. And the further north you go, the wilder it gets. Once you get north of Vancouver Island and into the channels and bays on the east side of Hecate Strait, you may find bays that go months without seeing a boat or a human.

And the tide runs very swiftly through the **Discovery Islands.** There are a number of routes: Seymour for the big cruise ships, Yuculta Rapids for small cruise ships, yachts and fish boats (they like the narrow channels,) and the narrowest channels in between, for even smaller craft, with crews willing to pick their ways through the rock piles.

But whatever the route, vessels must wait for slack water or close to it, for safe passage. To do otherwise risks getting capsized or swamped by the powerful whirlpools and rips.

It is almost as if nature set a gate across the route. At the very place where the busy south coast ends, and the wilderness begins. As if to warn the traveler of what lies beyond.

Johnstone Strait - Mile 218 - 264 - is probably the best known place in North America to see orcas. The good months are July and August, when the orcas are chowing down on migrating salmon as well as seals which also eat the salmon.

British Columbia orcas played a huge part in the worldwide change in human perception and understanding of orcas. In June of 1965, Bill Lechkobit, a B.C. salmon fisherman caught a big bull orca in his net, near **Namu, Mile 375**, and decided to try to keep it alive and sell it.

Seattle Aquarium owner Ted Griffin was very aware of the success that the Victoria Aquarium had with its captive orca, Moby Doll, and jumped at the opportunity to get one. He rushed up to Namu with a crew, built a floating underwater cage or pen, hired a tug, crossed his fingers and headed down to Seattle.

For the first day or so, an obviously distressed female orca with two young or calves, followed Namu's cage, squeaking and chirping in communication according to one watcher.

Griffin was very lucky, getting Namu safely to Seattle and installing him in a big tank in his aquarium with big viewing ports for the paying customers. As Moby Doll had in Victoria, Namu thrilled the customers, who quickly had to revise their perception of what an orca was.

Instead of an angry killer, audiences found a creature that was obviously intelligent, gentle, and even funny. Ted Griffin spent huge amounts of time with his

Top: Approaching Dent Rapids from west. There are three tidal rapids in this area: Dent, Guillard Passage, and Yuculta Rapids. In order to transit all of them in a single slack water period, southbound vessels will usually enter Yuculta bucking the very last of the flood, go through Guillard Pass at slack water, then ride the beginning of the ebb through Dent Rapids.

ORCA OR KILLER WHALE
Size: to 30 feet. Range: global. Distinguishing features: bold black and white markings, tall dorsal fin, especially on male. Before 1970 thought to be dangerous to man, but captured whales showed remarkable intelligence.

59

Top: part of a pod or family group of orcas, which usually travel and feed together as an extended family. The closest orca with the tallest fin is a male, the smaller one behind probably a female. Minden Pictures

Below: a big male or bull sea lion, and his harem of smaller females. All are likely prey to orcas.

new capture, teaching it tricks, and even putting on a neoprene wet suit and getting into the water with him. National Geographic ran a 28 page story on Griffin and Namu that went a long ways to dispel the myths many had about orcas.

But just 11 months later Namu died from an infection. Griffin, devastated, realized what a money maker Namu had been for his struggling business and set out to capture another one.

Unfortunately all the publicity about Namu and Moby Dall created sort of a wild west gold rush mentality about capturing orcas, and Griffin captured a whole school of orcas on the east side of Whitbey Island, and offered them for sale. Tragically, in the commotion, several of the captured orcas accidentally died.

This was not good publicity for folks who wanted to make a buck capturing orcas. Eventually the Washington state legislature became concerned and involved after an even more spectacular orca capture a few years later. This one occurred in an inlet so close to the actual capitol building in Olympia, Washington, that legislators could hear the helicopters! This was in the era of Earth Day and a swiftly growing awareness of the environment and the natural world, and shortly thereafter Washington, followed by British Columbia banned the capture of orcas. Unfortunately in the decade between Namu's capture and the bans, around 100 orcas were killed or taken from the Puget Sound-lower British Columbia orca population.

Orca awareness probably reached a peak after the

release of "Free Willy,' starring an orca whose real name was Keiko. Poorly housed in a Mexican aquarium after the film, Keiko's plight inspired a large number of supporters, and his life became an astonishing saga of high profile fund raising by schoolchildren all over the world up to millionaires like Craig McCaw, an interim home in an custom made Oregon aquarium tank, and eventually a high profile ride in a U.S. Air Force C-17 transport and finally to the fjord in Iceland, near where he had been captured some 25 years earlier. There had always been an element of worry if he could be successfully reintroduced into the wild after so long in captivity. But he was released successfully in the wild, where he survived for about 18 months before dying of pneumonia. At 27, he was old for a captive orca, but young for a wild one, many of whom live for 40 years plus.

Once, my wife and I came upon a sweet scene when we were exploring a very remote island, near the Alaska - Canada border: a mother seal and her two pups, napping in the sun on a rare sandy beach.

Then as we watched in shock, a twenty foot killer whale surfed into the beach on a big wave, gobbled up one of the sweet little pups, and wriggled back into the water to disappear into the next wave.

A pilot friend had a similar experience flightseeing some folks over Le Conte Bay near Petersburg. They were circling low over a flat small swimming pool-sized piece of ice with another mother seal, nursing her two pups, a postcard scene.

This time the orca slid completely across the ice, getting both pups in one bite but leaving a few bloody pieces behind

"Now, that's not something we see every day," said the pilot to the shaken passengers

Top: another traveling pod in Johnstone Strait, probably all males.
Above: more orcas? Nope, these are Dall Porpoises, which are frequently mistaken for orcas, as their coloring is similar and they also have noticable dorsal fins. The key thing to remember in distinguishiung them is that porpoises are much much smaller than orcas.
Porpoises are very fast swimmers and frequently like to accompany and play around the bows of traveling power boats

WATCH OUR DOCUMENTARY
"**Mile 375**: Namu." at
alaskacruisehandbook.com

Top: a potlatch at Alert Bay around 1910. All the stacked goods in the background will be given away. BCARS

WATCH OUR DOCUMENTARY
"Mile 270: Rainforest Culture" at
alaskacruisehandbook.com

Occasionally ships will stop near **Alert Bay**, **Mile 280** in order for passengers to see the big totems - actually that thing in the back of town that might look like a telephone tower is actually the world's tallest totem, 173 feet high.

Alert Bay is the center for the Kwakiutl Band of coastal First Nations, at one time the most powerful tribe along the southern coast of British Columbia.

Major events in First Nations life were often marked by a potlatch - a big celebration to which many tribes were invited. Many items were given to the guests at these potlatches as a way of the hosting tribe showing how wealthy they were. Before the arrival of the whites, the gifts were mostly food and craft items. But with more natives participating in the cash economy through work at canneries and sawmills, the potlaches became even bigger events with boats, canoes, sewing machines, guns, etc. given away. Thinking the natives were impoverishing themselves, British Columbia authorities banned potlatches in 1885, showing their total insensivity to First Nations culture, and driving the potlatches deeper and deeper into the island wilderness. Eventually the ban was lifted in 1951.

After Seymour Narrows the Inside Passage continues into **Johnstone Straits** for about seventy miles. This is sort of the Route 1 of the Inside Passage and you are apt to see watercraft including all manner of fishboats, tugs and barges, Alaska state ferries, etc.

Typically on summer afternoons the interior of British Columbia heats up and drawns in cooler ocean air via Johnstone Straits. The result is a strong westerly and small craft have learned to leave early to get through here before the wind picks up and makes for nasty traveling.

On the Vancouver Island shore at **Mile 264** is **Robson Bight,** a pebbly beach that for some unknown reason attracts killer whales in the summer and early fall, who like to rub themselves along the shallow bottom! The area is a protected preserve. Nearby Telegraph Cove, offers whale watching tours.

Most ships swing from Johnstone Strait north into Queen Charlotte Strait at **Blackfish Pass, Mile 275.** This is the beginning of wider and less sheltered waters. Many times ships will be in the area off the islands known as the **Deserters Group,** near **Mile 300,** at sunrise. I know that many travelers have put in a long day before getting on the ship in Vancouver, but dawns here can be spectacular go get up early and have a look! **Tip: If your cabin is on the starboard or right hand side of the ship, just leave your cabin curtains open and have a look out the window when you wake up.**

Small craft take a different route here - passing west of Cormorant and Malcolm Islands to stay in sheltered waters as long as possible. When northbound their usual anchorage for the night is the protected bight in the western shore of Hurst Island, **Mile 311** that has come to be called **God's Pocket.**

Top: looking east to the mainland across Queen Charlotte Strait, near **Deserters Group, Mile 315**.
Above: chart and dividers for measuring distance. All have been replaced by GPS and plotters which show position as a boat icon on a moving map!

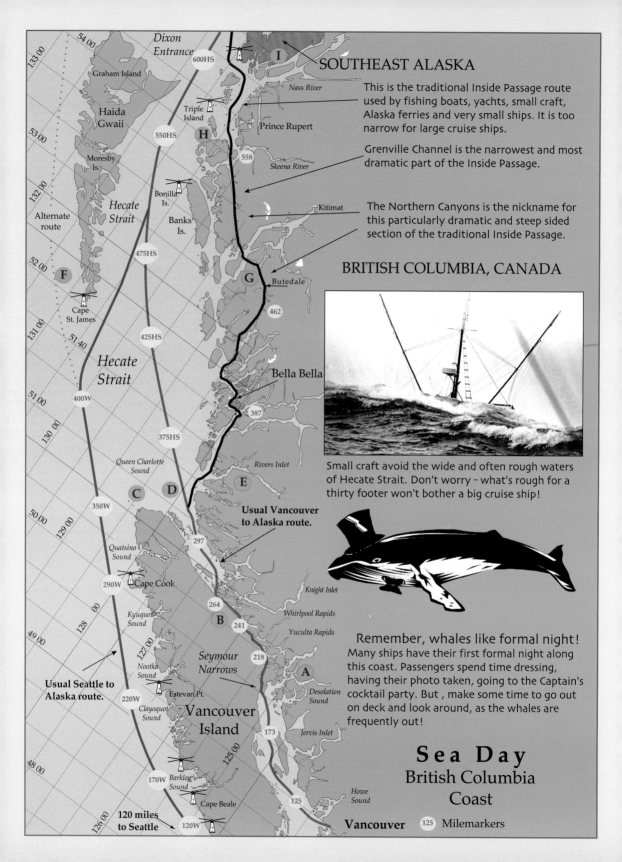

SOUTHEAST ALASKA

This is the traditional Inside Passage route used by fishing boats, yachts, small craft, Alaska ferries and very small ships. It is too narrow for large cruise ships.

Grenville Channel is the narrowest and most dramatic part of the Inside Passage.

The Northern Canyons is the nickname for this particularly dramatic and steep sided section of the traditional Inside Passage.

BRITISH COLUMBIA, CANADA

Small craft avoid the wide and often rough waters of Hecate Strait. Don't worry - what's rough for a thirty footer won't bother a big cruise ship!

Remember, whales like formal night! Many ships have their first formal night along this coast. Passengers spend time dressing, having their photo taken, going to the Captain's cocktail party. But , make some time to go out on deck and look around, as the whales are frequently out!

Sea Day
British Columbia
Coast

Vancouver   125 Milemarkers

Dixon Entrance

Graham Island

Haida Gwaii

Moresby Is.

Hecate Strait

Alternate route

Cape St. James

Hecate Strait

Bonilla Is.

Banks Is.

Triple Island

Prince Rupert

Nass River

Skeena River

Kitimat

Butedale

Bella Bella

Rivers Inlet

Queen Charlotte Sound

Quatsino Sound

Cape Cook

Kyuquot Sound

Nootka Sound

Estevan Pt.

Clayoquot Sound

Vancouver Island

Seymour Narrows

Knight Inlet

Whirlpool Rapids

Yuculta Rapids

Desolation Sound

Jervis Inlet

Howe Sound

Barkley Sound

Cape Beale

Usual Vancouver to Alaska route.

Usual Seattle to Alaska route.

120 miles to Seattle

600HS

550HS

558

475HS

F

425HS

400W

375HS

387

350W

297

290W

264

241

218

220W

173

170W

125

120W

462

I

H

G

E

C

D

B

A

ALONG THE WAY - BRITISH COLUMBIA COAST

A Discovery Islands - Desolation Sound Area: extremely scenic; the Sound is mostly a marine park, very popular with boaters for its very warm waters.

Tidal currents run so swiftly among the islands that safe passage is only possible at slack water - high or low tide - even for cruise ships. Small craft prefer the narrower more sheltered eastern passages, while larger craft including cruise ships use **Seymour Narrows, Mile 205.**

B This area of **Johnstone Strait** is particularly popular with orca whales, who chow down on the summer salmon runs. Near **Mile 264** are some beaches where the orcas swim into chest deep water to rub themsevles on the smooth pebble bottom.

C Triangle Island, near Mile 350W - Here the highest and brightest lighthouse on the entire coast was commissioned in 1910. Unfortunately they hadn't planned on the wind. The lightkeeper's dog blew off the cliff, and one storm blew the radio towers away and moved the office off its foundations against the generator building. Another storm blew the roof off the bunkhouse and the crews' clothes and bedding out into space. After just 8 years, the light was abandoned. Today, however, it is a major bird rookery. Each spring some 50,000 pairs of tufted puffins arrives, each to lay and incubate a single egg!

D The crossing of **Queen Charlotte Sound** was often a challenge for the many smaller vessels that travel up the coast every year.

Northbound boats would wait at **God's Pocket, Mile 310**, with their alarm set for 3 or 4 a.m. They'd wake up, 'sniff' the weather, and if it looked safe, head across before the wind got up.

E Rivers Inlet was once home to numerous canneries in the 1920s, '30s, and '40s until careless logging and overfishing depleted the mighty sockeye runs. Little remains of the big canneries today except for two that support themselves by operating as sumertime sportsfishing lodges.

F Occasionally in good weather ships from Seattle headed for Juneau will travel up the remote and wild outside coast of **Haida Gwaii** (formerly the Queen Charlotte Islands.) The islands are the traditional home of the Haida native tribe, who lived in numerous villages marked with lines of totem poles in front.

G In the middle of a stormy winter night in 2006 the BC Ferry **Queen of the North** steamed into the side of an island and sank. Fortunately the natives of nearby Hartley Bay heard the distress calls and saved all but 2 of the 101 passengers and crew. The officer on watch at the time of the collison was sentenced to jail.

H The pilots who accompany cruise ships in Alaska waters embark or disembark in this area.

I Still seeking the elusive Northwest Passage back to the Atlantic, English explorer George Vancouver had a particulary difficult time exploring these very long and winding inlets.

WOULD YOU GO TO ALASKA IN THIS?

OR THIS?

Top: the *Maggie Murphy*, circa 1920. It wasn't uncommon at all to see vessels like this picking their weather, just traveling on good days, and making it to Alaska without issues.
Bottom: *The Mad Dog*, winner of the 2016 Race to Alaska. Only wrinkle: you coudn't use or even have an engine. The first prize was a thousand bucks nailed to a bit tree just over the Alaska border. Second prize was a nice set of steak knives! NW Maritime Center

For many young people growing up on Puget Sound and hearing stories about Alaska and The North from those who had been, the urge to follow was strong. In the 1930s two eighteen year olds, Ed Braddock, and John Joseph Ryan salvaged a derelict 26 footer from the Tacoma mud flats, rebuilt it with the unknowing help from a nearby lumber mill, and set off the Inside Passage. They had barely made it 50 miles before one of the many flaws of their vessel revealed itself:

"First of all, the pilothouse proved to be utterly inhabitable. It had about two inches less headroom than was needed to allow either of us to stand erect when steering, the engine was right underfoot belching heat and fumes that rose up to smother the helmsman. Further, there was no danger that either fumes or heat would escape as the pilothouse had been puttied and nailed shut, sealing the pilothouse as tight as a mummy's crypt."
- John J. Ryan, *The Maggie Murphy*

Part of the Lure of The North was this: prior to 1974 when Alaska created the Alaska Limited Entry law, you could get a fishing license for a hundred dollars or so and make a pretty good season,with not much spent on fishing gear or nets. So anyone with a modest boat and a few hundred bucks could start a new life up in Alaska, and judging by the boats heading up the Inside Passage in those days, many did!

Of course before electronic navigation aids like radar especially, navigating the twists and turns of the Inside Passage was a challenge. Even in clear weather, there were many twists and turns where the careless or too casual navigator could easily end up on the rocks. One of the biggest issues was the very strong tidal currents, in many places running 3 or 4 mph. The good thing was that for the most part there was no surf or swells - the ocean waves that would quickly grind into pieces any ship that ran ashore.

The result was that many vessels had scrapes along these waters, but most weren't fatal or particularly serious. The above well-known fast steamer *Mariposa*, went ashore in Lama Pass, near **Mile 392.** Luckily the damage was minor, and though the passengers had a day or so of waiting before they were picked up by the next steamer. The *Mariposa* was refloated and repaired.

Radar alone, however, isn't foolproof. In 1982, I was southbound approaching Dryad Point, **Mile 400**, in thick fog. Our engineer had just taken the wheel, and I was about to take a nap, but decided to stand out on the back deck to see if I could hear the lighthouse foghorn as we made the right angle turn into Lama Passage. Quickly I realised that we weren't turning and were instead continuing into reef strewn Gunboat Passage. I walked into the pilothouse and asked him to show me where we were on the chart. He pointed to a place a mile behind us, and paled when I showed him where we actually were. Today, the ubiquitous GPS plotter makes navigation even easier, essentially like playing a video game.

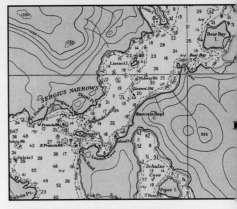

Top: *Mariposa* in Lama Pass, 1917. Above: Sergius Narrows, on the route from Juneau to Sitka. Another bad place: the tide runs here fast enough to suck the big Coast Guard navigation buoys completely under water, and an An Alaska state ferry, was swept into a rock here when the crew wasn't paying attention!

WATCH OUR DOCUMENTARY
"**Mile 400:** Trouble on Queen Charlotte Sound." at alaskacruisehandbook.com

Top: small salmon troller struggles to get across Hecate Strait.

From my 1975 logbook,
Oct 24:
"1230 - Egg Is. - sloppy, SE 20
1320 - Cape Caution, SE 25, 4' chop, wet going.
1500 - Pine Island - gale warning, wind here SE 40-45, very shitty going, had to tack downwind so as not to take seas on the beam.
1715 - God's Pocket - no room - full of Canadian trollers, laid alongside one fellow to fix our steering wheel.
1830 - Finally anchored, very narrow spot at SE end of Browning Pass. Steady 45 outside, water all white, glad to be inside! Two other boats in just at dusk looking mighty beaten up, one with plywood over a broken window.

WATCH OUR DOCUMENTARY
"Mile 310: In God's Pocket."
at alaskacruisehandbook.com

The little cove, **God's Pocket**, **Mile 340**, is the traditional jumping-off and arrival place for small craft crossing the 40 mile open water passage across lower Hecate Strait to sheltered waters beyond. For northbound small craft here's the drill: get ready the night before - tying down loose things, etc, and set your alarm for 3 a.m. When it goes off step outside and listen. If you can hear it rushing through the trees around the anchorage, go back to sleep!

Look for the **Pine Island Lighthouse** at **Mile 319**. Your ship may slow here to discharge (or receive, southbound) the Canadian pilots, who work with the navigational staff to guide the ship though the tricky channels inside of Vancouver Island.

Lighthouse families, particularly at Pine Island and the next lighthouse to the north, equally exposed **Egg Island**, did not have an easy life. A 50' wave from a 1967 winter gale smashed most of the buildings here and the staff with their children huddled by a campfire on higher ground until the storm had passed. Another storm smashed the Egg Island keeper's house into kindling; they were lucky to survive until help arrived.

Big ships in **Hecate Strait** usually pretty much run up the middle of the strait. Weather that might be nasty for a 50 footer wouldn't bother a big cruise ship. But in winter, it's a very different story. Once a big Alaska ferry got caught in a squall here while and rolled around so bad that a big truck rolled over when the hold-down chains broke. The motion was so bad that no one could get down there to secure it and it slid back and forth, breaking loose other cars and RVs. They were lucky a fire didn't start from the spilled gas, and when they got to their next stop, a tow truck had to get in there to pull out

all the smashed vehicles.

You may see the snow covered 10-11,000' tops of the coast mountains to the east, and you may see some lower land to the west.

On the west would be the **Queen Charlotte Islands or Haida Gwaii,** among the most rugged and thinly settled of the B.C. coast. They were originally settled by the Haidas, a First Nation tribe, who suffered the same ravages from disease and alcoholism as their mainland brothers. The islands are becoming favored by kayakers and adventure travelers seeking a true off the beaten path experience. Guides stress the remoteness of the land, and the importance of carrying adequate survival equipment and leaving a travel plan with a friend at home in case you don't return on schedule.

30 miles west of **Mile 480W** is **Skedans**, once the side of a large Haida village, now abandoned, but site of many old totems and other artifacts. It is a United Nations World Heritage Site.

From about 1910 to 1941, several whaling stations operated out of the Queen Charlottes, harvesting the schools of humpback, finback, sperm, and even the giant blue whales that migrated up and down the coast. It was hard, hard work with crude navigational equipment on an unforgiving coast:

Commercial fishing, logging, and a bit of tourism are pretty much the economic base of these islands. Most of the logs cut here are transported to mills at Prince Rupert or on Vancouver Island for processing. In the inlets and

Above: a big raft full of logs from Haida Gwaii. The waters of Hecate Strait were too rough for logs to be moved by traditional flat rafts towed by tugs.

Some barge are designed to be self-dumping - ballast tanks are flooded at the destination, the barge tilts and the bundled logs slide into the water.

Below: mortuary style totem - the bones of a deceased were sometimes placed inside. The style is particular to the Haida of Haida Gwaii.

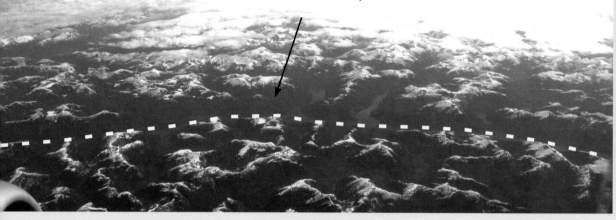

Top: view of Grenville Channel in the vecinity of **Butedale Cannery, Mile 473**. Bottom: view of Butedale from the top of the wooden penstock that brought water down to the turbines that powered the cannery.

passages between Vancouver Island and the mainland, the waters are sheltered enough for the traditional flat log rafts. However, this sort of raft could not stand the rigors of the rough ocean conditions of Hecate Strait, so an alternate raft design was developed, with hundreds of thousands of board feet of logs chained tightly together tightly enough to survive rougher conditions. Eventually big barges were used, complete with cranes to allow them to load themselves in remote inlets. With the addition of ballast tanks that could be flooded or pumped out as needed, these barges became self dumping as well—they'd get towed to their destination, then the tanks on one side would be emptied and the barge would tip all the logs into the water!

The islands suffered a hard blow in March of 2006, when their regular ferry, the *Queen of The North* hit a rock in the middle of a rainy, windy night and sank. Fortunately a few fishermen at a nearby First Nations village were awake with their radios on and immediately headed out in their boats to rescue the survivors who were shivering in life rafts. Two passengers were lost in the confusion of the sinking.

If you are northbound, this will usually be a formal night. Couples will spend time getting dressed; perhaps the ladies might get their hair done. Then there is the Captain's cocktail party as well as the all important formal portrait. But don't forget this is whale country as well. Today most ships carry naturalists who have a beeper. If the bridge staff spots a school of whales, they would often page the naturalist to come up to the bridge to do a running commentary. But if it's just one whale, and if an announcement would interrupt an important passenger activity, it might not be announced. Many times in Hecate Strait, I've been walking the deserted

outside decks and spotted whales, seeming eager for attention, while almost everyone else was inside, occupied with formal night activities.

So... remember to take time in your busy afternoon to take a stroll on the outer decks—the promenade decks on most ships are sheltered from the wind—and keep a sharp eye peeled for whales.

When cruise ships were small, say 300' feet and smaller, everyone pretty much took the traditional Inside Passage route, also nicknamed The Northern Canyons, instead of traveling up wide and sometimes windy Hecate Strait. See map on page 64. **The Northern Canyons begin at Boat Bluff Lighthouse, Mile 439.** (Photo on P. 65) The next hundred miles or so are among the most spectacular of the whole Inside Passage. The walls of the channels seem to rise vertically in places and waterfalls tumble down their flanks. In places there is not enough room for two ships to pass.

This region was especially popular with hand loggers because of the steepness of the slopes which made it easier for the men who worked alone or with a single partner, to slide the huge trees down into the water.

If you take this route, look for **Butedale Cannery,** on the west side of Fraser Reach at **Mile 473,** a traditional stopping spot for fishing boats. Once a complete little town all by itself, with neat rows of houses for administrators and their families, and bunkhouses for hundreds of workers, it was all powered by water from the lake in the hills behind it. Sadly, after the canning operations were transferred to Prince Rupert, the large cannery fell into disrepair and, now, like many old North Coast canneries, lies abandoned.

Top: Alaskabound salmon troller in Fraser Reach, in one of the most dramatic parts of the Northern Canyon. Above: two floating fishing lodges towed by a tug in Wright Sound, Mile 490. These lodges spend the summer in the area near **Hakai Passage, west of Mile 375,** hosting sportsfishermen who arrive by floatplane from Vancouver!

WATCH OUR DOCUMENTARY
"**Mile 455:** The Northern Canyons."
at alaskacruisehandbook.com

Top: Holland America ship *Zuiderdam*, near the narrowest part of the Inside Passage, **Mile 520**, where the channel is just about 1200' wide between the canyon walls. The sides of the channel are so steep that the ship could probably tie up to the trees! Above: the entrance to Grenville Channel seen from **Mile 498**.

WATCH OUR DOCUMENTARY
"Mile 485: Finding Bishop Bay."
at alaskacruisehandbook.com

Grenville Channel - see map on P. 64 - is the most dramatic part of the Inside Passage, deep in the mountain heart of British Columbia, and part of the area that I have named the Northern Canyons. Here the channel narrows to about 1200' at **Mile 522**, the sides rise back steeply to almost 4,000', and waterfalls cascade down the walls in several places so steep that small craft let the water fall on deck to fill their water tanks!

Rumor has it that the helmsman of more than one fishing boat, on watch and falling asleep here has been woken by branches slapping against the pilothouse windows, woke up, and steered back out into the channel without damage.

Sadly, in recent years very few ships take this route. Taking your ship up through Grenville takes a bit more fuel and a lot more attention on the part of the bridge staff, but the whole point of the cruise is to show passengers the dramatic beauty of the coast!

Fortunately when I was on the *Zuiderdam* in the spring of 2012, Captain Turner took us up through Grenville on just the most spectacular afternoon: Bravo Captain Turner!

The steep hills along this route were perfect for handloggers in the days before chain saws and large scale industrial logging. There was a pulp and shingle mill at **Swanson Bay, Mile 462** that supported a town of 500 by 1920. Today all that is visible from the water is the old brick chimney. The mill would often 'grubstake' hand

loggers with food and tool. The loggers, often working in pairs and exploring the coast in just a rowboat, would pick the steepest slope, set up camp, then cut trees so that hopefully they would slide all the way down and into the water. If they stopped on the way down it would mean a lot of work with axes and jacks to get them moving again. The handloggers would limb the trees, assemble them into rafts, then contact the mill, which would send a tug to tow the log raft to the mill. Only then would the loggers be paid.

These were the days of big trees and big men - no chain saws, eight foot diameter and larger trees, and sharp, sharp axes. To get above the swollen area at the base of the tree where it becomes the roots, the loggers would drive what they called springboards into the side of tree maybe eight feet up to stand on, climb up, and start chopping away.

There was another big pulp mill at **Ocean Falls**, east of **Mile 400**, basically, like all the remote mills and canneries, a whole little town unto itself with a dam for power, medical center, etc, all alone in the wilderness about 20 miles from the nearest town and only accessible by floatplane and boat.

Of course, the mill eventually became too expensive to operate, and the town was set to be demolished before a major effort by the residents managed to save at least a part of it. Today, the year round population is around 30, expanding to maybe 70 in the summertime.

The coast of British Columbia had perfect growing conditions for big, big trees. Before light one person chain saws came along after World War II, it took big men, and big axes to bring down the big firs, spruces, hemlocks, and cedars growing along the coast.

The drawing above shows a logger on a springboard high stuck into a tree high above an inlet on the Inside Passage. Christine Cox

Top: inside the Museum of Northern B.C.
Above: this is what jobs leaving looks like - logs being loaded directly from the water into an Asia bound ship in Prince Rupert harbor. Alaska at least has a law that logs must be processed into lumber before export.

Before the Grand Trunk Pacific Railway punched a line down the through the coast mountains to connect interior Canada to the sea at Prince Rupert, Port Essington, a cannery town on the Skeena River, 8 miles south, was the business center of northern British Columbia,

The railroad totally changed things. It was the first place north of Vancouver where a direct line from interior Canada reached the sea, and almost immediately exports, particularly grain and timber poured out, and imports from Asia came in. Having the railroad made "Rupert" (as it is known locally) a cheaper place to process fish as well. And as fish runs declined, and refrigerated tenders—fish buying & transport vessels—made it possible to bring fish from remote areas in to Rupert, the outlying canneries eventually closed—and most salmon came here. Today, Port Essington, once a booming town with several canneries, is a ghost town and Rupert is the regional center.

Sadly, Charles Hays, manager of the GTPRR, whose vision of Prince Rupert as a major port, never got to see his dream fulfilled. Returning from England where he had raised capital for the rail line through the mountains, he unfortunately chose to travel on the *RMS Titanic*. He was lost along with many, many others when it grazed an iceberg that sliced the magnificent ship open and sent it to the bottom.

Today Prince Rupert's economy is like much of

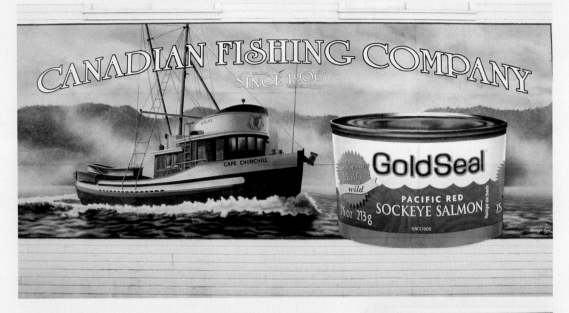

Southeast Alaska's was a few decades earlier: essentially dependent on commercial fishing and pulp mill employment, although port operations are a major employer as well.

Sensing the crowding of Southeast Alaska ports, and wanting to further diversify its economy, a modest cruise ship dock and terminal was completed in 2006, and a few ships began to schedule stops there.

A few blocks west of the new dock is the **Museum of Northern B.C.** with excellent displays on local First Nations culture and local history. A short walk away in downtown, behind the courthouse are the Sunken Gardens.

Today, almost all of all the hundreds of remote outlying canneries up and down the B.C. and Alaska coast are gone, abandoned or burned, most just pilings on a beach and buildings rotting in the forest. Fortunately at Prince Rupert, a group of concerned local citizens have preserved one, the old **North Pacific Cannery** on the Skeena River as a National Historic Site. Offered as an excursion to most visiting passengers, a visit is a remarkable glimpse into the past and a time when it seemed as if the salmon resource was, like the forest, endless.

There's also a great local cafe—**Smiles Seafood Cafe**— with wonderful seafood if you are looking for a colorful eatery.

Top: old cannery billboard. In its glory days of the 1930s and 40s, hundreds of small gillnetters fished the salmon runs on the mighty Skeena River delivering fish to 10 canneries scattered on both sides of the river near the mouth.

Above: great sign in old cannery.

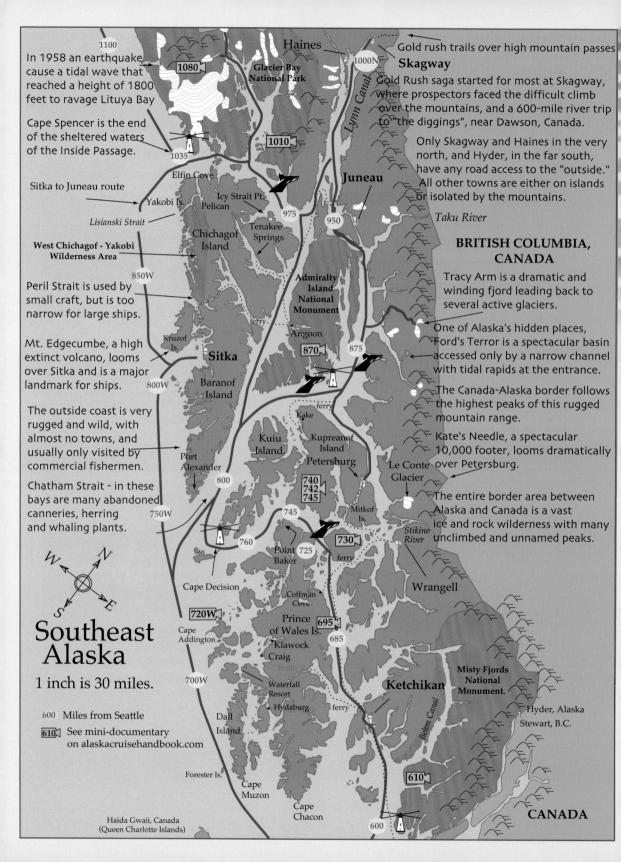

In 1958 an earthquake cause a tidal wave that reached a height of 1800 feet to ravage Lituya Bay

1100

1080

Cape Spencer is the end of the sheltered waters of the Inside Passage.

1035

Sitka to Juneau route

Yakobi Is.

Lisianski Strait

West Chichagof - Yakobi Wilderness Area

850W

Peril Strait is used by small craft, but is too narrow for large ships.

Mt. Edgecumbe, a high extinct volcano, looms over Sitka and is a major landmark for ships.

800W

The outside coast is very rugged and wild, with almost no towns, and usually only visited by commercial fishermen.

Chatham Strait - in these bays are many abandoned canneries, herring and whaling plants.

750W

Elfin Cove

Icy Strait Pt.
Pelican

Chichagof Island

Tenakee Springs

Kruzof Is.

Sitka

Baranof Island

Port Alexander

800

Haines

Glacier Bay National Park

1010

975

950

Admiralty Island National Monument

Angoon

870

ferry

Kake

Kuiu Island.

Kupreanof Island

Petersburg

740 742 745

745

Juneau

875

ferry

Mitkof Is.

730

ferry

1000N

Skagway

Gold rush trails over high mountain passes

Gold Rush saga started for most at Skagway, where prospectors faced the difficult climb over the mountains, and a 600-mile river trip to "the diggings", near Dawson, Canada.

Only Skagway and Haines in the very north, and Hyder, in the far south, have any road access to the "outside." All other towns are either on islands or isolated by the mountains.

Taku River

BRITISH COLUMBIA, CANADA

Tracy Arm is a dramatic and winding fjord leading back to several active glaciers.

One of Alaska's hidden places, Ford's Terror is a spectacular basin accessed only by a narrow channel with tidal rapids at the entrance.

The Canada-Alaska border follows the highest peaks of this rugged mountain range.

Kate's Needle, a spectacular 10,000 footer, looms dramatically over Petersburg.

Le Conte Glacier

The entire border area between Alaska and Canada is a vast ice and rock wilderness with many unclimbed and unnamed peaks.

Stikine River

Wrangell

N
W E
S

Southeast Alaska

1 inch is 30 miles.

600 Miles from Seattle

610 See mini-documentary on alaskacruisehandbook.com

Cape Decision

720W

Cape Addington

700W

Point Baker

725

760

Coffman Cove

Prince of Wales Is.

Klawock

Craig

Holl...

Waterfall Resort

Hydaburg

ferry

Dall Island

695
685

Ketchikan

Misty Fjords National Monument.

Behm Canal

Hyder, Alaska
Stewart, B.C.

Forester Is.

Cape Muzon

Cape Chacon

600

610

CANADA

Haida Gwaii, Canada
(Queen Charlotte Islands)

COMING TO ALASKA:
AN ACCOUNT OF ARRIVING IN ALASKA, IN MY OWN BOAT, JUNE, 1972

So we came to Alaska, on a lost and wild afternoon, caught in a tide-rip off a nameless point, in failing light, far from any help. The heavy westerly swell, the dirty southwest chop made it all I could do just to keep way on the boat, throttling over the big ones and diving deep into the troughs. The waves came from all directions, and even at dead slow, slapped against the windows, making the thick glass sag inward. Twice a big one roared over the stern, filling the trolling cockpit, and the boat wallowed deep in the water until it drained. *Kestrel* was just 50 yards away, and sometimes I could see half her keel as she came off a big one.

The shore wasn't far, and I looked long and hard at it. If the engine ever quit, we'd be broadside in a minute and probably swamp. I'd rather pour on the coal and put her bow in the trees; a rocky beach is better to walk home on than this crooked piece of water.

For three long hours we jogged in that lonely spot, barely making a yard. Only at very last light did the push of the tide ease up, the seas lay down. In the black, with seas breaking on the reefs on both sides of the entrance, our radar guided us into the furthest corner of Foggy Bay, Alaska. Our dog went up to the bow as dogs will, to sniff out a new place, and we found the rum and sat for a moment before cleaning up the debris.

From *Alaska Blues, A Fisherman's Journal,* by Joe Upton, Alaska Northwest Books, 1975

ALASKA HISTORY TIMELINE

30,000 BC - Migratory hunters move across land bridge from Asia, created by ice age.

8,000 BC - Ice age ends, migration slows.

1741 - Russian explorer Vitus Bering lands in Alaska, dies before returning, but sea otter furs they brought back start first resource boom. Russians quickly colonize much of Alaska.

1791-5 - British Navy Captain George Vancouver explores and names much of NW coast.

1799 - Capital of Russian Alaska is Sitka.

1867 - Secretary of State William Seward arranges purchase of Alaska from Russia and is rediculed for it; Alaska is nicknamed "Seward's Folly."

1896-1900 - Gold strike on a Yukon River tributary brings 100,000 prospectors and settlers.

1922 - Roy Jones makes first floatplane flight up the Inside Passage; bush travel changed forever.

1925 - A 674 mile dogsled relay brings diptheria vaccine to Nome, saves many.

1942 - Japan invades the Aleutian Islands; Alaska Highway begun to move supplies north.

1959 - Alaska becomes the 49th state.

1964 - Good Friday Earthquake

1968 - 10 billion barrels of oil are discovered at Prudhoe Bay on the Arctic coast.

1977 - First oil flows through an 800 mile engineering feat, The Alaska Pipeline.

1980 - Alaska National Interest Lands and Conservation Act (ANILCA) passed, establishing many parks and settling Native land claims.

1989 - Tanker *Exxon Valdez* rams Bligh Reef, Prince William Sound, creating a massive oil spill and years of work for hundreds of lawyers.

Reindeer, brought over from Siberia to alleviate winter hunger, thrived in Alaska. UW Nowell 38

The coast, like British Columbia, is deeply indented with inlets winding back into a mountainous and forbidding interior. The islands, large and small, form a maze of channels. In the northern part, glaciers lie at the head of most of the inlets discharging ice year round.

A vast part of the area is thickly forested, without settlements or towns, little changed since the arrival of white men. Almost all the land is owned by the Federal Government and little is available to individuals

There are a few towns, none large. Each has a few miles of roads, but for the most part, they aren't connected to each other and travel between is by boat or plane.

Scattered in little coves and harbors far from the towns are a few roadless fishing communities that still enjoy a quieter existence. Except for the storekeepers and the fish buyers, the residents mostly fish for salmon or host sports-fishermen. In summer they are scattered - from the bay in front to up and down the coast. Summer is a busy time - with boats from far

and near, hustling to make a year's pay in a few short months.

But then comes the fall - the outside boats straggle back to Washington State, and by the first of November, the locals are pretty much tied up for the winter. The days get short, the sun disappears between thick clouds. Weeks might pass with only the mail boat or a float-plane setting down to break the monotony.

Despite the short days and the gloomy weather, many of the local residents prefer the winter. Salmon season is a rush, and winter can be a welcome change, with time to work on cabin or boat, visit with neighbors, or just sit and read. It's not a fast paced life, but there's enough to do to just keep going. Many of the residents have spent time in the larger towns and wouldn't think of moving back.

Top: view from path above Mt. Roberts tram station, looking south down Gastineau Channel.

"Southeast Alaska is the closest you can get to actually living underwater."

- Ray Troll, Ketchikan

In Southeast Alaska, the size of some small states, thousands of islands are divided by tide swept channels. To the east the border runs along the highest peaks of the coastal range; to the west the North Pacific Ocean beats on a rugged coast with just a single town: Sitka.

The land is not friendly. The forest starts right at the water's edge and is almost impenetrable. In the roadless communities residents often find it easier to take an outboard skiff over to a neighbors just a hundred yards away rather than brave the spiny devils club and thick undergrowth in the forest.

In summer, the days are long, sunlight often until ten or eleven at night near the June summer solstice. People stay up, working or fishing, 16, 18, 20 hours a day. But then comes the long winter with the sun over the mountain at 3 in the afternoon, not to reappear until 9 or so the following morning. And those are the hard days.

But even from the earliest days, it was a land that drew hardy people: fishermen, trappers, loggers, cannery workers, tugboaters, card sharks. And drinkers.

In the early days, most everyone made their living

Top: the snowy mountains of Baranof Island loom above Chatham Strait.

Above: friends and big halibut, Point Baker, 1975.

Top: Young homesteader and his cabin, Port Protection, 1973. This Chicago school teacher came up to Alaska, worked for a bit as a logger, then built this cabin for his family and settled into a new life as a commercial fisherman.

Above: hunting and gathering is still an active lifestyle here. Deer hunting trips to remote islands are a regular part of life. UW Thwaites 0098-1

with their hands. As much as anything perhaps, this is what appealed to a certain type of people from 'down south,' or the 'lower 48.' That here was a land where if you were strong, and you worked hard, you could make your place. Single men, with perhaps not much to recommend them except for maybe a certain bullheaded strength would say goodbye to friends and family and 'head up North.' Then maybe a few years later they'd stop back home again, obviously a modest success from their labors 'up North,' and maybe looking for a bride, for as The North had many things in abundance that might attract a man, like fish and trees and land, women were not among them.

For much of the 20th century, the economy of Southeast Alaska had three elements - fishing, logging, and tourism. It was a good mix, with the mills providing a good base of employment in the wintertime when fishing was pretty much over until spring. Then in summer all the towns would boom as seasonal workers for the canneries and fish boats rolled in for the fishing season. Starting in the 1970s, when the Japanese economy entered the high growth mode, prices paid to Alaska fishermen rose, sometimes even weekly. Fishermen had new boats built and shiny new pickups rolled around town.

Then the 1980s and early 1990s brought sort of a double whammy. After many years of allowing logging practices that were damaging salmon streams and fish production, the Forest Service drew up stricter rules and the big mills at Sitka and Ketchikan closed. Then the Japanese economy took a big tumble, taking fish prices down with them, and fishermen and processors quickly reigned in their spending.

Today in most of the coastal towns that a cruise passenger might see, tourism is pretty much the biggest game in town, (except for the capital, Juneau, with its many government jobs) and many residents hope for the return of the days when their economy was more balanced.

Top: Peril Strait, north of Sitka. The tide runs so strongly here that it sometimes sucks the big Coast Guard buoys underwater. The Alaska ferry *Le Conte* hit a rock here and came close to sinking in 2004; human error....

Above: the new economy - a big cruise ship tied up in downtown Ketchikan. A few years earlier, one of the big ships actually knocked off part of the Tongass Trading Company!

Herring skiff at **Kah Shakes Cove, Mile 625.** "Hurry up and wait" is the motto in the herring business—often the fleet will arrive in late March and wait for several weeks while the herring roe or eggs ripens or matures. Then, with spotter planes buzzing around the 'fishing period'—often as short as 12 hours—starts and hundreds of these strange craft set their gillnets for the wily herring.

Above: herring fly aboard in a gillnet, where they are quickly shaken out.

There aren't any duty free shops clustered around this border: it's a lonely, windy spot, exposed to the wind, wracked by tidal currents. The prudent mariner hurries across. Look for the high ridge of snow-covered peaks to the east. They effectively seal off Southeast Alaska from any land connection, except in the very north at Haines and Skagway, and tiny Hyder, pop. 100, far up Portland Canal. Fortunately the larger (population 500) town of Stewart, B.C. is just two miles away and residents can share shops and services. The 2001 movie, Insomnia, was filmed near here.

Study the map carefully here. This entire area, with many winding inlets that all had to be explored, was very difficult for Vancouver and his men.

In the 1920 and 30s, there were several canneries in this area, at **Hidden Inlet** and **Nakat Inlet**, east of **Mile 600**. Today the old canneries have mostly disappeared into the forest, just leaving old pilings and rusty machinery on the shore, and the whole area is essentially wilderness, all part of the **Misty Fiords National Monument.**

Look for salmon gill-netters, typically fishing Sunday noon through Wednesday noon. If the weather is calm, you may also see fish packers (they're larger) making their rounds among the fleet, buying fish. Many vessels remain the summer here, remote from any town or cannery, getting water, groceries, fuel, and supplies from the tenders, or fish packers, that service the fleet.

Just a decade or so ago, fishermen would just throw

their fish into their dry fish hold and deliver them at the end of the day. Today all Alaska salmon processors are working hard to improve the quality of their fish, and encourage their fishermen to ice their fish. To this end, a barge with a generator and an ice-making machine is usually anchored in **Foggy Bay, Mile 622**, to serve the fishermen in this area.

The salmon fishery in Alaska is huge - each season more than 3,000 salmon fishing boats work the vast Alaska coast. Many come up from the Puget Sound area as there actually aren't enough fishermen in Alaska to catch all the salmon. Some of these fishermen leave home with cases of jars of fruit and vegetables that their families have put up for them from the garden at home. With a typical fishing period of just three or four days a week, there's plenty of time on the weekends. Crab and salmon are so abundant here, that some fishermen will set up little processing operations aboard their boats and refill the same jars with crab and salmon to be consumed all winter!

Top: gillnetters and their nets, near **Tree Point Lighthouse, Mile 608.**

Above: my wife, Mary Lou, and Ethel Hamar, a Haida native, look over garnets they picked off the rocks near Garnet Point.

ORCA TALES

One summer when my wife and I were running a fish buying boat on the Garnet Point run, we had an afternoon to explore and anchored our big 70 footer just east of the **Lord Islands, mile 602,** and motored ashore in the skiff.

Possibly we were the only human visitors in decades - the islands were remote and tiny and there were far more sheltered anchorages just a few miles away.

And so wild! The trees were bent and sculpted by the winter storms, the underbrush thick as a wall, but with exquisite tiny beaches on the west side, hemmed in on both sides by rock bluffs. My wife and I could tell at once that it might be a good place to look for the highly sought after glass balls - old Japanese net floats. We started onto the beach then stopped, not wanting to disturb the two obviously very young seal pups sunning just above the surf line.

Then as we watched, stunned, a big orca surfed in on a wave, headed like an arrow for the pups. He snatched one up with a single snap of his big jaws, as the other quickly wriggled further up the beach. Then, when the next big sea washed around him, the orca wriggled back into the water and disappeared. And all probably in less than 30 seconds. Our mouths hung open; we were amazed.

KETCHIKAN

OOSTERDAM
ROTTERDAM

Visitor to child: "How long has it been raining?"
Child: "I don't know. I'm only four."

Don't be fooled by the restaurants and jewelry boutiques along the waterfront here; until relatively recently, this was a full on rough and tumble logging and commercial fishing town. Right where the cruise ships now tie up used to be a big sawmill and a three story smoky sawdust burner, and canneries, cold storages, and fish processors lined the waterfront. Fishing boats, headed up to Alaska from the lower 48, and bound for other parts of the remote Alaska coast would always stop here to let the crew wet their whistles. And the next morning the skipper would just hope that they all made it back aboard.

Saturday nights in those days were particularly rough. Out in the channel floatplanes would start to land, big twin-engine Grumman Geese, and the slow, lumbering Stinsons, bringing in loggers from Prince of Wales Island and Tsimshian Indians from the village of Metlakatla. Then the fishing boats - big seiners and tenders - would start to arrive from the outer districts, the crews with a few bucks in their ass pockets, ready for a big night, drinking and carousing at Dolly Arthur's and the other

Top: downtown - at heart a fishing town, many residents look out over the activity in Tongass Narrows.
Above: at the Logging Show.

87

brothels along the boardwalk at Creek Street, known as the only place in Alaska where the fish and the fishermen both came to spawn.

The first whites arrived in the 1870 to salt salmon, Next, as the technology to put fish in cans was developed, the first of many canneries were established. In the early days of the salmon fishery, almost all fish were caught by floating fish traps—elaborate mazes of logs and netting, either anchored to the bottom or hung from thick pilings, and placed along the routes of migrating salmon. The canneries and the fish traps were mostly owned by big fish companies from Seattle. This out of state ownership caused deep resentment among many Alaskans and was one of the key factors in the push for Alaska statehood that was finally achieved in 1958.

Of course, the entrepreneurial spirit flows strongly in Alaskans, and so Alaskan fishermen made it a point of honor to steal as many fish from the traps as they could. When one new cannery, that eventually grew into one of the largest salmon companies in Alaska with many canneries, started up, observers at the time noted that they had neither seine boats—another way of catching salmon—nor owned any fish traps, but somehow had plenty of fish to can: all reportedly stolen from the fish traps of the Seattle owned companies.

The history of Ketchikan is deeply inter-

Ketchikan and Sitka are probably the best places if you want to try and catch a salmon. DK photo

twined with the three major native tribes of the region, the Tlingits, Haidas, and Tsimshians. Natives traditionally fished commercially and worked in the canneries as well as the sawmills. When the whites arrived, there were numerous native villages throughout the area, but over time some of these settlements were depopulated primarily because of the diseases that the first whites brought to the area.

Big industry came to town around 1950, in the shape of the big pulpmill out at Wards Cove, eight miles north of downtown.

Conceived as a way to utilize some of the vast spruce and hemlock forests of the region, and generate good paying, year round jobs (most fish and fish processing jobs were seasonal) the mill got a sweet deal from the U.S. Forest Service, and quickly became the largest employer in town.

But by the 1960s and 70s, salmon fishermen began to complain that logging practices like driving bulldozers down the middle of salmon streams and indiscriminate clear cutting were reducing the salmon runs on which they depended. The mill operators wanted to cut when and how they pleased, were backed up by the Forest Service, and for years there was ill feeling between these two factions in town.

Eventually the pendulum swung the other way: the Forest Service made stricter salmon protections and the mill closed.

A few years after the mill closed, salmon prices took a big tumble as well when the economy of Japan, our largest seafood customer, hit the skids. This hit the coastal communities, where there was little work except for fishing and processing, very hard.

About the same time, the cruise industry was beginning a major expansion, building much larger ships, and building lodges and infrastructure to transport, entertain, and house their passengers after they left the ships. Within a few years major changes came to Ketchikan, Skagway, and Juneau, the major cruise ports, as entrepreneurs created new excursions to offer the many new visitors off the ships, as well as new shops. The rapid growth was not without its blemishes as Caribbean based chain jewelry stores began to drive smaller, local stores out of business. Additionally, the downtown shopping areas on the main streets that used to be primarily focused on services and products for locals became primarily oriented to visitors. These stores would close up quickly after the last ships of the season, leaving deserted streets with window after window, covered over with plywood for the winter.

Over time, many residents hope that economy that is more balanced between tourism, fishing, and timber will return to the region.

Top: the new and the old; a salmon tender - that takes fish from fishing boats in remote areas to processing plants, and a Celebrity cruise ship.

Bottom: excursions in all these coastal towns come in many flavors. You might even ask a cabbie where you could see a bear, and find yourself at the dump!

The good thing about all the major towns in Southeast Alaska is that they're small and the ships usually tie up or lighter passengers ashore right in downtown.

In Ketchikan, there's plenty to see on foot within a few blocks of the ship, and lots of variety if you want to walk a little further, as well as regular city buses if your feet get too tired to walk back!

The big **Southeast Alaska Discovery Center** downtown has excellent historical exhibits, a bookstore, coffee shop, and theatre showing a free regular feature on native culture. Adjacent is **The Great Alaska Lumberjack Show**, highlighting loggers competing in axe work, tree climbing, etc.

Another block or so of walking takes you to **Creek St.**, the old red light district, today transformed into one of the more unique and eclectic shopping and eating areas of Alaska. The creek was handy - in prohibition days, bootleggers would slink up in the black of the night at high tide, paddle under the establishments, give the secret knock, and trapdoors would open and eager hands change cash for booze. A short walk to the north is the **Tongass Historical Society,** and to the east the **Totem Heritage Center.**

A really nice two mile walk, one way, is along the waterfront to the south past cannery row and the Coast Guard Station to **Saxman,** a native village with an excellent collection of totem poles, a clan lodge with the Cape Fox Dancers performing when the ships are in, as well as a carving shed. Of the three totem pole collections around Ketchikan, I like Saxman the best, because it is in an actual native village, and one gets a true sense of the struggle to make it in a fishing and logging economy.

Also the walk along the shore is a great place to look for bald eagles and see how many of the waterfront places have a plane in their backyard. There is a city bus that stops at the bottom of the hill at Saxman - schedule and fare posted inside the little tribal museum on the right just up the hill - if you want to rest your feet on the way back. If you are up for a longer walk, consider the trip up to **Deer Mountain Trail**, entrance near Creek St.

Back in town a good place to catch some lunch is the **Westmark Cape Fox Lodge** - take the tramway that operates from Creek Street.

On a bluff just south of downtown, the dining room offers a dramatic vista of the busy waterways and islands in front of town. At sea level just south of Creek St, is the unpretentious **New York Hotel and Cafe**, looking out on the boat harbor and the cruise ships beyond.

Most of the galleries and gift shops are located between the tunnel on Front Street, and Creek St. If you walk along the waterfront to the north past the tunnel, you'll find plenty of authentic Alaska to look at, especially along the water side.

Take some time to look around at the boats in the small boat harbors on both sides of the downtown docks where the cruise ships tie up. On most of the US coasts, boats this size - 40' and under - would be mostly be used for day fishing, the crews returning home at night to sleep in their own beds. But in Alaska with the fishing grounds often many hours from the nearest town, these boats are homes for their crews - often couples, sometimes with young children, for months at a time.

Top: totem and lodge at Saxman, 2 miles south of downtown Ketchikan. Right: carver Nathan Jackson works on a totem in the carving shed at Saxman Village.

Opposite page: inside the Southeast Alaska Discovery Center a display of a native village circa 1800, with salmon fillets inside a smoker and on a drying rack outside.

ANNAH C

Top: fish packer or tender loading salmon from a fish trap, to be delivered to a cannery in Ketchikan. Tongass Historical Society

Above: pile driver scow abandoned in a slough near Waterfall Resort, which was previously a major cannery. The crews lived aboard the scow while they drove pilings for fish traps.

If there were one burr under Alaskan's saddles, spurring the push for statehood, it was the fish traps. Made of netting and hung from big log frames or from pilings, the traps caught migrating salmon. Alaskans deeply resented that the traps and canneries were mostly owned by distant Seattle companies.

Each trap had a watchman, often a tough, hard bitten Alaskan, but occasionally a green college kid. The fish pirates would approach the fish traps at night and threaten or, more commonly, pay off the watchman, and make off with a load of fish. Few Alaskans frowned on this, feeling that the Seattle-owned canneries were stealing their resource to start with.

"The cannery told me to keep that kerosene lamp burning in the shack all night long, so it would look like I was awake; that sometimes kept fish pirates away. But that if push came to shove, they told me that it was better to let them have what they wanted instead of getting shot."
- Fish trap watchman.

Another way to steal fish was called "crick robbing" – the practice of fishing in closed areas, particularly the mouths of streams, where salmon often congregate by the thousands. To deter such robbing, "fish cops" patrol in boats and floatplanes, and college students are often hired to camp on major salmon streams, count the fish going up, and deter creek robbers by their presence.

Actually, all of the lower southeast mainland and islands of Southeast Alaska are part of the **Misty Fiords National Monument,** essentially a vast wilderness, with few visitors except in the summer.

Excursions to Misty are available both by boat and plane. The most frequently visited spots, like Rudyerd Bay to the right, are about a five hour round trip. These trips are extremely popular, so consider booking early.

The other option is to visit Misty by floatplane. When the visibility is good, the view from a seaplane above Misty can be truly spectacular.

Misty is busy in the summer with planes, kayakers, and tour boats, but in the winter, it's pretty much deserted except for two or three boats that fish the deep inlets and fiords for crab, shrimp, and halibut. Imagine what a week's trip in that awesome country would be like for them, probably without seeing another boat the whole time.

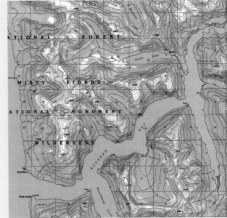

Top: anchored near the head of Rudyerd Bay in Misty Fiords, a guide on the *Wilderness Adventurer* gives some kayaking tips.

Above: a topographical map shows the winding nature of the heart of Misty Fiords.

Top: over the entrance to Rudyerd Bay in the heart of Misty Fjords National Monument.

Lower: Punchbowl Cove, a particularly steep-sided part of Rudyerd Bay.

On a recent June morning, a friend picked me up at Ketchikan's New York Hotel at 4:30 a.m. for a flight over to Misty Fiords before the ships came in and the air got crowded. Perhaps because my friend had been an ER doctor in Ketchikan for more than a decade, he gave me a more detailed emergency briefing than any other floatplane pilot I'd traveled with. More than anything else, he focused on what to do if the plane flipped in a rough landing:

"First, you'll probably break at least one arm, so practice opening your seat belt and the door with your other hand... Remember the floats will be over your head, so don't hit them when you swim to the surface." Next, he had me practice with both hands turning around and getting the emergency air bottle out of the seat pocket behind me, good for 5 minutes of breathing. Then he showed me how to push the button on the GPS emergency beacon, and repeated that my job was to get out, not to save him.

A few minutes later it was throttle up and we were rattling over the short harbor chop as we lifted off.

Will I catch a fish? At each cruise port excursions offer opportunities to go out into the salt water after the wily salmon. Typically the boats are modern, comfortable cruisers with heated cabins, toilets, and able to take parties of up to six. Depending on the season and where the "bite" is, vessels may run an hour or more to get to the fish.

Most sports fishermen here like to target king and silver salmon. Kings, running up to 60 pounds and larger, (if you catch a king over 50 pounds, it is a big event...) are generally caught from May through August with the best fishing generally in the first half of the season. Silvers run smaller, typically 6 to 12 pounds, and are available mid-June through September. Pink salmon, much smaller and less desirable to the sportsman are primarily caught by net and canned.

If you're not experienced, don't worry, there are a lot of fish in Alaska, and charter skippers are quick teachers.

But remember, it's not all about the fish—as much as anything else, going out on a charter boat for a day is an opportunity to get out close and see, up close and personal, some of the most abundant marine life and most dramatic scenery you will find anywhere. Whales, dolphins and eagles are all common sights for the charter fishermen so bring your camera.

What to do with your fish? In all towns, services are available to freeze, smoke, store, and ship your fish.

Top: trolling skiff towing lures for silvers or cohoes.

Above: "June Hog," a large Columbia River King salmon, frequently caught in Alaska until Depression Era dams were built. CRMM

Top: The ex-king crabber *Aleutian Ballad* offers visitors and Deadliest Catch fans a taste of commercial fishing for king crab... without the terrible weather!

Above: want to see bears? The Neets Bay excursion might be a good choice, or.. ask a taxi driver. He might take you to bears feeding at a salmon stream.. or ... maybe.. the dump!

Just a sample - changes annually.
Misty Fjords - by air or sea, or a combination.
Bering Sea Fishermen's Tour (on vessel above)
Coastal Wildlife Cruise
Wilderness Exploration and Crab Feast
Sea Kayaking
Rainforest Wildlife Sanctuary Hike
Neets Bay Bear Watch and Seaplane Flight
Rainforest Ropes Course and Zipline Park
Bear Creek Zipline
Adventure Kart Expedition
Back Country Zodiak Expedition - U Drive
Flightseeing and Crab Feast
Totem Bight Park and Town Tour
Totem Bight and Lumberjack Show Combo
Saxman Native Village tour
Town and Harbor Duck Tour
Motorcycle Tour (as driver
Sportsfishing Expedition
Sportsfishing & Wilderness Dining (of your catch!)
Alaskan Chef's Table
City Highlights Trolley Tour
Mountain Point Snorkeling Adventure
And, as they say, many more.....

Important note: if the tours available through your cruise line or ship are sold out, often similar tours will be available on the dock near the ship.

1 **"It's not too bad,"** the manager at the logging camp radioed the pilot of the Beaver floatplane, "you guys have come out here in worse stuff than this."

But it was - gusty winds and violent rain squalls make it very difficult to land safely, unload the freight and load the full load of anxious passengers.

2. To Harris Lake Pass - arrive after 40 minutes of tense flying in the few dozen feet between the trees and the low clouds, the big Beaver getting tossed violently by gusty winds. Pass blocked by low clouds.

3. Trocadero Pass - solid clouds at 300 feet make the pass too dangerous to attempt. Passengers occasionally vomiting. Pilot beginning to worry about having enough fuel.

4. Harris Lake Pass - back for another look at this pass, usually the easiest way to get across the relatively low mountains on Prince of Wales Island, but still the clouds press too low to the ground.

5. Attempt the unnamed pass at the head of Big Salt Lake, but blocked by clouds and fog. Passenger in seat next to pilot leans over to say, "I can't take too much more of this." Pilot thinking he'll have to land at native village of Klawok to spend the night.

6. Trying Harris Lake Pass one last time before giving up, pilot finds clouds have lifted just.... enough to tease him into trying it. But then clouds closed in suddenly and plane had to be quickly turned around. Halfway through the turn, pilot spots the water of Kassan Inlet, dives into the hole, and is through the Pass and safely over the water again; Ketchikan just 15 minutes away.

Adapted from Chapter 1 of *Seaplanes Along The Inside Passage*, by Gerry Bruder.

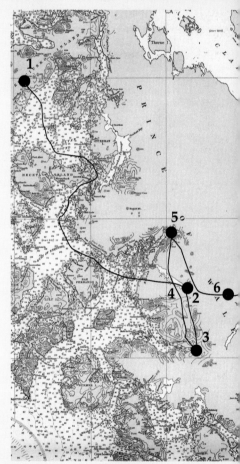

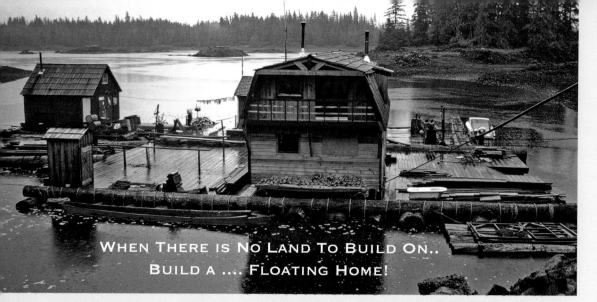

WHEN THERE IS NO LAND TO BUILD ON..
BUILD A .... FLOATING HOME!

AND IF YOU FIND SOME LAND, JUST DRAG IT ASHORE!

Top: a floathome in **Coffman Cove**, west of **Mile 705** in 1982. Note the traditional dugout canoe (red hull, lower left). The mother of this family was a Haida Alaska native and wanted her family to experience some of her culture so they built this canoe in the traditional way. Her children used the cedar canoe to commute to school at the logging camp across the Cove.

As they got older, they probably would have really liked to have had a nice fast aluminum Lund skiff, like other kids around the Cove!

Above: Eventually some nearby land became available and the family bought a hilltop lot, beached the float, hired a bulldozer to drag their home off the float and up to its new home overlooking the cove where it used to float!

The ironic thing about this coast is this: all that gorgeous waterfront land.. and (hardly) any that you can buy! Basically most of the land is owned by the State of Alaska or Federal Government.

But for this entrepreneurial Alaskan couple, that wasn't a problem. They found a sheltered cove that they liked - near a logging camp where there was a school for their children and possible work as well.

In those days the big plywood mill at Sitka and the pulp mill in Ketchikan were going full blast so there was a steady traffic of floating log rafts getting towed up and down nearby Clarence Strait. On occasion the rafts would break up in a storm or a bundle of logs would escape in rough weather. The result was that the shores were littered in places with big spruce, cedar, and hemlock logs. So, after getting a permit from the Forest Service to get the logs, this couple started pulling the logs off the beach - a big job in itself - these logs are typically sixty feet long, three or four feet in diameter, and weigh several tons.

Next was assembling the logs into a raft and building a small platform to support a portable sawmill to start sawing the logs into planks. Next they planked over the whole raft - another big job as you can see how big the raft is - and started building their house!

Now living in a floating home is different from living in a regular home. For instance, while this family was building the big house, they lived in the very small one on the left. And with two young and rambunctious boys, sometimes on rainy days, the mom, needing a little quiet time for herself, would send the boys out to fish, in the outhouse.

North of Ketchikan you'll pass out into Clarence Strait. To the west the big land mass is Prince of Wales Island, actually the third largest in the US. POW, as it is called locally, was pretty much ground zero for a huge logging effort starting in the 1950s. Actually, it was logging practices on POW, damaging salmon streams that essentially were the cause of the new regulations that led to the closing of the Ketchikan pulp mill at Wards Cove in the 1980s.

Today, some logging still continues, but to a much lesser degree with some of the logs being shipped to Puget Sound, and others to small local sawmills.

In a sense Prince of Wales is making the transition to the new Alaska economy - more based on recreation than commercial fishing and logging. 25 years ago Craig, on the west coast of the island, was a rough Native town where commercial fishing was pretty much the main economic activity. Today Craig features a number of sport-fishing lodges and has a surprising amount of second home construction. Much of this has been spurred by the paving of old logging roads and daily ferry service from Ketchikan to Hollis, on the east coast of Prince of Wales Island.

If you see some small fishing skiffs around **Mile 686**, they'll be from **Meyers Chuck**, one of a handful of roadless fishing communities scattered throughout the region.

Top: **Cape Decision Lighthouse** at **Mile 775** is at the south end of Kuiu Island, 60 miles long, with a population of around a dozen. In the distance is Cape Ommaney, the south end of Baranof Island.

Bottom: boat work at Sitka. Throughout coastal Alaska fishing, both sports and commercial fishing produce a significant portion of total revenue.

Passengers up on the bow of the *Sapphire Princess* look for spouts marking the location of whales as they approach Snow Passage, about four hours after leaving Ketchikan.

At **Mile 722**, about three hours after leaving Ketchikan, your ship will transit narrow **Snow Passage.** The constricted channel often creates tide rips that will bunch herring together and attract humpback whales. Get your binoculars and go out on deck, preferably up near the bow where you can see both sides of the channel. Most ships carry a naturalist and in addition most captains are alerted to the possibility of whales here, so the presence of whales is likely to be announced. But different ships have different protocols. If there are passenger activities, and there's just a single whale blowing occasionally, it might not be announced.

If you're really fortunate and have strong binoculars, you may be able to observe bubble net feeding, a method used by humpback whales to herd fish into compact, easy-to-eat schools. The whales circle beneath the herring, exhaling slowly. The circle of bubbles serves to contain or herd the fish, and the humpbacks then surface in the middle, with their mouths open.

Whales, like humans, are mammals, air breathers. After a period underwater, the must surface to breathe. As they do this, they blow out a spout of water vapor that may be easily seen, making whales easy to spot from several miles away.

The buoy, on the right side of the ship (northbound) in the narrowest part of the passage, at **Mile 722** is a favorite hangout for big sea lions. These guys, weighing up a ton apiece jump up onto the buoy to sun themselves!

Top: gillnetters working on their nets
inside protected Wangell Harbor. The
Stikeen supports a number of salmon
runs.

Bottom: ready for the Stikine: floatplane and kayaks in Wrangell Harbor.

Off the beaten path, about 25 miles southwest of
Petersburg, Wrangell's history stems from its
position at the mouth of the Stikine River.
This small town was the busiest spot in Alaska when
the hordes bound for the Stikine and Cassiar gold rushes
poured through in 1861 and 1873, bound up the Stikine,
the natural route into the interior. But when the rushes
were over, Wrangell settled back down into a small fishing and logging community, with many Chinese coming
to work in the canneries and the first sawmill constructed
in 1888.

But it is still the river that is the biggest draw. It is on
the main migratory route north for many species. April is
especially dramatic, when 1500 plus bald eagles congregate to feed on the hooligan (a small oily fish) run, and
8-10,000 snow geese pass through on their way north
to nest in the grassy tundra of western Alaska. The 160
miles of river between Wrangell and Telegraph Creek,
Canada, are especially dramatic, and raft, floatplane,
or jetboats are a great way to explore. Another visitor
option is a boat trip to the **Anan Creek Bear Observatory**, about 30 miles south. When the fish are running, the
bear are waiting for them and it's an impressive sight.
Short on time? Consider a floatplane trip and ask the
pilot to swing over Petersburg, Wrangell narrows, and
LeConte Glacier. Wrangell was hit especially hard when
the Alaska Pulp Corporation sawmill, the town's largest
employer, closed in 1994. Unlike Ketchikan and Sitka,

Top: Chief Shakes tribal house on Shakes Island, walking distance from downtown.

Bottom: "Deadliest Catch" King Crab... in.. Wrangell? Yes.. see text on right!

that also had big mills that closed, Wrangell did not have a strong visitor and tourism industry to fall back on. So when Wrangell Seafoods failed a decade or so later, it was an especially hard blow. Fortunately, Alaska's biggest seafood company, Trident, bought the plant and made major upgrades. Around the same time the town began cleaning up the old sawmill site, purchased the largest boat lift in SE Alaska and redeveloped the site as a major boatyard. It was a big hit and the town has high hopes that over time, it will be a major part of the local economy.

Southeast Alaska also has a king crab season, albeit a short one. I found a 58-footer unloading crab in June directly into big plastic lined cardboard boxes, rather than going into the adjacent processing plant, which struck me as odd. But then that evening, as I was getting into the Alaska Airlines 'combi' - a 737-400 fitted out with cargo hatch/pallet tracks forward and passenger cabin aft, I saw the big boxes of live king crab being loaded as well. The entire catch was being flown live to Seattle, where they would be put into a live tank in some restaurant!

Around Town:
Klondike Bikes - 907-874-2453
Sunrise Aviation - 800-874-2319
Star Cab - 907-874-3622
Alaska Charter & Travel - 888-993-2750
Fish Wrangell - 907-874-2590
Breakaway Adventures - 888-385-2488
Muskeag Meadows Golf - 907-874-4653

Stikine Inn - 888-874-3388
Wrangell Hostel - 907-874-3534
Sourdough Lodge - 800-874-3613
Places to eat:
For the view: Stikine Inn
Where the locals eat: Diamond C Cafe
For more: www.wrangell.com

Once a twisting, shallow slough, **Wrangell Narrows**, N. of **Mile 730** was in such an convenient place as a shortcut—saving 70 miles off the trip between Ketchikan and Juneau—that eventually the waterway was dredged, widened, and marked with 60 markers and buoys.

Even so, it is still a considerable challenge at night or in fog. The problem is that the region's big tides—the water level rising or falling as much as 23 feet in six hours—create very strong currents.

In the fog and in the black the prudent mariner is best served by anchoring up off the south entrance, or tieing up to the docks in Petersburg to wait better conditions. But canneries want their fish and ferries have schedules, and sometimes they meet in the middle of the Narrows:

"I hate to go through them Narrows in the black and the fog, but the cannery wanted the fish, so we had to go. Then right in the narrowest place, the radio blasts in my ear: 'This is the Alaska ferry *Matanuska*, southbound at marker 16. Northbound traffic please advise.' The *Matanuska*? Just a mile ahead, and him with the tide pushing him on? I called him right back, and mister, I could hear the tension in that man's voice:

'*Matanuska* back. Yeah... I see you on my radar... but you'd better pull over and let us by... it's pretty damn tight here.'

"We were right below Burnt Island Reef, and I could see his target on the radar getting bigger and bigger all the time. So I just slowed down and pulled over into the shallows. I'd rather put 'er ashore on a mud bank than get T-boned by a 400-foot ferry!

"I slowed right down until I was just idling into the current, and looked out into the black, trying to see him. You know how it is with that radar: when something gets really close, it just disappears into the sea clutter in the middle of the screen and you can't really tell exactly where it is. Well, the ferry did that and I was just bracing myself to hit either the shore or him, when I saw him—just a glimpse of a row of portholes rushing by fast in the night, the big tide pushing him on, and then he was gone. Man, I don't know how them fellows do it, but I know I wouldn't have liked to been him that night."

—An Alaskan tender skipper

AFOGNA

Top: the Petersburg waterfront is a busy place when the salmon are running. Here the fish buying vessel *Afognak* unloads plastic totes of iced fish, while a seiner waits its turn out in Wrangell Narrows.

Below: fresh Alaska spot prawns just out of a shrimp pot.

If you are on an Alaska ferry or a small cruise ship, chances are you'll travel through Wrangell Narrows to Petersburg. Set in one of the most dramatic landscapes in the region with **10,000' Kates Needle** rising spectacularly behind, the town is known as Little Norway for its original descendants, who settled here after coming from the old country.

With strong shrimp, salmon, crab, and halibut resources close at hand and icebergs very conveniently drifting right into the boat harbor from **nearby Le Conte Glacier,** it was a commercial fisherman's dream. Eventually, three salmon canneries, a shrimp processor, and a cold storage plant served the needs of its fishermen.

Until about 1985, the Petersburg fishermen mostly worked the nearby waters of Southeast Alaska. With markets for Alaska seafood expanding with the robust Japanese economy, Petersburg fishermen and a locally owned cannery, Icicle Seafoods, made a major expansion into fisheries in the remote areas of western Alaska, particularly the Bering Sea and Bristol Bay.

When many seafood markets weakened in the 1990s with the major slump in the Japanese economy, Petersburg fishing companies were mostly able to survive, while some others in Wrangell, Ketchikan, and Juneau had to close their doors.

Today, while tourism plays a huge part in the economy of most towns in the region, here it is conspicuously

absent. The harbor isn't large enough for the big ships, and candidly, the town fathers prefer to concentrate on what they know best: fishing. Nevertheless, small cruise ships—100 passengers and less—often stop here, as does the Alaska ferry.

If you do visit, stop by the harbormaster's office, just off main street, with canneries on either side. There you can pick up a town map, etc.

Two big events are the **Little Norway Festival** celebrating Norwegian Independence Day in mid May, where traditional costumes and crafts are in evidence, and Fourth of July, a bit more raucous, as the fishing fleet is usually in town.

Hammer Slough is close by with the **Sons of Norway Hall** and **Sing Yee Alley**, an excellent place for local crafts, and the **Clausen Museum** celebrating local commercial fishing.

A nice stroll is just along the waterfront, north out of town. On the right you'll see the homes fishermen and processors built overlooking Frederick Sound and the entrance to Wrangell Narrows. From their view homes it was a short walk down to either the boat harbor or 'cannery row.' Not a bad life.

Top: big money: workers sorting salmon roe or egg sacs. Once a cannery superintendant joked to me that he might have to get a guard to ride shotgun on the forklift when it was moving roe. Above: proud of his Norwegian heritage, a worker with a stack of salmon egg containers at a Petersburg fish processing plant.

105

Top: two salmon trollers head out for the morning bite in Sea Otter Sound.

Right: memorial plaques in a Petersburg waterfront park.

Above: spoons, or trolling lures.

Opposite page top: the big packer *Trailblazer* unloads one seiner while another waits their turn.

Opposite bottom: fish splash and struggle in a gillnet.

Ole Sjonning Husvik
1890 - 1961
"Ya, vi ha it god in America"

Ky Michael Thomassen
"Fishing is not a matter
of life or death, it is
more serious than that."

Steven D. Bergman
1959 - 1993
My glory was
I had such friends.

In the summertime, almost all the fishing vessels you will see will be engaged in some form of salmon fishing.

Purse seiners are typically 58' long, have a crew of four or five, and can be recognized by the net piled on the stern, a large power block at the end of the boom and a large skiff.

Gillnetters are smaller, usually 35-40' long, and are operated by one or two people. The net, a floating fence in the water with corks on top and leads on the bottom, is rolled on and off a large reel on the back deck.

Trollers are the boats with the two really tall poles, vertical for traveling and at 45 degrees for fishing. They tow a number of lines, attracting silver and king salmon with bait or lures.

Packer or tenders are support craft, often big steel boats, that purchase fish from smaller gillnetters and seiners, and transport them to processing plants in refrigerated sea water.

107

EMILY JANE

FRIGIDLAND

SECRETS OF THE
OLD TIME FISH BUYERS

Top: tenders or fish buying vessels un-loading salmon from smaller gillnetters in Chilkat Inlet, near Haines. The bigger boats also provide fuel, water, limited groceries, and maybe even an occasional shower for the gillnetter who may spend weeks without going into a town.

Above: secrets of the oldtime fish buyers: lower your whole grocery cart down to your boat instead of trying to carry bags down the ladder!

When the summer salmon fishing season is in full swing, the Petersburg waterfront is a busy place, with perhaps fifteen big tenders (fish buying vessels) and maybe 30 seiners, vying for dock space along with maybe 40 gillnetters. Plus, the tenders especially, are usually in town for less than 24 hours, so it behooves their crews to get as much done when the boat is actually alongside the dock, instead of trying to climb over three or four boats with your laundry, groceries, etc.

In 1981, my wife and I were running a big tender for the first time, and a gal on another tender filled us in on one of Petersburg's special attractions: the dock hoist. For in that small fishing town, the main grocery / clothing / hardware store was just down the street from the Icicle Seafoods cannery that we were working for. Each week, when we left the remote area where we were buying fish, our fishermen would give us their grocery lists, so we always had two or three shopping carts of groceries to get.

The trick, we quickly learned, was to buy all our groceries while we were tied alongside the dock for the hour or so that it took to pump our fish up from our refrigerated hold and into the cannery. We'd take our shopping carts right out of the store, down the street just a block, and into the cannery complex and out onto the dock hoist - a boom mounted winch - and then instead of taking the groceries down the ladder one bag at a time, we'd use the hoist to lower the whole full shopping cart right down to the boat!

LANDING THAT GREAT ALASKA FISHING JOB

Each spring hundreds of young men walk the docks of the fishing fleet spread out across Washington and Alaska. The crews are all busy - painting, overhauling their nets, repairing equipment.

The young walkers stop at each boat, waiting for an opporunity to speak to the skipper, to ask if they might need an extra hand for the season.

It is a frustrating exercise: the skippers are busy trying to get their boats ready and headed out for the season. The process can take days, even weeks, but those who persevere know that sometimes guys get sick, or don't show at the last moment.

And the word on the docks is this: many of the guys at the top of the industry, the skippers of hi-liners, the owners of fishing companies, started just like this: walking the docks. Looking for that summer full of adventure and even a bit of danger, with a big paycheck at the end.

I was one of those guys way back in '1965, 19 years old, walking the docks. It was a deeply discouraging time, but finally a tip led to my first Alaska fishing job.

It changed my life forever.

Top: A purse seiner lifts a bag of salmon over the rail. In a good year, a crewman on a top boat might earn $50,000 in a two month season. DK

Above: many women work aboard Alaska fishing boats.

EXPLORING:
LE CONTE BAY

In a little visited bay east of Petersburg the first glacier that actually makes it all the way down to the saltwater drops its ice.

Off the beaten path with a shallow bar blocking the entrance, only a few small ships ever venture this way. But for those who do, the reward is exquisite: ice in all shapes and hues of blue, ever changing.

Each fall filmmaker Dan Kowalski, and I would try to get in there for a few days. Get in the skiff with the cameras, try to capture the drama of the ice in that wild and lost spot. Sometimes there would be a sudden booming or splashing in the silence: a truck or house-sized berg falling into the water from the hidden glacier face.

One evening we wanted to stay, but couldn't find a place to drop our anchor where a berg wouldn't surprise us in the night. So we set out across the bay at dusk, with a big moon filling the bergs around us with this mysterious light as we dodged them in the last of the daylight.

Picked our way to the anchorage in the black, and shut the engine down. And as we ate, carrying all the way across the strait to us, again and again, the dull thunder of falling ice.

Top: morning off a tiny dot of an island, but secure and away from the ice! Above: picking our way through the bergs in the failing light.

THE GILLNETTER'S LIFE

Each spring 400-500 small (30'-45') gillnet vessels set out from Alaska and Puget Sound ports for the long salmon season in Alaska waters.

For the Seattle and Puget Sound based boats, it's long indeed. They leave home in early May if they want to start their season fishing for king salmom, often not returning until close to Halloween, depending on how bad the weather is coming down the coast. However, as these things go, it is a fairly relaxed fishery; often the boats are owned by a couple, perhaps even with children.

Fishing periods are tightly regulated, usually only Sunday noon through Wednesday noon. (Although it can be lengthened or shortened depending on salmon abundance.)

This allows the crews to have four days off between fishing periods (also called "openings"), perfect for exploring, setting out crab pots, or just relaxing. Most of the fishing areas are remote and distant from the nearest town. Many boats stay in the remote areas for the whole season, getting their groceries, fuel, water, etc. from the fish buyer that makes weekly round trips to town.

Top: my crew picking red salmon in Bristol Bay, western Alaska, our son on the right. Middle: picking, Sumner Strait, Mile 742. Bottom: often these vessels are operated by a husband and wife.

LIFE IN A ROADLESS COMMUNITY
POINT BAKER
MILE 742

Imagine: cheap waterfront land and good fishing close at hand. This was the situation at the remote and roadless communities of **Point Baker** and nearby **Port Protection** (south of **Mile 745**) in the early 1970s. A person could get an acre-sized waterfront lot on a sheltered cove, with the right to harvest a substantial amount of timber each year from the adjacent forest to use for lumber. So if you couldn't afford store-bought lumber, you could build your house from the nearby trees and make enough cash fishing salmon from a skiff to support a family.

A floating store/bar/fish-buyer at Point Baker served the needs of the hundred or so souls settled around these two coves on the edge of the vast woods. The mail and freight boat came once a week, supplemented by the occasional floatplane. Families with gill-netters or trollers tried to make a trip to town—Wrangell or Petersburg, each about 40 miles away, a long day's round trip—every few months to stock up on supplies a little cheaper.

Behind the shore was the forest—thick, almost impenetrable. For the most part walking was so difficult everyone traveled by outboard. At Point Baker, especially, one's traveling decisions were dictated by the tide. Have a whiskey warmup some snowy winter afternoon with your groceries at the store? Stay too late and the trip

Top: fisherman's homestead, Point Baker, 1972.

Above: Bob Anderson pulls the herring gillnet: fresh bait!

113

"Downtown"
Point Baker

Author's
Cabin

"Suburbs"

Top: Point Baker aerial view. We called
the cove by my cabin "Port Upton"

Above: typical small salmon trolling
skiff. Often powered by a small gas
engine ordered from the Sears catalog,
and towing two lines, a good fisherman
could make enough in four months to
carry him through the long winter.

home might be a nightmare: wading along the shallow
channel, towing your skiff behind you, lifting, scraping it
over the thin places, picking your way with the flashlight
through the snow, and hoping your batteries last until
you make it home.

In summer, the main activity was gillnetting and
trolling for salmon, and in the evenings the floats in the
two communities were crowded with boats from all up
and down the coast. Many of the 'outside' boats returned
every year with their friends, and the floats were a whole
little very congenial community.

With low costs for entering the fisheries before limited
entry (after 1972, Alaska initiated a limited entry salmon
license system) the area was particularly popular with
young folks fishing open skiffs or other small boats.
These folks would either live on their boats, set up camps
on the beach, or perhaps rehabilitate an abandoned cabin
for the summer.

Often booze, marijuana, and the like were mailed to
these remote communities. The mailboat usually arrived
Thursday night around midnight. So Friday meant that
folks you rarely saw might emerge from the woods or
arrive by skiff to pick up their stash and supplies!

AN ALASKAN RETIREMENT

My neighbor, Old Flea, was pretty much a fixture around Point Baker in the 1970s. "Been a baseball player down south..." one story had it, "was a handlogger back in the day..." All I really knew was that he had been a handtroller at Point Baker for as long as anyone could remember, that he lived in a tiny cabin on the back channel to Port Protection, and that he was a regular at our colorful floating bar.

A lot of young folks were coming to Port Protection and nearby Point Baker in those days. Hand trolling was an inexpensive way to enter commercial salmon fishing. The newcomers were mostly a long-haired bunch, shunned by the older, more conservative members of the community. But not Flea. He welcomed the new blood, became sort of The Patriarch of the hand troll fleet. And was so generous. He had his monthly Social Security check and his cabin was all paid for. Often, one or another of the young couples that came to Point Baker to fish would be down on their luck. It would be Flea that would take them in, take them fishing with him each day, show them the best places for the biggest king salmon, how to rig their gear. And until they got on their feet, give them his fish money.

He had a regular schedule. When the 'bite' was over for the day, he'd sell his fish - the bartender was also the fish buyer - and you'd see him headed home, beer in hand... Not a bad retirement at all.

Top: Flea and his hand trolling skiff, Point Baker, 1974. Chugging along with its Briggs & Stratton engine, Flea would head out every morning to catch the bite, just like clockwork, to return in mid afternoon to sell his fish at the Point Baker Bar and fish buying station.

Bottom: Flea and one of the many young friends he took out fishing with him.

115

BUILDING A HOME IN THE NORTH

When I arrived at **Point Baker, Mile 742** with my former wife on our 32-foot gillnetter in the spring of 1972, the flavor of the place was compelling. The older residents welcomed younger blood, and the salmon fishing in Sumner Strait was great. We found an island, on a private cove, with a gorgeous western exposure and view, for $17,000. After the season, in our houseboat on Seattle's Lake Union, we made plans for a cabin. But as our money dwindled, so did the size of our new-home-to-be until whatever roof we could get over our heads for $1,500 would have to be it. We settled on a 12-by-16-foot box with a half loft, 275-square-feet: tiny.

With tight-fisted determination, we scoured garage sales and discount building suppliers. At a second-hand store we found a big diesel oil range for $35; at another, all our windows and doors for $175. In my tiny floating shop I prefabbed a Formica kitchen counter top, complete with sink and drawers. We got plywood, nails, and shingles, all on deep discount, and purchased a 16-foot cedar skiff with a 10-horsepower 1958 Evinrude outboard. Tool by tool, fitting by fitting, we packed the supplies aboard my 32-foot gill-net vessel and skiff to tow north.

Shortly after arriving in Point Baker, the mail boat arrived with our pickup truck-sized bundle of lumber, The plan had been to tow the tightly strapped bundle of lumber through the narrow back channel to our seclud-

Our cabin. The water supply was rainwater from an old oak whiskey barrel. It tasted like a very light whiskey and water.

116

ed cove and house site. But it was so green and dense, it wouldn't even float. It was what was locally called "pond dried." So we had to set it temporarily on the dock and then haul it in our skiff, load by load to our island.

In the two weeks before the salmon season began we struggled: the wood was so wet it splashed when your hammer missed the nail. My one and only hand saw bent on the first beam we cut. It rained every day; every night we would take the skiff back to our boat at the Point Baker dock, heat up something quick, and fall, exhausted, shivering, into our sleeping bags.

And created something exquisite: out of every window was the water. As we ate at the driftwood table, we could see eagles swooping low over the cove. There were curious seals, and most marvelous of all, a pair of humpbacks that hung out in the tide rips by West Rock, off the mouth of our cove. On still nights, we could hear the sigh-like breathing of the whales as they surfaced and exchanged fresh air for stale.

We called our little cove Port Upton. We dragged big logs off the beach, got more lumber from town to build a big float to work on our nets. Just us and our friends in that wild and remote cove.

When the first snow came one November evening, the fire in the wood stove crackled cheerily, our kerosene lamp shone out on the vast and wild world beyond the windows.

It was magic.

Top: out the window.. Someone once told me that if you were a fisherman and could look out your window and see your boat, you were living your dream. We could and we were.

Middle: the float at Port Upton

Bottom: a humpback just outside our little protected cove.

JUNEAU NATIVE FESTIVAL 2010

119

Every two years the native tribes gather in Juneau to discuss issues of mutual concern, perform tribal dances, share experiences and generally celebrate their rich culture. Many of the activities are open to the public. The parade, seen here, is the largest public display of native culture and traditional costumes that you are liable to see anywhere!

"To pull the anchor in the pale predawn off another lifeless cannery and slip out into the empty strait, this is my bell, ringing, ringing."

— my fishing journal, 1974

Top: looking west from the native village of Kake, the snowy hills of Baranof Island loom over Chatham Strait.

Bottom: an old timer at Port Alexander, Mile 790, remembers the old days when the harbor was full of boats and fish buyers and that little settlement was the only light for many miles.

For much of the last century, **Chatham Strait,** which begins at **Mile 775** was a beehive of activity. Between the salmon, herring, and whaling plants, almost every bay in this canyon-like region was home to some sort of commercial activity, frenzied during the summer fishing season, and sleepy in winter, with usually just a caretaker and his family keeping a watch on things. Then the herring and the whales disappeared, and refrigerated tenders allowed consolidation of the salmon canneries into towns like Petersburg and Ketchikan.

For the small craft traveler today, it is almost spooky to travel in Chatham Strait, to anchor and go ashore and wander in the ruins, rarely encountering another traveler.

One of the few settlements remaining is **Port Alexander, Mile 792.** With a good harbor, fish buyer and a store, and good fishing at **Cape Ommaney**, it's a popular spot in summer. In its heyday, the 1920s and 1930s, it was Alaska with a capital A, as the *Maggie Murphy* boys noted:

"It became the number one trolling port in the territory, a wide-open, carefree, money-kissed little place."

—John Joseph Ryan, *The Maggie Murphy*

When they walked into town, they were halted by an elderly man who told them, "Boys, it's illegal to walk on

the streets of Port Alexander sober."

In those days, many trollers worked out of open boats, some without motors, rowing as they towed their lines through the water. A little tent city sprang up each summer. But by the late 1940s the party was over, the great runs rapidly diminishing as the newly-built dams on the Columbia River, 1,200 miles south, prevented the big kings from reaching their spawning grounds.

At **Port Conclusion**, **Mile 790**, three miles north of Port Alexander, in August, 1794, Captain Vancouver anxiously awaited the four overdue cutters and yawl boats that were filling in the last blank places on his chart. Finally the boats hove safely into sight during a rainstorm on the 19th.

Then with grog for all hands, and cheers ringing from ship to ship in a remote cove halfway around the world from England, there ended one of the most remarkable feats of navigation and exploration in modern times. In three summers of exploring and charting this unknown coast, through persistent fogs, swift currents and occasional thick ice— losing just one man to bad shellfish— Vancouver had disproved the ages-old notion of a Northwest Passage back to the Atlantic. In doing so, he charted, explored, described and named much of the Northwest coast. It was nothing less than a stunning achievement.

He was 38 years old.

Top: The old store at Killisnoo Island served the workers of a busy whaling plant.

Above: an old blower waits for workers who will never return.

123

Hidden in **Thomas Bay**, 20 miles northeast of Petersburg, lies **Baird Glacier**, slowly receding back into the mountains.

Wanting to see a glacier up close, the *Wilderness Adventurer*'s big inflatable skiffs dropped us off in the boulder strewn flats about half a mile from the ice. A short walk brought us to the terminal moraine, a ridge probably 50 feet high that showed where the glacier finally stopped its advance probably a few hundred years earlier.

As the glacier had advanced, it had scraped gravel, dirt, and boulders from the land it advanced over pushing them in front of it. When it finally stopped and reversed, the moraine was left to mark its furthest progress.

Hiking over the top of the moraine, we came upon this otherworldly landscape of boot sucking mud, odd shaped ice holes where sun heated boulders had melted their way down, and the ice itself.

Wow! With the sound of dozens of streams loud beneath us, cautiously we advanced across a sort of living geology lesson. For clearly seen on the valley walls was the trim line where the top of the glacier had been at the peak of its advance. It was clear at that time that the surface of the glacier had been at least 80 or 100 feet higher than at present, a lot of ice to have disappeared in a relatively short time period.

125

WHAT HAPPENED TO ALL THESE PLACES?

Top: a victrola sits half full of records it will never play again at a homestead at **Harbor Island, near Mile 900.** In the bushes nearby were the rusting cages of the foxes that the family raised for furs in the 1940s. A friend grew up here. He told me that when there weren't enough salmon running to feed the foxes, his father would send him and his brother to the sea lion rookery at nearby Point Astley to kill a few, saw them into pieces they could carry and bring them back for the foxes.

On a wonderfully fair summer evening, back in fish buying days in the 1970s, we dropped the anchor in the protected anchorage at **Cape Fanshaw**, east of **Mile 870**. Launched the skiff, motored in to the beach to walk around this exquisite abandoned homestead. An orchard's apples ripened on the trees, deer tracks evident in the soft ground. We explored in awe, marveling at the site: a protected anchorage, southwest exposure, gardens gone wild.

The original owners were gone. Someone, probably a traveling skiff fisherman, had squatted for a while, maybe even the summer before, judging by the recent plastic in the windows. On the beach was an old boiler, on the shore, pillings. Clearly there had been more than a homestead here; perhaps in earlier days there had been a fish processing plant as well.

35 years later I came again, this time with filmmaker Dan Kowalski, to video some of what was there and what

AN OF THE DEEP
WHALE 15 FEET LONG

I had felt. Before we came around the point, I was thinking that maybe there was a lodge there now, that it was probably private land, and that surely someone would have taken advantage of such a promising spot.

We found the trees tall and dark, the settlement, the homestead that seemed just to wait for settlers in 1975, gone. Only by exploring the thick underbrush did we find the old house: the trees pushing up through it.

Why? I wondered. I'd seen it before—a fox farm on Harbor Island—see opposite, and abandoned settlements up and down the Inside Passage, only flowering shrubs in the spring or bright decidious trees in the fall, standing out sharply in the endless miles of evergreens along the shore to reveal them.

Years before, I'd rooted among the drawers in the old superintendant's office in the abandoned big cannery at Butedale, B.C. , found a RCMP report of an old settler, found shot by his own hand, in a remote homestead that gave me a clue. There was no note; but the circumstances made the reasons plain: lonliness and failing health.

These little places needed a critical mass of settlers, it seemed to me. Without it, the dark long winters were simply too much.

Watch: Mile 870 - The Salmon Coast at alaskacruise-handbook.com; the first part was filmed here.

Top: a sperm whale at Port Armstrong, Mile 800, around 1910. MOHAI

Bottom: sometimes when fish companies stopped operating a cannery like this one at Waterfall, Prince of Wales Island, it was cheaper just to abandon the place, even with buildings full of supplies and equipment, than send up crews and boats to strip it out and bring it south. When they "jerked their watchman," locals knew that it was open season on what was left!

Top: what's wrong with this picture? (except for no life jackets.. we were too casual back then..)

Well... what we didn't realize at the time—that's my wife out there... is that big icebergs like this are very unstable and can easily capsize without warning. The issue is that most of the iceberg is underwater and melting faster than the part in the air. Plus when an iceberg this size capsizes, even if it doesn't hit you directly, it could easily create a wave that could capsize a small boat like this one.

Opposite: as the maps and charts show, the sides of Tracy are very steep. Look carefully at the photo and you can see the striations - the horizontal scars created by rocks embedded in the glacier as it ground its way down the fjord.

Many ships enter **Tracy Arm**, **Mile 900**, around 6 a.m. so they can get to Juneau for a port call in time for passengers to go on their shore excursions

If yours does: get up early! The entrance, particularly that first right angle turn is truly spectacular, as the light can be exquisite at that time of day.

Traveling up Tracy Arm (the entrance is five miles northeast of **Mile 900**) is like going back through geologic history. The fjord's dramatic walls lose their vegetation until they become bare shining rock, shaped and ground smooth by the ice. In many places the mountains plunge vertically into the water, which is more than a thousand feet deep.

John Muir was genuinely moved by the power and the beauty of the glaciers when he came by native canoe in around 1870, and he was able to communicate some of this enthusiasm to the native paddlers. Once, when they had paddled most of an afternoon up Tracy Arm, frustrated with the narrow and ice-choked channel, they turned yet another corner and found what he had come to seek, the glacier itself. While Muir stood in the canoe, sketching the glacier, several huge icebergs calved off, thundering into the water of the narrow fjord. "The ice mountain is well disposed toward you," one of the natives said to Muir, "He is firing his big guns to welcome you."

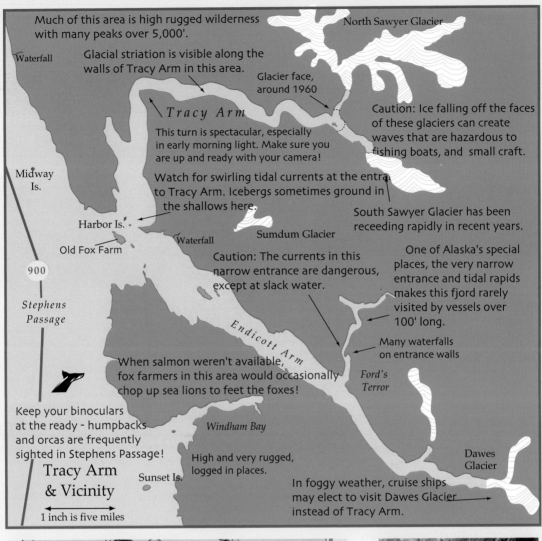

Much of this area is high rugged wilderness with many peaks over 5,000'.

North Sawyer Glacier

Waterfall

Glacial striation is visible along the walls of Tracy Arm in this area.

Glacier face, around 1960

Tracy Arm

This turn is spectacular, especially in early morning light. Make sure you are up and ready with your camera!

Caution: Ice falling off the faces of these glaciers can create waves that are hazardous to fishing boats, and small craft.

Midway Is.

Watch for swirling tidal currents at the entra to Tracy Arm. Icebergs sometimes ground in the shallows here.

Harbor Is.

Old Fox Farm

Waterfall

Sumdum Glacier

South Sawyer Glacier has been receding rapidly in recent years.

900

Caution: The currents in this narrow entrance are dangerous, except at slack water.

One of Alaska's special places, the very narrow entrance and tidal rapids makes this fjord rarely visited by vessels over 100' long.

Stephens Passage

Endicott Arm

Many waterfalls on entrance walls

When salmon weren't available, fox farmers in this area would occasionally chop up sea lions to feet the foxes!

Ford's Terror

Keep your binoculars at the ready - humpbacks and orcas are frequently sighted in Stephens Passage!

Windham Bay

Dawes Glacier

Tracy Arm & Vicinity

Sunset Is.

High and very rugged, logged in places.

In foggy weather, cruise ships may elect to visit Dawes Glacier instead of Tracy Arm.

1 inch is five miles

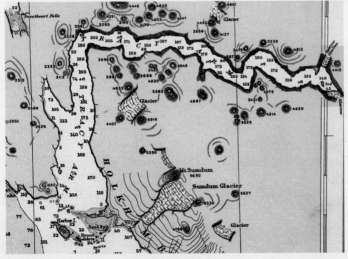

I was mighty glad to see my buddy, Dan's boat when pilot Jacques banked in over **Harbor Island**, at the entrance to **Tracy Ar**m, 90 miles south of Juneau. I hadn't spoken to Dan for a week; he was bringing his fishing boat up from Petersburg and out of cell phone range. If he wasn't at the rendevous, it would be ugly. But Jacques slid in for smooth landing and and Dan and I were off for a photo session in the dramatic fjord called **Fords Terror**, southeast of **Mile 900**.

Now Dan and I are very experienced - between us we have 50 plus years of experience on Alaskan waters. We know how careful you have to be around icebergs, how their center of gravity changes as they melt, how they can capsize without warning...

So... at the entrance to Ford's Terror was this totally spectacular iceberg, maybe 200 feet long with a graceful arch perhaps 40 feet high, the biggest one I had ever seen: stunning. We assumed, from its position near the entrance to the narrow inner basin that it was grounded: sitting on the bottom, and therefore stable.

Jumping in the small outboard powered inflatable skiff with our cameras, we circled that gorgeous iceberg in awe, stopped the engine and drifted, close to the arch, but not underneath. It was a Zen-like experience: we could feel the ice's cold breath on our faces, hear the slow hiss of bubbles rising from from its submerged mass beneath us. The blue translucent arch just towered over us, seemingly lit from within. The sea was still; in the distance was the whisper of a waterfall tumbling down the canyon wall: it was magic.

Then there was this rumble that we felt through the water more than heard. Dan turned to me with a smile, "The iceberg is talking to us."

Just then the iceberg broke in half at the top of the arch, almost directly over our heads. Our cameras both hanging from our necks, stunned into inaction, we just stared as the nearer half toppled toward us, as if in slow motion, smacking into the water a few feet behind our outboard motor. Only when the other half toppled away from us, and the previously underwater part started to emerge from the water, pushing our inflatible back, rolling water into the boat, did we have the presence of mind to start the motor and dart away, lest an emerging ice projection catch our skiff and flip it.

"OK," Dan said to me when we could breathe again, "what was the worst that could have happened? We'd be in the water, our cameras would be ruined, but we could have flipped the skiff back over, and paddled back (a half mile) to the *Sue Anne* and warmed up..."

Or not...

So.. take it from a couple of really experienced guys: don't get close to icebergs if you are in small craft!

THE BAD ICEBERG
AT FORDS TERROR

Exploring:
Dawes Glacier

In August, 2014, we traveled aboard the *Wilderness Adventurer* up to the head of Endicott Arm through the ice as far as the ship dared. And then we launched the kayaks to explore even further. For us in our little kayaks, with the roar of the waterfalls on both sides of the Arm, and occasionally deep thunder as another thousand ton berg fell into the bay was truly humbling.

Sept 5, 1973: Just at one, traveling dead slow, with little water under us, we passed the rapids in the creek-like entrance to Fords Terror. Hardly spoke a word for the next mile, so overpowering was the scenery. The sun went over the mountain at 4:30, and the evening came early and chill. At dusk, flight after flight of ducks came in low and fast, to settle on the water near the shore with a rush of many wings and soft callings.

"The night was chilly, with northern lights again. Stood out on deck and watched, until the cold drove us in. Yesterday and today, the places we visited make us feel tiny indeed.

"September 6, 1973: First frost! The stove went out in the night, and we woke to find the dog nestled in between us. To go out onto the frosty deck on such a morning, with the still glassy basin around, and the dark forests and frozen hills above— words can't tell it, pictures can't show it.

"Our cup seems pretty full just now."

- from my journal

Surrounded by high mountains and dramatic scenery with many glaciers, Juneau is an excellent place for fightseeing by floatplane or helicopter.

There is no road access to Juneau; Alaska state ferries are the only way you can 'drive' to Juneau. Very rugged terrain along Lynn Canal north of Juneau makes road construction very challenging. A campaign is underway to fund and build a road 35 miles further north to a proposed ferry landing opposite Haines. Further north almost vertical rock walls block the route to Skagway.

20 miles to end of road.

Eagle Harbor

The Mendenhall Glacier, a 30 minute bus ride from the cruise ship docks, is the most accessible glacier in Alaska. The lake in front of the glacier often has many icebergs.

The graceful steamer Princess Kathleen drove ashore here in 1912 after a navigational error. All 412 passengers and crew climbed ashore, but shortly afterwards the popular ship slid into the deep water and sank.

Tee Harbor

Lena Cove

Mendenhall Glacier

Mendenhall Lake

Auke Bay

Visitor Center

Raft trips start in the lake and travel down Mendenhall Creek

Auke Bay

Juneau Area

1 inch equals 4 miles.

Norris Glacier

Taku Glacier

airport

In the shadow of a steep mountain with a large glacier field, Juneau has much colder winters than Ketchikan or Sitka.

Whale watching area

Small craft passage at high tide.

Main helicopter base for flightseeing trips.

← To Perseverence Trail & Last Chance Basin

JUNEAU

GO WHALE WATCHING!
Juneau is probably the best place on your cruise to take a whale excursion.

Mt. Roberts Tramway

Douglas

To Skagway 50 miles

Gastineau Channel

Abandoned cannery

Sunny Cove

Taku Inlet

Jaw Pt.

DOUGLAS ISLAND

To Glacier Bay 75 miles

ADMIRALTY ISLAND

Cooper Pt.

Early native village site.

Greely Pt.

Bishop Pt.

Brown bears frequent this beach

Gold Rush steamer Islander hits iceberg in 1901 and sinks here with miners and their gold. 44 perished and 141 survived.

Fl. 6 sec.

waterfall

JUNEAU

A bear? Behind the espresso stand? No roads in or out? (you have to come by boat or plane...) What kind of a state capital is this? Probably different from what you're used to...

Almost surrounded by high mountains and with a vast ice field—larger than Rhode Island—to the north, Juneau winters are substantially colder than Ketchikan or Sitka. Tlingit natives had fish camps near today's downtown, but wintered in a more temperate and sheltered area near Auke Bay.

In 1880 Kowee, the local Tlingit chief, led two prospectors, Joe Juneau and Richard Harris, up Gold Creek, which runs through today's downtown, to Silver Bow Basin. The men found ample nuggets and quartz laced with gold, and Alaska's first gold rush was on.

However, the easy to find streambed gold was quickly gathered up, and a new kind of enterprise was formed to follow the gold underground. This industrial scale, deep hard rock mining was very different from other Alaska gold rushes where individuals or small groups of men worked creeks and beaches with essentially hand tools.

At Juneau, high grade ore was quickly exhausted and massive stamp mills were built to extract gold; it wasn't uncommon for 20 or more tons of ore to be dug and processed to yield a single ounce of fine gold. The tailings—the crushed rock that was left, were dumped along the

Top: tram landing station with Auke Bay and Lynn Canal in the distance.

Above: upstairs in a Juneau gallery, a native Tlingit woman shows a piece of her tribal art.

135

Top: Renee Hughes and the giant air compressor at the Last Chance Mining Museum. Above: hardy gals ready to dip!

shore, creating the flat land on which today's downtown Juneau was built on. At peak capacity, the big stamp mills of the Alaska-Juneau mine, still visible above the cruise ship docks, could crush 12,000 tons of ore a day. Working conditions were dangerous and - the entrance to the big Treadwell mine was nicknamed the "glory Hole," for all the miners—sometimes one a week—that went to glory there. Eventually the gold played out, the tunnels—by then deep under the channel—filled with water, and today all that's left are ruins of the old stamp mill on the hill above the cruise ship dock.

But the gold is still there and a 21st century style mine—designed with minimal visual and environmental impact—is being built on a slope above Lynn Canal, above 45 miles north of Juneau.

The gold made Juneau the economic capital, so the legislative capital was moved there as well from Sitka in 1906. As the gold played out, government jobs, both state and federal, assumed a dominant role in Juneau's economy.

Because of these government jobs, economic life in Juneau is much less seasonal than in other Alaska coastal towns which are more dependent on tourism and sport and commercial fishing. For this reason, the impact of the growing cruise ship industry sets a little less easy with Juneau residents. Cruise ship captains have learned that if they want to avoid an angry call from the harbormaster, they need to keep their deck public address systems off as they pass Douglas (across the channel from Juneau) as they approach and leave town. Another source of an-

noyance to locals is the noise created by the flightseeing helicopters and float planes, which echo up off the steep rock walls behind town. In order to avoid the air pollution that occurs when four or five big thousand-footers are running their generators in the harbor, cruise operators have installed dock wiring to allow their ships to operate off local hydroelectrical power while in port.

Like most cruise ports, the shops and galleries are concentrated right near the docks, and passengers will be pleasantly surprised at the peaceful pace of life on the streets if they take the time to walk up and out of the downtown commercial district.

The **Mt. Roberts Tramway** operates from right by the main cruise ship docks. Another good stop close to the docks is the **Taku Fisheries Ice House**, at the south end of the main downtown dock complex. This is an active fish processing facility with boats unloading and taking ice, as well as a great seafood restaurant and retail shop with some excellent smoked seafood products.

Shopping: North Franklin Street, which runs right past the cruise ship docks, is the main passenger shopping venue. If you are at all interested in Native Alaskan Art, I recommend taking some time in the art galleries here. Sometimes you have to look a bit for the best buys; I found a wonderful carving of an Eskimo lodge on the dusty bottom shelf of one of these galleries for $500, an unusual item and an excellent value.

Mendenhall Glacier: If there ever were a reason for the "See it before it melts," motto used by some travel agents, it is this glacier, as it is receding rapidly. The shuttle ($8 one way) or the city bus ($2, but drops you a mile from the visitor center) are the way to go, allowing you to explore the glacier at your leisure.

Whale Watching: A special mention should be made of the whale watching excursions operating out of Auke

Top: this waterfall is about a 20 minute walk from the Visitor Center at the Mendenhall Glacier.

Above: gold panning up in the Last Chance Basin, in the hills behind Juneau. Even today, visitors can usually pan a bit of gold from the sands here.

Bay. There are usually resident populations of both killer and humpback whales in nearby Lynn Canal, and this tour has an excellent record of finding them and many passengers have reported seeing humpbacks bubble feeding or breaching on these tour boats.

Red Dog Saloon: If you're looking for a colorful spot for a modestly priced pub food style meal, stop in at the Red Dog Saloon, right on North Franklin, about two blocks from the tram station. With sawdust on the floor, banjo playing and rustic decor, it's full of local flavor. Other favorites are the **Hangar Bar** and **Tracy's King Crab Shack**, both close to the docks.

Top: Cruise ship dock area around 1930, when the big buildings held the stamp mills that crushed thousands of tons of gold ore each day in preparation to separating the gold out.

Lower left: A small streamboat ready to carry passengers around the harbor.

Opposite top left: Zipline over the old Treadwell Mine.

Opposite top right: Big humpback tail seen from one of the whale watching boats in Lynn Canal.

Opposite lower right: The Flume Trail is a mellow walk behind downtown.

JUNEAU EXCURSIONS
(CHANGE OFTEN; CHECK WITH YOUR SHIP)

Mendenhall Glacier Explorer
Mendenhall Glacier & Salmon Hatchery Tour
Original Alaska Salmon Bake
Underground Juneau
Rainforest Garden
A Taste Of Juneau
Guide's Choice Adventure Hike
Dog Sled Summer Camp
Gold Panning & History Tour
Glacier View Bike & Brew
Rainforest Canopy & Zipline Expedition
Mountain Zip & Rainforest Bike Ride
Juneau Sportfishing Adventure
Juneau Fly-Out Fly Fishing
Juneau Steamboat Cruise
Photo Safari By Land & Sea

Alaska's Whales & Rainforest Trails
Whale Watching & Wildlife Quest
Mendenhall Glacier & Whale Quest
Whale Watching & Orca Point Lodge
Mendenhall Glacier Float Trip
Glacier View Sea Kayaking
Mendenhall Glacier Canoe Adventure
Taku Glacier Lodge Flight & Feast
Pilot's Choice Ice Age Exploration
Mendenhall Glacier Helicopter Tour
Four Glacier Adventure By Helicopter
Extended Helicopter Glacier Trek
Glacier & Dog Sled Adventure By Helicopter
Dog Sledding On The Mendenhall
Custom Hummer Adventure

THE HILLS ARE HONEYCOMBED WITH TUNNELS!

HOIST
1-2 ....." STOP IF IN MOTION
2 .3 ...." BELLS LOWER
7 ....." MEN ON RUN SLOW
ACCIDENT HOIST OF
3-2-1 ....." LOWER BY VERBAL ORDE
READY TO SHOOT

ENGINEER SHALL AFTER SIGNAL 3-2-1 RAISE BUCKET O
CAGE TWO FEET AND LOWER AGAIN AND SHALL REMAIN AT
POST UNTIL FINAL SIGNAL IS GIVEN AND COMMAND EXECUT

LEVELS

1-1 BELLS	1ST LEVEL	4-1 BELLS	11TH LEVE
1-2 ....."	2ND "	4-2 ....."	12TH
1-3 ....."	3RD "	4-3 ....."	13TH
1-4 ....."	4TH "	4-4 ....."	14TH
1-5 ....."	5TH "	4-5 ....."	15TH
2-1 ....."	6TH "	5-1 ....."	16TH
2-2 ....."	7TH "	5-2 ....."	17TH
2-3 ....."	8TH "	5-3 ....."	18TH
2-4 ....."	9TH "	5-4 ....."	19TH
2-5 ....."	10TH "	5-5 ....."	20TH

RULES GOVERNING SIGNALS.

RULE I. IN GIVING ORDINARY SIGNALS MAKE STROKES ON BELL A
REGULAR INTERVALS SIMILAR TO "READY TO SHOOT" 3-2-1 BELLS, EAC
BAR (-) MUST TAKE THE SAME TIME AS EACH STROKE OF THE BEL

RULE 2. WHEN MEN ARE TO BE HOISTED OR LOWERED, GIVE SIGNAL
MEN ON, RUN SLOW" 3 BELLS, MEN MUST THEN GET ON BUCKET O
CAGE, THEN GIVE SIGNAL TO HOIST OR LOWER, 1 OR 2 BELLS.

RULE 3. AFTER SIGNAL "READY TO SHOOT" 3-2-1 BELLS, ENGINEER MUS
IVE SIGNAL THAT HE IS READY TO HOIST BY RAISING AND LOWERING
UCKET TWO FEET. MINERS MUST THEN GIVE SIGNAL "MEN ON" 3 BELLS
FUSE GET ON BUCKET OR CAGE AND GIVE SIGNAL TO HOIS
ER THAN DEPTH OF BUCKE

Literally hundreds of miles of tunnels were drilled in the hills behind Juneau and even the channel in front in the search for gold. Large rooms were created as the ore was excavated, with pillars supporting the ceiling and the rooms and pillars of levels above them. As the richer ore was depleted, mine operators began to shave down the pillars to recover the richer ore within them. Bad move; the mining of pillars in the Treadwell Mine, underneath Gastineau Channel, led to a hole opening up right at the edge of the water, as the tide was coming up! The salt water ran into the mine with such force that the escaping air blew the elevator house totally off the mine, which was never reopened. Luckily no one died.

FLYING THE
JUNEAU ICE FIELD

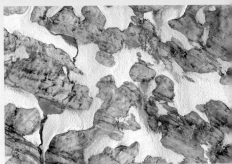

Behind Juneau is a vast ice-field with fascinating shapes and colors. Flightseeing excursions are offered both by the big new turbo Otter floatplanes and by helicopter. The tours come in several flavors - the helicopter excursions usually land and encourage passengers to explore the top of the glacier on foot. Additionally, you may choose to take a helicopter to a dogsledding camp set up on the glacier and experience dogsledding first hand.

The floatplanes offer both a scenic flight and one combined with a salmon dinner at a waterfront lodge.

SITKA

Top: with no dock big enough for big ships, passengers come ashore here by lighter. Right: one of the domes at St. Michael's Cathedral. Above: inside the Cathedral.

Consider yourself lucky if your ship stops here. The lack of a downtown cruise ship dock, and a slightly off the beaten path location make for a much more mellow downtown environment than you will find in other major Alaska cruise ports. Additionally, Sitka is easily your most historic port.

When Juneau was woods and snow and Ketchikan was a summer village of the Tlingit people, Sitka residents enjoyed theater, fine wines, and all the riches that the sea otter trade provided her Russian residents.

It was a trade based on the sometimes unwilling participation of the native people. In the Aleutian Islands, for example, the Promyshlenniki, as the Russian fur traders were called, had no qualms about destroying whole villages if the Aleut residents didn't quickly obey them.

At Sitka, the proud Tlingit people cared little for the Russians, and in 1802 they destroyed the first Russian outpost, north of the present town site. Two years later the Russians returned with three ships and many Aleut mercenaries in kayak-like bidarka boats. Finally routing the Tlingits, the Russians reestablished Sitka on the site of the Tlingit village, Shee Atika.

For much of its Russian history, Sitka's leader was Aleksandr Baranov, who established schools for the Tlingits and made Sitka the trading capital of the north-

Top: Mt. Edgecumbe, an inactive volcano looms over Sitka. On a recent April's Fool's Day, a local character loaded up a helicopter with old tires, flew up to the top of the volcano, lit them on fire, and flew back to town to spread the word: "She's gonna' blow!"

Above: teen selling cookies on the street - Sitka has a much more low key and less crowded flavor than Juneau or Ketchikan.

west coast. These were prosperous years when Sitka was the busiest port on the entire west coast of North and South America.

Fortunately for the Americans, the Russians' enlightenment didn't extend to conserving the valuable fur resource, for once the sea otter had been slaughtered almost to extinction, financial reverses made the Russians willing to sell Alaska to the United States for $7.2 million, about 2 cents an acre, which they did in 1867.

After the Americans took over, Sitka slowly evolved into a sleepy fishing and logging town until World War II when the Japanese invasion of the Aleutians triggered a massive navy operation near the site of the present airport, with a huge influx of sailors.

In more modern times, Sitka's economy pretty much depended on the big plywood mill out in Sawmill Cove, and commercial fishing. The closure of the mill in 1992 was a substantial financial blow. But instead of languishing, Sitka experienced sort of a slow renaissance based on the arts, and to a lesser degree, tourism.

Today, having missed the booms and busts of the gold rush, Sitka, way out on the ocean side of Baranof Island, is the cultural center of Southeastern Alaska. Yet Sitka offers more than museums and vistas:

Go fishing; If you have any inclination to try for a salmon or halibut, Sitka is an excellent place to go out on

Top: snowy owl at the Alaska Raptor Center. Left: the New Archangel Dancers perform when cruise ships are in town. Below: totem in the Sitka National Historical Park.

145

one of the charter vessels. The city's unique position on the outside coast and the strong runs of king and silver salmon make the chances of getting a fish here very high. Such a trip is also an opportunity to see close-up the dramatic coast of Alaska and its sea life and wildlife.

Jet boats: Advances in vessel design and propulsion have made an unusual experience available at Sitka: the high-speed jet boats. Propelled by water jets (essentially large pumps) rather than conventional propellers, these impressive craft allow passengers to travel quickly to places such as Salisbury Sound, 25 miles north of town. The abundant wildlife populations make it likely you'll see a whale, bear, or sea otter (today protected).

The Sheldon Jackson Museum: In his travels through the state as education agent, Dr. Jackson acquired a remarkable collection of native art and historical artifacts. Even if you have seen other such displays, you will find this collection unusually complete and worth seeing. The Aleut and Eskimo exhibits are particularly fascinating, with material such as rain gear made of walrus intestines.

Alaska Raptor Rehabilitation Center: A place where injured hawks, falcons, owls, and eagles (mostly eagles) are cared for, this volunteer-run facility lets visitors view the dramatic birds close-up.

Sitka National Historical Park: If you didn't get to Totem Bight or Saxman at Ketchikan and want to get a good view of totem poles, this is a close-to-downtown opportunity to do so. Set among trees in a dramatic walk along the shore, the 15 totems are "recarves" of poles collected from Prince of Wales Island at the turn of the century. Cedar totems have a life of about 100 years outside exposed to the elements.

The Russian Bishop's House and St. Michael's Cathedral: Both downtown, these are culturally rich elements of Sitka's Russian period. The Bishop's House is the original 1842 structure; the cathedral is a replica of the one destroyed by fire in 1966 (much of the artwork was saved).

Top: Castle Hill, a short walk from downtown, offers a great view. Lower: consider renting a kayak and exploring the nearby islands.

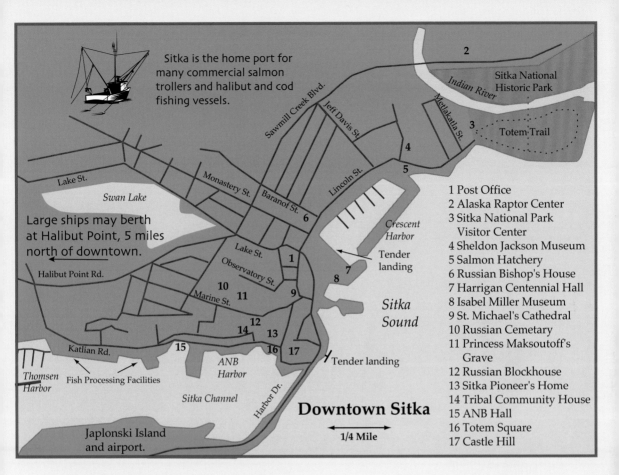

Sitka is the home port for many commercial salmon trollers and halibut and cod fishing vessels.

Sitka National Historic Park

Indian River

Totem Trail

Sawmill Creek Blvd.

Jeff Davis St.

Mellakatla St.

Lincoln St.

Monastery St.

Baranof St.

Lake St.

Swan Lake

Large ships may berth at Halibut Point, 5 miles north of downtown.

Halibut Point Rd.

Lake St.

Observatory St.

Marine St.

Katlian Rd.

Thomsen Harbor

Fish Processing Facilities

ANB Harbor

Sitka Channel

Japlonski Island and airport.

Harbor Dr.

Crescent Harbor

Tender landing

Sitka Sound

Tender landing

Downtown Sitka

◄—► 1/4 Mile

1 Post Office
2 Alaska Raptor Center
3 Sitka National Park Visitor Center
4 Sheldon Jackson Museum
5 Salmon Hatchery
6 Russian Bishop's House
7 Harrigan Centennial Hall
8 Isabel Miller Museum
9 St. Michael's Cathedral
10 Russian Cemetary
11 Princess Maksoutoff's Grave
12 Russian Blockhouse
13 Sitka Pioneer's Home
14 Tribal Community House
15 ANB Hall
16 Totem Square
17 Castle Hill

SOME SITKA EXCURSIONS

Russian America History Tour
Russian America & Raptor Center Tour
Sitka Nature & History Walk
Sitka Bike & Hike Tour
Advanced Bike Adventure
Tongass Rainforest Hike
4x4 Wilderness Adventure
Sitka Sportfishing
Wilderness Sea Kayaking Adventure
Dry Suit Snorkel Adventure
Sea Life Discovery Semi-Submersible
Sea Otter & Wildlife Quest
Sea Otter Quest & Alaska Raptor Center
Silver Bay Nature Cruise & Hatchery Tour
Wildlife Quest & Beach Trek
Alaska Up-Close Exclusive Cruise Adventure

Opposite: Bishops and parisoners around the model of the cathedral, 1842. Tlingit chief, around 1880. Tommy Joseph, Carver at the Sitka National Historical Park. Below: inside the carver's workshop at the Park. Historical photos from E.W. Merrill Collection, Sitka NHP.

Building the boats: After making it over the passes, the next step for the Klondikers was to cut down trees, saw them into boards, and build crude boats. Then when the lake ice melted, they had to float and paddle down 500 miles of the Yukon River to Dawson and the Klondike Country. The first part included several violent rapids where boats and men were lost.

Carcross

CANADA

Water route to the Klondike

Lake Bennett

Haines Highway connects with Alaska Highway

ALASKA

Gold Rush Trails

Klondike Highway to Alaska Highway

Chilkoot Pass

Skagway

White Pass & Yukon Route RR

Dyea (abandoned)

White Pass

Haines

The Passes - Canada required that all those headed for the Klondike carry a year's food (about a ton) with them. For most prospectors, this meant many backbreaking trips up over the pass, shuttling their supplies to the border checkpoint.

Chilkat River

1014N

High rugged mountains

Proposed ferry dock

The Road - Many Juneau residents yearn for a road to somewhere. (The only road connection is by ferry.) However the proposed road only runs up Lynn Canal to another ferry dock, as the last miles to Skagway is blocked by almost vertical rock walls.

Muir Inlet

Eldred Rock Lighthouse

990N

Glacier Bay National Park

High and rugged with many glaciers.

Passenger Tip - The landscape of upper Lynn Canal is very dramatic. When you leave Skagway in the evening, spend some time with your camera on an upper deck; the views can be spectacular!

Glacier Bay

Lynn Canal

Proposed road

Salmon Cannery

Berners Bay

Excursion Inlet

960N

Present road ends here

Pt. Retreat Lighthouse

JUNEAU TO SKAGWAY

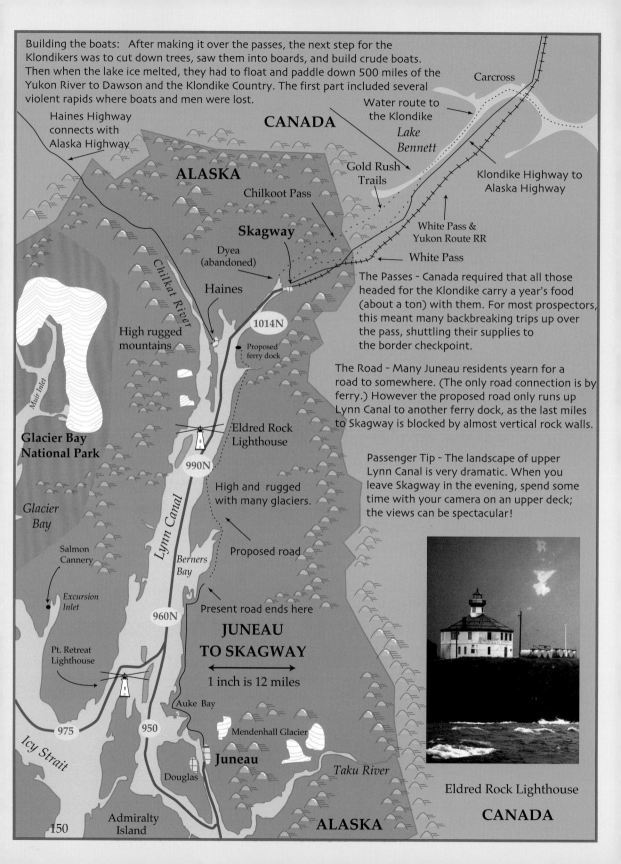

1 inch is 12 miles

975

950

Auke Bay

Icy Strait

Mendenhall Glacier

Eldred Rock Lighthouse

Juneau

Douglas

Taku River

CANADA

Admiralty Island

ALASKA

CHAPTER 4
WHERE HISTORY LURKS

LYNN CANAL TO SKAGWAY AREA
MILE 900 TO MILE 1000N

There's a dramatic change in the landscape as your ship enters Lynn Canal north of Juneau. The mountains are higher, the vistas starker: glaciers seem to overhang the water in little cirque valleys.

And it wasn't just the landscape, but the weather as well. Lynn Canal and Chatham Strait, to the south, form a 200 mile long wind tunnel for the wet North Pacific lows sweeping up from the ocean and the cold Arctic highs pushing down from Siberia and the Alaska interior. Sometimes, especially in the fall, there would hardly even be a break between systems, and weatherbound fishermen in Auke Bay would catch a ride out to the shore by Pt. Lena to get their grim weather forecast: row after row of nasty looking grey bearded seas rolling down the canal.

The bottom here is littered here with the pieces of two of the finest steamers to travel north, both belonging to the Canadian Pacific Railroad. First was the *Princess Sophia*. At around 1 a.m. on October 24, 1918, the gold miners and the crews from the 10 Yukon River paddle-wheelers aboard the *Sophia* were probably still celebrating. They'd left Skagway a few hours earlier, the rivers freezing up, their season over, the bright lights ahead.

But up in the pilothouse, the atmosphere was anxious. The captain had seen **Eldred Rock Light**, **Mile 994**, at midnight through the snow but navigation on such a

Top: "Old 73" still makes regular runs from the Skagway docks!

Below: GPS map on a plane headed into Skagway shows the ruggedness of the country around town.

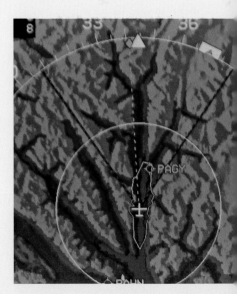

Top: and it didn't break in half! The *Princess May* survived this scrape in Lynn Canal with hardly a scratch. But possibly her survival encouraged the captain of the *Princess Sophia* (see story) to keep his passengers on board, hoping that they would float off. PSMHS Bottom: tragedy in the making: the *Sophia* on the rocks: there were no survivors.

night relied on something called "time and compass." The skipper would calculate from the engine revolutions how fast his vessel was traveling. Taking his course line from the chart and making allowances for the wind and the tidal currents, he would steer until his time ran out, that is, when he should be at the next point of reference.

On that bitter night in 1918, with blowing snow and limited visibility, the next checkpoint after Eldred Rock was Sentinel Island Light, 28 miles away. Over such a distance, a steering error of one degree would put the vessel a half-mile off course.

Sometime around 2 a.m., as her skipper was groping through the snow and trying to see the Sentinel Island Light, the *Sophia* drove her whole length ashore on Vanderbilt Reef. Fortunately the rocks cradled her, and there was no need to try and launch lifeboats on such a rotten night.

By first light a rescue fleet was standing by: the *Cedar, King and Winge, Estebeth, Elsinore*, and others. But a gale was howling so it was decided to wait until better weather to evacuate the passengers and crew.

It proved to be a tragic mistake. In the late afternoon, the northerly began to blow with renewed fury, and the rescue fleet was forced to seek shelter in a nearby harbor.

Darkness came with driving snow and bitter wind.

Roaring down the canal, the wind caught the *Sophia's* high exposed stern, driving her off the reef, ripping open her bottom, and sending her into the deep water beyond. There was time for one desperate radio call: "For God's sake come! We are sinking." In the morning only her masts were above water, her 343 passengers and crew drowned in the northwest coast's worst maritime disaster.

Thirty-four years later, miscalculation of a course change drove the graceful *Princess Kathleen* ashore at **Lena Point, Mile 956**. Her passengers were more fortunate. They climbed down ladders to the rocky beach and watched the favorite of all the Alaska-run steamers slide off the rocks and disappear into deep water.

On the east side of Lynn Canal, at around **Mile 980N** look for what remains of the old mining settlement of Comet. Behind it, in the vicinity of Lion's Head Mountain is a highly mineralised area, with several old abandoned mines. A project at the old Kensington Mine, is being developed. The mining company promised a low environmental impact operation; however part of the tailings will be dumped into a nearby lake, angering local commercial fishermen and environmentalists. Whether or not the mine can successfully operated without any adverse environmental impact will be a critical test of the idea of balancing development and natural resource protection.

Top: Eldred Rock is the very prominent Lighthouse at **Mile 998N**. Bottom: Pacific salmon die after spawning and attract many scavengers! The eagles around Haines come for the salmon spawning in the Chilkat River.

Top: barracks and officer's quarters at Port Chilkoot, once an Army base.

Bottom: mural showing what happens here in the fall - salmon die after spawning, attracting literally hundreds of bald eagles.

The spot that looks like a New England village at **Mile 1012N** is Fort William H. Seward, better known as Port Chilkoot. Decommissioned after World War II, it is now part of the city of Haines, just to the north, and offers a variety of cultural activities.

Haines, until the Skagway to Whitehorse, Canada highway, was completed in 1979, was the only town (except for tiny, tiny, Hyder far south) in southeastern Alaska with a road that went anywhere (it connected to the Alaska Highway). Today it is rich with Tlingit culture and is especially known for the dramatic fall migration of bald eagles that feed on Chilkat River salmon.

Few large cruise ships stop here, but if yours does or you want a refreshing change from the congestion of Skagway when the big ships are in town, there is a foot ferry over to Haines. You'll find a nice path from the dock along the shore to a very laid back town with some great views overlooking Lynn Canal. If your ship does stop, there is usually a kayaking excursion as well as a trip down the Chilkat River, usually by big inflatable rafts.

Groups have taken the kayaking trip reported a really good experience, getting up close to sea lions, etc.

Just to the west of town, over the hill, is the mouth of the Chilkat River. Here it winds through an ever changing landscape of islands and sand bars. In Tlingit, Chilkat means 'winter storage container for salmon,' which pretty much sums it up - salmon runs continue here into late fall. The presence of so many fish attracts the largest

collection of bald eagles anywhere. Haines markets itself as The Valley of the Eagles and has a festival, usually in early November, when typically there are three or four thousand eagles hanging out along the lower river, chowing down on the carcasses of chum salmon that have spawned and died. The river excursion takes you lazily right through the heart of this. In summer, of course, there aren't as many eagles, but there still are plenty.

If you haven't seen totem carving up close, the native cultural center on the south side of Port Chilkoot has an ongoing totem carving project. Also **The Port Chilkoot Distillery** is a small low key distillery with a tasting room offering vodka, gin, absinthe, and bourbon

Haines is also a pretty good place to bike - there are bike rentals as well as bike tours. If you're on your own, ask for the road to Cannery Cove. It's very scenic - with glacier hung mountains over the inlet. And if you want to get to Skagway, just jump on the Chilkat Express, a short walk to the left as you get off your ship in Haines. It's just a 30 minute trip to a totally different world.

Top: got a thing for hammers? There's a whole hammer museum here!

Above: carver in the workshop at the Alaska Indian Arts Center at Port Chilkoot.

Top: braided channels in the lower
Chilkat River: ideal grounds for
spawning dog salmon, and the eagles
waiting for the fish to spawn and
die...

Right : inside the Alaska Indian Arts
Center at Port Chilkoot. Notice the
many eagles in the trees in the diora-
ma; it is really like that in the fall!

WHY JUNEAU ISN'T GETTING A ROAD ANYTIME SOON....

You may already know that the only way in or out of Juneau is by boat or plane. In recent years, however, there has been a movement to build a road north along the east side of Lynn Canal. It would run about 40 miles north to connect to Skagway, where there is a road up the valley that connects with the Alaska Highway in Canada's Yukon territory.

Like most things Alaskan, there are strong feelings on both sides of the issue. Juneauites would love a road and it would open up the Juneau hospitals for Skagway and Haines residents, as well as bringing 80,000 or so more visitors and their RVs to a city of 31,000 that might have 10,000 cruise passengers visiting on a five ship day. Definitely a mixed blessing there...

But the biggest challenge is simply the landscape: almost vertical in places, with many well established avalanche chutes, it would be hugely expensive to build, and expensive to maintain in the winter. Plus it wouldn't even go all the way - but simply to a ferry dock a few miles from Haines.

Of course, the lawyers love this one - several lawsuits have been filed and the state's environmental impact statement was possibly headed for the US Supreme Court, unless cooler heads prevail..

Someday, there may indeed be a road out, but no one is really sure when.

Top: Alaska ferry in Lynn Canal opposite Haines.

Below: aerial view of the same part of Lynn Canal; you can see why building a road along the shore would be such a challenge!

157

Mushers, Alaska.

THE GOLD RUSH
HOW MANY STRUCK IT RICH?

"HO" FOR KLONDIKE

"Sixty-Eight Rich Men on the Steamer Portland"
"Not a man has less than $5,000. Some of them have over $100,000"
"Big strikes made by tenderfeet"
"Fortune seemed to smile on the inexperienced."
"Strikes in the Yukon the greatest ever known."

Such were the headlines in the July 17, 1897 Seattle Post-Intelligencer that spread across a depression ravaged country like wildfire. In those days, to a family struggling to keep food on the table and coal in the stove, $5,000 was a fortune, $100,000 riches beyond imagination. The dimensions of mysterious Alaska and the Yukon had just began to enter American consciousness, primarily through John Muir's exciting discovery of Glacier Bay just 20 years before.

But the part that electrified struggling men all across America and Canada was that most of the rich men coming out to tell their stories had gone in as inexperienced "tenderfeet," with no more knowledge of Alaska, the Klondike, or gold mining than the average midwest sodbuster or eastern factory worker.

Desperate people see what they want to see; most didn't read the small print, at the end of the article that started with "GOLD! GOLD! GOLD! GOLD! splashed across the front page. "They attribute their success to "lucky strikes," and aver that thousands of people will rush to the Yukon valley in the next year or two, and after undergoing great privations and hardships, will probably return broke in health and finances."

And so they came, from all parts of the country, from all walks of life, fixated on finding the gold that would transform their lives. First to Seattle, where the water-

Opposite page: look at these faces aboard a Gold Rush steamer. UW]
[Thwaites 0394-1286

Top: home made boats on Lake Bennet, the men waiting for the ice to thaw so that they can head downriver to Dawson and the Klondike.
AMRC b64-1-43

Above: getting there could be bad; a Gold Rush steamer at Skagway.
UW15549

Top: jealous wellwishers crowding the docks as another dangerously overloaded ship gets ready to head north from San Francisco for Skagway. UW 14504

Bottom: the news that went around the world. At the time the US and much of the world was in a recession and perhaps as many as a hundred thousand men left home, work, and family to try and get in on the allegedly easy pickings in the Yukon. MOHAI 19084

GOLD! GOLD! GOLD! GOLD!

Sixty-Eight Rich Men on the Steamer Portland.

STACKS OF YELLOW METAL!

Some Have $5,000, Many Have More, and a Few Bring Out $100,000 Each.

THE STEAMER CARRIES $700,000

front was a frenzied marketplace of merchants hawking their supplies to eager men with their family's savings in their pockets.

A Gold Rush fleet was rushed into service. Some were older, tired ships, operated by unscrupulous owners wanting to get in on the Gold Rush frenzy. Overloaded and pushed into dangerous weather, several didn't make it and were lost. For the tens of thousands who came north during the Gold Rush years, upper Lynn Canal represented the last easy miles of their journey to the diggings.

As you enter **Taiya Inlet** at **Mile 1,014N** from Seattle, imagine yourself at the crowded rail of a ship like the *Queen* or the *Victoria* in the fall of '97, jostling for your place with hundreds of other Klondikers, looking out through a snow squall, trying to get a glimpse of what lay ahead. There is but an hour or two before you must put on your pack, get the boxes and sacks of your "outfit" (a year's worth of supplies) ready to unload, and step out into the cold and whatever fate had in store for you.

"Them days it was every man for hisself. The faster a boat could get out of there, the sooner it could get back to Seattle or Vancouver and pick up another load of suckers. A man shipped his gear at his own risk. If he didn't get his stuff off the beach before the next tide, it was just his hard luck. No one else done no worrying about it."
- Monte Hawthorn, in *The Trail Led North*

160

O n C h i l k o o t   P a s s

The snow clears, and a cold and cheerless sun shines on as bleak and unfriendly a landscape as you've probably ever seen. The mountains rise vertically out of the water; with hardly a beach. The chatter of the crowd fades as all look at the mountains and what lies ahead.

For those in the first wave in 1897, there were no wharves. Most gold seekers unloaded their outfits from steamers onto lighters–shallow-draft barges. If the tide was up, the lighters took you right in to shore. If it wasn't, the lighter got as far as the flats and you had to cross 100 or 200 yards of sand and mud to get to shore. Many had brought animals and staked them out with their piles of boxes and gear while they made the first trips across the flats to shore.

Some weren't familiar with the big tides in the northern fjords of Alaska. They rested, perhaps, after lugging their first load up the beach, and visited with others about what they might expect in the rough-hewn town, visible through the snow, and hiked back to find their outfit underwater, their animals drowned. Few were really prepared for the rigors of that journey, or the true nature of the gold country.

For most of the hundred thousand or so who came north in 1897 and 1898, their Gold Rush experience had three phases. The first was often the hardest: the passes. The mountain wall that lay between the salt water of up-per Lynn Canal and the edge of the Yukon had but two routes over it: Chilkoot Pass and White Pass.

Top: The infamous "Golden Staircase" at Chilkoot Pass in 1897.

Bottom: Prospectors on barge coming ashore in Skagway. The ships didn't wait for high tide to make it easier. As one Klondiker put it, "They had to get back and pick up another load of suckers..." UW La Roche 380

Top: how the wealthy traveled to the Klondike - on big steamers like this one in Five Finger Rapids on the Yukon River. This was a particularly challenging set of rapids; the *White Horse* either had enough power or the current wasn't running at strength. For sometimes boats have to run a cable through the rappids, tie it to a tree and pull yourself through with your winch while you are also running the engine full speed ahead.

UW21255

Another dangerous spot, Miles Canyon, was even narrower and some steamers put hay bales along the sides of the hull to protect it from hitting the canyon's almost vertical rock walls.

The most powerful image from '97 and '98 is the long line of climbers, each bent with his load, on the steps cut into the ice on Chilkoot Pass. At the top lay the Canadian border and the North West Mounted Police. No one could pass without a year's supplies, about 1,000 lbs.

Wealthy men hired porters, but most just carried it all up themselves, load by backbreaking load, caching it at the top and hoping no one would rob them before they got back. A solid stream of upward-bound men filled the steps. If you wanted to rest, you stepped off to the side, but when you wanted to get back in, you had to wait for a gap in the line; it was that crowded. By 1898 cable tramways could carry your gear over the pass for a fee, but the men in the first wave had only their feet.

Down the other side from the summit was Lake Bennett and after that it was the boats and the rivers. They were 50 miles from salt water, but there were another 500 to the gold country. Arriving in winter, the men camped on the shore, cut down trees, whipsawed them into planks and built boats, and waited for the ice to melt to launch their boats and begin the journey:

"Some leaked, some didn't steer. They had lots of things wrong with them. But a lot of the boats, made of whipsawed lumber, had beautiful lines and sailed as pretty as anything I ever did see on the Columbia. Yes, sir, that was an expedition, that fleet of boats getting ready to set out from Lake Bennett, come spring of '98."

—Martha McKeown, The Trail Led North

The trip became a journey of true epic proportions. Some 6,000 boats started: down the canyons and through the rapids they came, some capsizing or breaking up; the survivors trying to hitch a ride with the next boat that had room. The wealthier switched to Yukon steamers as soon as the river got wide enough, but all were heading for Dawson Creek and the last phase of the epic saga: the diggings.

But for most, only disappointment awaited them. The best claims were staked before most of the gold seekers even had left home. Many who started north gave up before they got to the Yukon. Only half who made it staked a claim. Just a very few struck it rich. Most found some kind of work in Dawson City or in the diggings, made a little money, and moved on.

Yet their adventure transcends time. All experienced the powerful drama of The North. Those who returned to the lower 48, even penniless, brought back stories and memories to entertain generations of breathless children and grandchildren.

Spring 1898: the next stage of the epic journey begins as the ice melts and the many waiting boats begin their long river journey. UW Hegg 227

Below: For some, the challenge of The North - the cold, the difficult conditions, was simply too much, like this quote from The Trail Led North:

"..he was setting there in the middle of the road talking to himself... He looked plumb played out. He never seen us, he just went on talking to himself..." Christine Cox drawing

Skagway

Surrounded by high mountains, at the end of a narrow windy fjord, this town was where the Klondikers left the (relative) comfort of the ships and faced the difficulties of the trail.

..."Them days it was every man for hisself. The faster a boat could get out of there, the sooner it could get back to Seattle or Vancouver and pick up another load of suckers. A man shipped his outfit at his own risk. If he didn't get his stuff off the beach before the next tide, it was just his hard luck. No one else done no worrying about it."

- Monte Hawthorne, in Martha McKeown, The Trail Led North

1. Railroad depot,
2. "Soapy" Smith's Parlor,
3. Red Onion Saloon,
4. Arctic Brotherhood Hall,
5. Town Hall and Trail of '98 Museum.
6. Skagway Fish Co.
7. Gold Rush Cemetery

9 Miles to abandoned townsite of Dyea and start of Chilkoot Trail

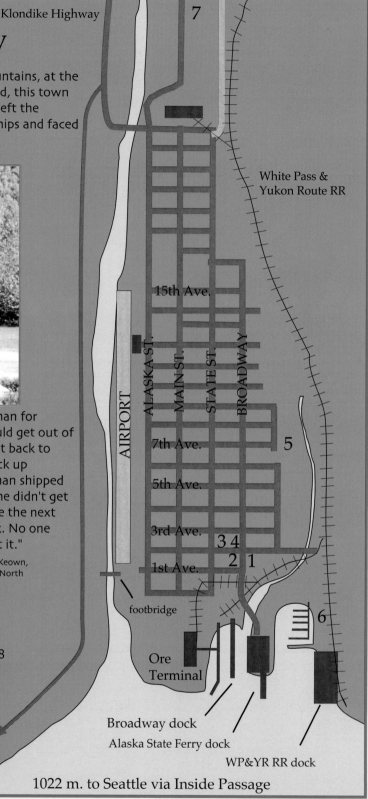

Klondike Highway

7

White Pass & Yukon Route RR

15th Ave.

ALASKA ST.
MAIN ST.
STATE ST.
BROADWAY

AIRPORT

7th Ave.

5

5th Ave.

3rd Ave.

3 4
2 1

1st Ave.

footbridge

6

Ore Terminal

Broadway dock

Alaska State Ferry dock

WP&YR RR dock

1022 m. to Seattle via Inside Passage

Skagway

Occasionally in the early 1970s my commercial salmon fishing buddies and I would travel up to Skagway for the weekend, when fishing was closed around Haines, around 15 miles south. The merchants were thrilled to welcome our group of 20 or 30, kept their shops and restaurants open late for our business. Dust blew in the empty streets, or if the Alaska state ferry was in, perhaps a few dozen visitors wandered around. It was definitely sleepy.

This isn't what you'll find today. If you come by cruise ship, you'll probably arrive with eight or ten thousand other visitors to a town with perhaps 825 permanent residents.

Yet surprisingly, this town still retains its charm and the ghosts of the men who passed through in the epic Gold Rush that essentially put Alaska on the map still walk these streets.

As much as anything that kept the turn of the 20th century buildings intact – Skagway essentially was built between 1897 and 1900 – was the weather. Buildings that would have rotted away without maintenance in rainy Ketchikan, simply last longer in this much drier, sunnier climate.

But it is the drama of '97 and '98 that fills this town. Skagway blossomed for but a few years, lawless and

Top: the train winds along near the top of White Pass.

Below: the Klondikers didn't have the luxury of the train - look to the left of the train as you near the top, and you will see the old foot path taken by so many men bent over with their loads.

rough, then almost disappeared.

The gaunt-faced men have passed through to whatever fate The North had in store for them. But the town the boom built at the jumping-off place for the Klondike remains, looking much as it did in 1897 and 1898, when some 80 saloons and many professional women were anxious to serve the lonely men on the trail north.

Today, Skagway offers a unique experience to visitors. Even the vegetation is different from the rest of Southeast Alaska, because the town is under the influence of the harsher temperature extremes of the interior instead of the milder, cloudier maritime climate elsewhere in the region. Some of the native craftwork available here, especially of ivory, is truly excellent.

Note: Only ivory harvested by Native carvers in accordance with federal regulations may be sold legally. Make sure to get a export/transit permit if you buy ivory and plan to transit Canada on your way home. You'll need it to bring the ivory into the United States.

If Skagway's your last stop and you've saved your shopping until the end, you're in luck, the density of shops, particularly jewelry shops (their website, Skagway.com lists 17...) equals that of any other town on your cruise.

Shopping's great, but make sure you take some time between your excursion if you take one, and shopping, to just walk around town, get a sense of the place and of the

drama that took place here.

A good place to start is the Gold Rush National Historical Park Visitor Center, on the water side of downtown in the White Pass and Yukon Route Railroad station. It gives a great overview of the Gold Rush saga, as well as being in the train station for the WP&YR RR, which is fascinating just by itself. The town of Skagway also operates its own visitor's center, in the restored and very dramatic Arctic Brotherhood Hall, with its 10,000 or so nailed on pieces of driftwood, probably the most distinctive building in all of Alaska. The Fraternal Order of the Arctic Brotherhood constructed this hall and at least another in the Yukon Territories as a social and cultural organization to further the interests of the miners. It grew to have substantial political muscle as well. being an early advocate for more political power for Alaskans to manage their own affairs locally rather than through Washington, DC.

Pick up a copy of the walking tour map at the AB Hall. It's got directions up to the Gold Rush Cemetery, the Trail of '98 Museum, and other points of interest. It's definitely worthwhile to walk around with the map as your guide. The hike to Lower Dewey Lake (3 hrs. RT) has a

167

Skipper and Nils at Bites on Broadway, a wonderful spot for coffee drinks and amazing pastries!

steep stretch at the beginning, but then flattens out for a very pleasant walk.

Of course, Skagway's signature hike is up the old Chilkoot Trail, followed by so many of the men of '98. This is way, way more than a pleasant stroll; more like a grueling 4-5 day epic, and that's in summer, not in the depth of winter with the poorly insulated clothing of the day and 1,000 pounds of gear to pack over the summit. If you start up the trail, think about this: many of the men who took it made a dozen or more trips back and forth to ferry their loads if they couldn't afford to hire a native porter to help them.

One good way to see the old trail is an excursion combining a hike up the first few miles with a raft trip back down the river to Dyea. Skagway and Dyea boomed together, but today only Skagway remains, primarily because of the railroad and the docks quickly constructed there. (The tide flats at Dyea were almost a half mile wide on a big low tide, a long, long, way to carry your gear in multiple trips.)

What's interesting about Dyea is this—today the ruins seem really far from the water even at high tide. As it turns out, the land used to be much lower, and hence the water much closer. But as the glaciers that used to cover this whole area thousands of feet deep had only receded recently (well, maybe 10,000 years earlier) the land was experiencing 'glacial rebound' to the tune of about a half

to three quarters of an inch a year–enough to lift the land 6-7 feet since the Gold Rush and push the waterline back considerably in that flat river delta.

Just renting a bike downtown for a few hours is also a pretty mellow way just to explore the town and surrounds. The 10 miles out to Dyea is a pretty nice ride, but at least in 2005 much of the road was unpaved and though we loved the free tour by a ranger around the old townsite, we were really glad when a kind driver offered to run us up to "the top of the hill." (Which was most of the way back to Skagway.)

The helicopter excursions that operate out of near the waterfront are a good way to see the dramatic landscape as well as the Chilkoot Trail. There are a number of different variations most of which include a landing on top of one of the nearby glaciers and a chance to walk around. If you're ready to dig deep and have never been around dog teams, there is an excursion that includes a dog sled ride. The dogs get really excited then the choppers land and they know that they will be on the trail

Bottom: the Park Ranger at Dyea explains how glacial rebound has pushed the waterfront so far away.

soon!

Save some time at the end of the day to drop in to one of the local watering holes like the Red Onion Saloon, where a lot of the Klondikers tipped a few before they hit the rugged trail. If you want a bit more local color, try Moe's Frontier Bar, between 4th and 5th. Another highly recommended spot is The Skagway Fish Company, located by the small boat harbor out near the Railroad docks.

But most of all, try and take a few moments to think about the men who came, in the fall of 1897, and walked these streets and prepared for the obviously difficult challenges ahead. And the Skagway of those days was very very different from the cheerful busy place you'll encounter. By all accounts it was a grim place full of hard men.

Right: another gem - an Aleut hat, in Dennis Corringtons free museum.

SKAGWAY EXCURSIONS
(THESE CHANGE OFTEN; PLEASE CHECK WITH YOUR SHIP)

Skagway & The Dangerous Days Of '98
Klondike Summit & Liarsville Experience
Klondike Summit, Bridge, & Salmon Bake
Historical Tour & Liarsville Salmon Bake
Skagway's Original Street Car
To The Summit
Experience The Yukon
White Pass Scenic Railway
Best Of Skagway
Klondike Scenic Highlights
Delectable Jewell Gardens
Deluxe Klondike Experience & Rail
    Adventure
Alaska Garden & Gourmet Tour
Yukon Jeep Adventure
Horseback Riding Adventure
Klondike Bicycle Tour
Rainforest Bicycle Tour

Klondike Rock Climbing & Rappelling
Alaska Sled Dog & Musher's Camp
Chilkoot Trail Hike & Float Adventure
Glacier Point Wilderness Safari
Glacier Lake Kayak & Scenic Railway
Dog Sledding & Glacier Flightseeing
Glacier Discovery By Helicopter
Heli-Hike & Rail Adventure
Alaska Nature & Wildlife Expedition
Remote Coastal Nature Hike
Takshanuk Mountain Trail By 4x4
Eagle Preserve Wildlife River Adventure
Chilkoot Lake Freshwater Fishing
Wilderness Kayak Experience
Skagway's Custom Classic Cars
Glacier Country Flightseeing

Trimline or previous
top of glacier

ONTO THE ICE:
SKAGWAY HELICOPTER EXCURSION

Finally I bit the bullet and sprang for the $250 chopper excursion out of Skagway to the glaciers behind town. It was a lot of money for me.

But it was a stunning experience, not only on the glacier itself but also the ride in and out were extremely dramatic. The highlight was simply landing and getting out and walking around on top of that glacier and looking down into the crevasses. Plus it was a geology lesson - the trimline on the sides of the canyon showed the height of the glacier probably just a hundred years earlier: probably 70 or 80' higher!

KLONDIKE GOLD RUSH 1897-98

THE NOME NUGGET
DIPHTHERIA EPIDEMIC THREATENS

DEATH RACE BEGINS

DOG TEAM STARTS WITH STRICKEN NOME ANTITOXIN SERUM

SERUM RELAYED 674 BY TWENTY DOG TEA

TOGO NOT BALTO REA HERO SAYS L. SEPPAL

DENNIS CORRINGTON'S
IVORY MUSEUM

If you want to see some unique Alaska Native art, don't miss Dennis Corrington's Ivory Museum - in the back of his shop on Broadway and 3rd. When Dennis was a boarding school principal in the 1960s, often, in the summer, he would go out to visit his students at their homes in remote native communities. Asked to bring hard to get supplies, he was often paid in carved ivory, as the cash economy still hadn't reached there.

Developing a deep interest in Alaska Native art, he eventually set up a store in Skagway, both to sell art, but also to showcase some of the more unique pieces he had collected. The walrus tusks on these pages have been decorated with Alaska history scenes by the same scrimshaw technique used by the crews of whaling ships on the bones and teeth of sperm whales. Dennis travels regularly to visit carvers he has met over the years and bring back their best work.

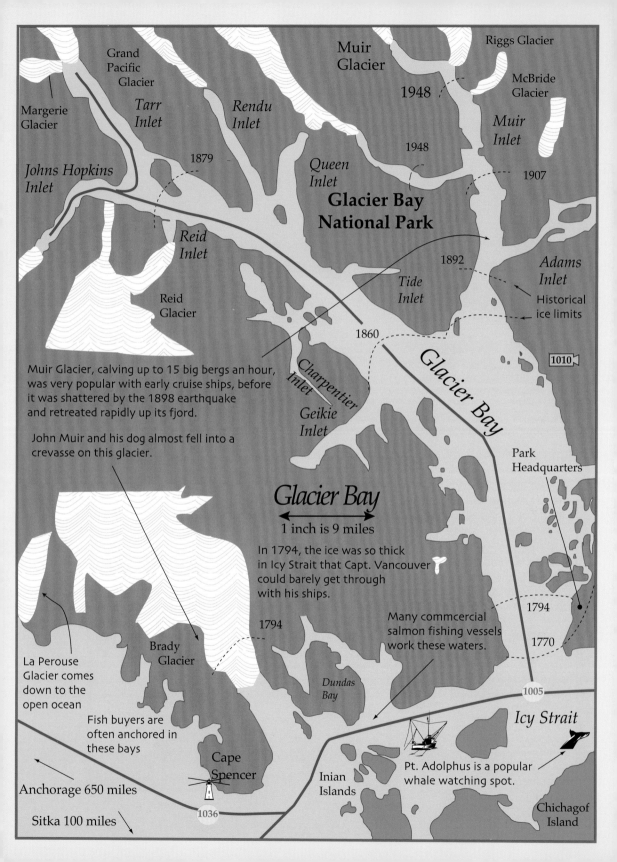

Grand
Pacific
Glacier

Riggs Glacier

McBride
Glacier

Muir
Glacier

1948

Margerie
Glacier

*Tarr
Inlet*

*Rendu
Inlet*

*Muir
Inlet*

1948

Johns Hopkins
Inlet

1879

*Queen
Inlet*

**Glacier Bay
National Park**

1907

*Reid
Inlet*

1892

*Adams
Inlet*

Reid
Glacier

*Tide
Inlet*

Historical
ice limits

1860

1010

Muir Glacier, calving up to 15 big bergs an hour,
was very popular with early cruise ships, before
it was shattered by the 1898 earthquake
and retreated rapidly up its fjord.

*Charpentier
Inlet*

Glacier Bay

John Muir and his dog almost fell into a
crevasse on this glacier.

*Geikie
Inlet*

Park
Headquarters

Glacier Bay

1 inch is 9 miles

In 1794, the ice was so thick
in Icy Strait that Capt. Vancouver
could barely get through
with his ships.

1794

Many commercial
salmon fishing vessels
work these waters.

1794

1770

1794

La Perouse
Glacier comes
down to the
open ocean

Brady
Glacier

*Dundas
Bay*

1005

Icy Strait

Fish buyers are
often anchored in
these bays

Cape
Spencer

Inian
Islands

Pt. Adolphus is a popular
whale watching spot.

Anchorage 650 miles

1036

*Chichagof
Island*

Sitka 100 miles

"This spacious inlet presented to our party an arduous task, as the space between the shores on the northern and southern sides, seemed to be entirely occupied by one compact sheet of ice as far as the eye could distinguish."
-George Vancouver, A Voyage ...

This was Vancouver's Lieutenant Joseph Whidbey looking east to Icy Strait from near the entrance to what is today Glacier Bay. The Strait was completely choked with ice and appeared to be impassable. To the north, the bay was closed by "compact solid mountains of ice, rising perpendicularly from the water's edge." Glacier Bay didn't exist; it was solid ice.

A month or so after this discovery, Vancouver and his men finished their three summer exploration of the Northwest Coast and determined that there was no ice free Northwest Passage back to the Atlantic. They headed off to England around Cape Horn. And Glacier Bay disappeared into the mists of time for some 80 years.

The Tlingits, of course, from the nearby village of Hoonah, and the Chilkats, hunted seals in Glacier Bay and had found that often the best hunting was on the very edge of the ice, where seals would often go to calve and nurse their pups. So it is very likely that during this period, if the ice had been receding, they would have been moving north with it, setting up hunting camps in Glacier Bay, but leaving no written

Top: Lampugh Glacier; note the kayakers and the fresh ice fall behind. Don't know how comfortable I would feel camping there.

Bottom: Margerie Glacier; the yacht gives a sense of how big it is.

Top: This splash from a falling iceberg is about 200 feet high!

Below: lichens are the first to grow in the bleak landscape left by receding Johns Hopkins Glacier.

records. Then in 1877, an explorer, Charles Wood, seeking to climb **Mt. St. Elias**, entered a now much bigger Glacier Bay and noted he had to travel 40 miles to reach the ice front. While there, he stopped at a Tlingit seal hunter's camp and recorded another bit of information that gives an insight to the ice's rapid recession. The chief, around 30 years old, said that within his lifetime the whole area around them had been solid ice.

This was startling: it meant that within that relatively short period of 30 years, 10 or 20 cubic miles of ice had disappeared. What caused such a great recession of the vast ice sheets during this period—some earlier version of global warming? No one really yet knows, but events in the late 1890s suggest substantial seismic activity in the Glacier Bay area. As these events were to prove, earthquakes seem to have the ability to shatter the ice in glaciers. Where such glaciers face the water, they will calve off immense amounts of ice after an earthquake, causing them to recede rapidly.

The modern history of Glacier Bay really began in October of 1879, when **John Muir,** a noted naturalist and early preservationist, left Wrangell by canoe with a missionary friend, and three native paddlers. He had heard rumors of ice mountains in Alaska and had come to find out for himself.

He had neither gore-tex nor fleece; his canoe was overloaded, and the route was one today's kayakers probably wouldn't even attempt at that time of year. They paddled west through Sumner Strait, up through Rocky Pass (Keku Strait) and across Frederick Sound to follow the west shore of Admiralty Island north. Their canoe was small, the waters big. When they'd finally crossed the choppy seven mile stretch of open water between Kuiu and Admiralty Islands, his chief paddler told him he hadn't slept for days worrying about it.

On they came, through Chatham and Icy Straits. As they traveled, the youngest native, Sitka Charley, told Muir he'd hunted seals as a boy in a bay full of ice and thought he could show Muir the way.

Muir was skeptical. Sitka Charley said the bay was without trees and that they'd need to bring their own firewood. The other paddlers, in all their lives throughout the region, had never seen a place without firewood.

They came to a bay cloaked in fog and storm. Sitka Charley became uneasy; the bay was much changed, he said, since he had seen it before. Even Vancouver's chart, a copy of which Muir so much relied upon, failed them, showing only a wide indentation in the shore.

Fortunately, they found a group of natives hunting

Top: Muir Glacier was the premier destination for early cruise ships, calving icebergs at a rapid rate. Plus passengers were invited to go ashore and climb up! American Geographic Society

Below: in his first trip in 1879, Muir traveled in a native canoe with frightened native Tlingit paddlers. Christine Cox

179

Top and bottom: the closer you get to a glacier, the more austere the landscape becomes.

seals and staying in a dark and crowded hut. One of the men agreed to guide them, and northward they paddled, off the chart and into that astonishing bay that had been birthed from the ice almost within their lifetimes.

The weather got worse and Muir's paddlers wanted to turn around:

"They seemed to be losing heart with every howl of the wind, and, fearing that they might fail me now that I was in the midst of so grand a congregation of glaciers, I made haste to reassure them that for ten years I had wandered alone among mountains and storms, and good luck always followed me, that with me, therefore, they need fear nothing. The storm would soon cease and the sun would shine to show us the way we should go, for God cares for us and guides us as long as we are trustful and brave, therefore all childish fear must be put away."
—John Muir, *Travels in Alaska*

So on they went, camping in rain, on snowy beaches, pushing farther and farther, only glimpsing the vastness and grandeur of the land.

Finally Muir climbed the flanks of one of the mountains just as the clouds passed, and he gazed, stunned, at the grandeur and the size of the many-armed bay that was revealed below him, full of slowly moving ice.

When the party headed back, the lateness of the season was evident. Each morning before they reached Icy Strait, the ice was frozen a little thicker, and the men had to cut

a lane for their canoe with an axe and tent poles.

Muir's descriptions of his time in Glacier Bay are some of the shining icons of Alaskan literature:

"Then setting sail, we were driven wildly up the fiord, as if the storm wind were saying, 'Go then, if you will, into my icy chamber; but you shall stay in until I am ready to let you out.' All this time sleety rain was falling on the bay and snow on the mountains; but soon after we landed the sky began to open. The camp was made on a rocky bench beneath the front of the Pacific Glacier, and the canoe was carried beyond the reach of the bergs and berg waves. The bergs were now crowded in a dense pack against the discharging front, as if the storm wind had determined to make the glacier take back her crystal offspring and keep them at home."

—John Muir, *Travels in Alaska*

After Muir's discovery and powerful writings about what he'd seen, the bay soon became one of the premier sights of the Western Hemisphere, and a regular stop for steamers such as the *Ancon*, the *Idaho*, and the *Queen*.

For many of the early steamer excursions, the ship's boats took passengers ashore where they would climb on top of the glacier itself to walk around amongst the crevasses!

The destination of those early trips was Muir Glacier,

Top: steamer *Queen* at Muir Glacier around 1895. In those days passengers would go ashore by skiff and climb ladders up to the top of the glacier and walk around. Imagine the reaction of the Park Service if you tried it today! American Geographic Society

Top: waiting for the big splash - the leaning tower at the middle of the photo is a tall as a six story building. After a long wait it finally toppled with a loud boom and the huge splash seen P. 178.

the face of which was an ice cliff towering above the decks of the approaching steamers and calving up to 12 icebergs an hour.

"The Muir presented a perpendicular ice front at least 200 feet in height, from which huge bergs were detached at frequent intervals. The sight and sound of one of these huge masses of ice falling from the cliff, or suddenly appearing from the submarine ice-foot, was something which once witnessed was not to be forgotten. It was grand and impressive beyond description."
—Fremont Morse, National Geographic, January, 1908

The 1899 Earthquake. At midday on September 10, 1899, as he was waiting for lunch at his salmon saltery in Bartlett Cove, now site of Glacier Bay National Park headquarters, August Buschmann was surprised to see his trunk come sliding across the floor at him. Moments later, the cook's helper came running into the building, frightened. He had been up on the hill at the native cemetery as the ground started to heave around him, and he thought the dead were coming to life.

The earthquake shattered the front of Muir Glacier and others, and within 48 hours Glacier Bay was a mass of floating ice so thick that ships could not reach the saltery at Bartlett Cove for two weeks. Icy Strait filled with ice, making Dundas Bay, ten miles to the west, inaccessible.

It wasn't until the following July that the steamer

Queen ventured close enough to Muir Inlet to see what had happened. The bay was still full of ice; only by picking their way along the shore west of Willoughby Island could they make any progress. The closest they could get to Muir Glacier was ten miles; the rest was solid ice.

Hidden behind a fleet of icebergs, Muir Glacier commenced a rapid retreat up the inlet; today the face is 25 miles north of where Muir found it in 1879.

Usually large cruise ships travel up the west side of Glacier Bay, often slowing or stopping to allow passengers a good view of **Reid Inlet**. Next to the north is the entrance to **Johns Hopkins Glacier**, very active in recent years, and the outgoing stream of ice is often so thick that ships often do not enter, for fear their propellors would contact ice pieces large enough to damage them. Additionally, seals use the ice flows in this inlet to birth their pups. During the period when they are actively birthing pups, ship traffic is prohibited here.

However, while seal activity is the thickest in the inlet itself, you are apt to see seals, and perhaps even with their pups on ice flows anywhere in Glacier Bay, so be sure to have your binoculars ready whenever you leave your cabin in this area.

Then most big ships will travel up and stop as close to **Margerie Glacier** and **Grand Pacific Glacier** as they can. In recent years there has been less ice here than John Hopkins, and ships are often able to approach fairly closely.

Top: Lampugh is 'grounded,' meaning it has receded back out of the water, although in this photo, parts of the glacier are still calving small pieces into the salt water.

Botttom: an 80' yacht in front of Margarie Glacier gives a sense of how high the glacier face is.

The most commonly seen whale in Alaskan waters is usually the humpback, large ones running up to **60 feet long!** A whale that big might weigh 40 tons. But the good thing is that they are generally easy to see and reasonably plentiful.

The key to seeing them is simply to look for their very visible spout, actually a plume of water vapor they emit when they breath out. As they are mammals, breathing air like we do, they must surface to breathe, often after being underwater for as long as 15 minutes (though 3-5 minutes is more common). This spout looks like a puff of smoke and can be seen easily from several miles away. Typically, a humpback will "sound" or dive deep for a longer time, then, surface, spouting, and then swim slowly, taking a few breaths on the surface, before sounding again.

Humpbacks here have an annual cycle familiar to many folks here: Alaska in the summer and Hawaii in the winter. Here, they are pretty much focused on fattening

themselves up on schools of herring.

A particularly dramatic behavior is called bubble feeding, when a group of whales work together to circle a school of herring, exhaling as they swim to essentially create a curtain of bubbles which serves to concentrate the herring in the middle. Then when the moment is right the group surfaces dramatically in the middle of the school, mouths all open as they gulp in tons of herring!

Another very exciting and fairly common behavior is breaching, when a whale shoots up, sometimes entirely clear of the water and crashes back down, sometimes with a loud boom. Reasons for breaches aren't entirely clear, though whale researchers suspect that they may be trying to shake loose parasites clinging to their skin.

Where to look for whales: Captains often stay in touch with other captains so as to steer their ships toward whale encounters, as long as it is not too far off their route. Also many cruise ships employ a naturalist who could be paged to the bridge in order to give a narrative over the ships PA system if whales are sighted. However, there are many activities aboard the big ships, and if there is a revenue generating activity going on like Bingo or an art auction, whales might not be announced.

So.. if you really want to see whales.. keep your binoculars with you and keep a sharp eye on the waters around the ship!

Opposite top: dramatic breach, alaskastock.

Opposite lower: a humpback spouts in the narrow waters of Kootznahoo Inlet. I watched as the big whale followed a school of herring with the tide into the narrow inlet, chowed down, and then when the tide started to ebb, let the current gently ease him back out into open waters.

Top: nice humpback whale seen close to a whale watching boat operating out of Juneau.

WILDLIFE IN GLACIER BAY

Top: whale breach by Duncan Kowalski. Opposite top: brown bear chowing down on mussels along the shore in Glacier Bay. Opposite lower left: seals on iceberg. Icebergs, protected from most predators, are a popular spot for seals to have their pups. Opposite lower right: see the mountain goats? Pretty hard to see; look for white specks on upper hillsides that seem to be moving.

Below: sea otter with pup on top. This is the critter that started the otter pelt rush that brought the Russians to Alaska and the Northwest coast.

Glacier Bay has traditionally been a good spot to see humpbacks and other whales, so be sure to have your binoculars with you on deck and remember to keep a sharp eye peeled. Your ship will have a naturalist, but there may be whales that he or she doesn't see.

Another good spot for whale watching is **Point Adolphus**, **Mile 1000**, directly south of the entrance to Glacier Bay. Your Captain may query the local whale watching boats and if he gets a report of sightings he may take a loop through before continuing on his course.

I was here in 1997 on the *Dawn Princess* when our Captain got a tip and, taking a loop through, spotted a group of humpbacks and let our ship drift, in hopes they might come closer. Regulations require big ships to keep a quarter of a mile away from whales, but in this case, after we stopped, the whales swam right over to us. I was on deck seven, the promenade deck, and had my camera handy as our fascinated group peered over the rail as the pod of five big humpbacks moved closer and closer until they were almost directly below where we were standing!

I had seen humpbacks blow at a distance before, but this time they were close enough to hear their distictive 'trumpeting' when they exhaled after a long dive. This was actually too close as their breath was bad, bad, bad!

Like other roadless towns around Southeast Alaska, Tenakee, 50 miles southwest of Juneau, was built around good fishing. With strong salmon runs and plentiful crab in nearby Chatham Strait, and a local cannery, Tenakee was a busy place for most of the 20th century.

Just ask Rosie, seen above. Her Blue Moon Cafe was the center for all the action in those years. Maybe too much action. "Why they alla time wanna fight?" she said, remembering the boisterous action when the fishermen and cannery workers and loggers were all in town and her cafe drinking at once.

Those days are gone. The cannery closed in 1976, and town slowly became a sleepy, more and more seasonal community as the years went by. Fortunately there are just enough families living year round to keep the school going, a critical part in community life.

What's unique about Tenakee compared to most other roadless communities in Southeast Alaska is its layout. The long line of homes and gardens spread out along the north shore of Tenakee Inlet, allows most to have a view of the water, if not waterfront and that wonderful southwest exposure.

Plus there's the hot springs: a community building built over a pool of delightfully hot and clean water: a great way to get through a long Alaska winter!

SMALL SHIP CRUISE;
A WEEK ON UNCRUISE'S
WILDERNESS EXPLORER

Day 1: Joined our 75 passenger ship in gorgeous Sitka, motored north through narrow Olga Strait to drop the hook off deserted and mysterious looking Magoun Islands.

Day 2: Wow: all hands kayaking and exploring in the inflatables this morning. A few seals, lots of eagles, but best was just ghosting slowly along the dramatic shoreline, while our guide explained what we were looking at. Through Peril Strait in the afternoon to lonely Takatz Bay.

Day 3: Explored Takatz Bay in the kayaks this drizzly morning after a good group stretch on the back deck. But what a spot: the bay winding back deep into the wilderness and what do we see but two big brown-

ies maybe waking up from a long winter's sleep.

Up wide and empty Chatham Strait in the afternoon back to supper in Pavlof Bay. Did we want to paddle after supper? You bet! So off we went and there was another big brownie, digging for mussels on the beach!

Day 4: Seal Bay, Chicagof Island: a little stiff tonight - we picked the most strenuous of the day's offerings: a "Yak and Whack" - paddle 4 miles, grab a bite in the beach, then bushwhack (there is no trail) for a couple of miles before paddling back. Whew.. glad that drinks are free on these rigs....!

Day 5: Inian Islands exploring by inflatable. This is the very wild and rugged outer coast, exposed to the full power of the North Pacific, the shores stripped of vegetation a full fifty feet above the water by the power of the winter storms. Saw exquisite and elusive tufted puffins and California sea lions that were a little too curious for my liking - something about a 1000 pound critter with sharp teeth approaching right next to the rubber tubes of our boat!

Day 6: Glacier Bay: Wow... But sobering as Grand Pacific Glacier, which was active and calving just a decade ago is retreating and dirt covered. Luckily the 100' high wall of its neighbor, Margarie Glacier, was exquisite in shades of blue, and even occasionally calving small bergs.

Best for us was launching the kayaks and paddling through the ice off of Lampugh Glacier on a total bluebird day! Wrapped it up with great birdwatching at the Marble Islands and an evening ashore at Bartlett Cove.

Day 7: Exploring Funter Bay by kayak and ashore with our naturalist guide, Alison, whose easy manner and amazing eye showed us some exquisite flowers we would have otherwise missed. Her excitement ("Be still, my heart," sez she..) at finding a rare Calypso Orchid was contagious.

Day 8: Juneau: bummer - back to the busy real world. Thank you so much UnCruise!
See UnCruise.com

A CRUISE SHIP AND A
ZIPLINE AT A CANNERY?
WHAT WOULD THE
OLD-TIMERS HAVE SAID?

ICY STRAIT POINT

Top: Hold on tight; the zipline here is the longest of its kind in the world, 5,330' long and with a 1330' vertical drop. Six riders can zip at once, and at one point you are almost 300' above the cannery with a spectacular view out to Icy Strait, Port Frederick, and your ship. Other excursions include a Hoonah bike tour, wildlife and bear watching expeditions, a forest/nature tram ride, salmon sports fishing, flightseeing over nearby Glacier Bay, Tlingit dancing and a wild Alaska seafood cooking lesson/meal. Photos courtesy Icy Strait Point.

Opening its doors for the first time in 2003, Icy Strait Point is unique among Alaska cruise ports as ship visits are limited to one at a time, and the facility–a renovated cannery next to a Tlingit native village–is surrounded by wilderness. If you've cruised Alaska before, you know how congested the other towns can get with four or five ships in port at once, so making a visit here is a welcome change.

The new dock (2017) means passengers can walk directly ashore to the old cannery complex and dock where there is a museum, cafe/restaurant, and numerous shops. Cannery life was a major cultural and economic element in coastal Alaska and this is an excellent chance to get a close look. There are walking trails around the site and additionally there is a shuttle bus to nearby Hoonah, the largest Tlingit village in Alaska. The facility is owned by a native corporation and the richness of Tlingit culture is a strong element throughout.

Icy Strait Point is located in Port Federick, just across Icy Strait from the entrance to Glacier Bay.

Left top: Hoonah Cold Storage. Commercial fishing is a major activity here.

Right top: Hoonah around 1900. Then as now, commercial fishing was the major activity here.

Opposite lower right: what's unusual about this zipline is that it is four parallel lines, allowing users to 'race' each other to the bottom.

To Seward

Whittier

College Fjord

Prince William Sound

Many salmon gillnet vessels operate in the remote Copper River delta area. Marketed as Copper River salmon, the early sockeye run here fetches very high prices in restaurants and to fishermen.

Cape Hinchinbrook

1480

Columbia Glacier

Valdez

ALASKA

Gulf of Alaska

1380

Cape St. Elias, with a 500' spire just off the lighthouse is a major landmark and a spectacular sight at dawn, when most northbound cruise ships pass it.
Have your camera ready!

Cordova

Copper River

Cape St. Elias

1310

· Katalla

With many peaks over 10,000', this part of the Alaska coast has been nicknamed "The roof of North America." Mt. St. Elias, at 18,008 feet, dominates vistas here and seems to loom over the coastal lowlands.

Bering Glacier

UP THE GLACIER COAST
Cape Spencer, Mile 1036 to
Cape Hinchinbrook, Mile 1380

W N

S E

Cape Yakataga

1250

Icy Bay

1220

Mt. St. Elias 18,008'

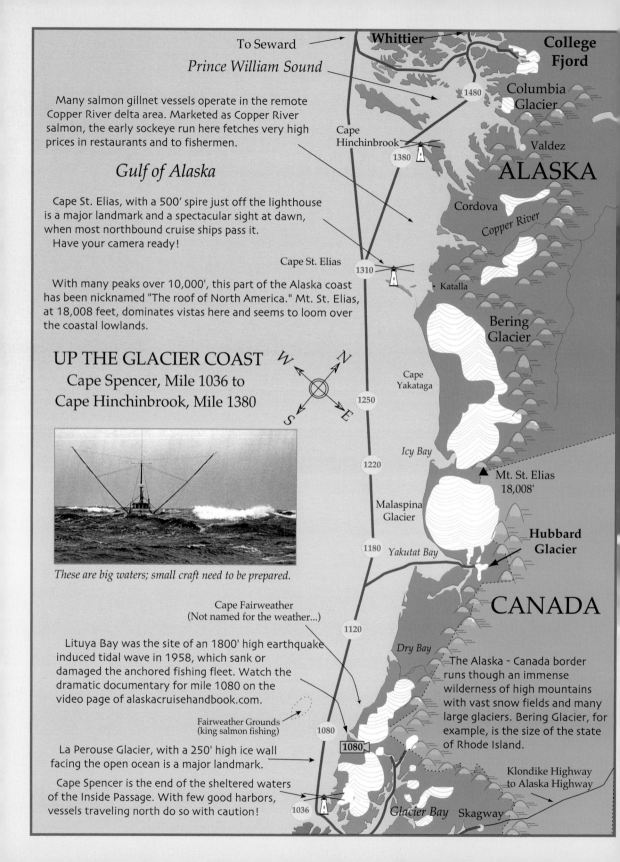

Malaspina Glacier

Yakutat Bay

1180

Hubbard Glacier

These are big waters; small craft need to be prepared.

CANADA

Cape Fairweather
(Not named for the weather...)

1120

Lituya Bay was the site of an 1800' high earthquake induced tidal wave in 1958, which sank or damaged the anchored fishing fleet. Watch the dramatic documentary for mile 1080 on the video page of alaskacruisehandbook.com.

Dry Bay

The Alaska - Canada border runs though an immense wilderness of high mountains with vast snow fields and many large glaciers. Bering Glacier, for example, is the size of the state of Rhode Island.

Fairweather Grounds
(king salmon fishing)

1080

La Perouse Glacier, with a 250' high ice wall facing the open ocean is a major landmark.

1080

Klondike Highway to Alaska Highway

Cape Spencer is the end of the sheltered waters of the Inside Passage. With few good harbors, vessels traveling north do so with caution!

1036

Glacier Bay Skagway

"We thought it was an iceberg at first, way out past Spencer - you used to see 'em out there sometimes—but then when we got closer, we could see it was a big crab boat. But ... wasn't she iced over! Just like one big hill of ice, with some rigging and antennas sticking out of the top, and ragged pieces of plywood covering where the pilothouse windows were broken out. Pretty soon we could see the crew was all out on deck, knocking off the ice with baseball bats and shoveling it over the side as fast as they could. It gets bad out there..."
- *Crab Fisherman Russell Fulton*

Mariners tread cautiously here. Gone are the harbors with easy access when the wind blows. (Except for a few bays just north of the Cape.) This is the outside coast: bold, rugged, with few harbors, and backed by the stunning and rugged St. Elias Range. Take the time to go on deck with your binoculars. In North America, only Alaska has a coast like this.

If the coast of British Columbia had been like this, the development of coastal Alaska would have been very different. The myriad harbors and sheltered passages of the Inside Passage allowed very small craft to travel to Alaska. Many would never have dared head north if their only route was outside, along a coast like this.

Top: our crabber, the *Flood Tide* after a bitter wind flowing down the Copper River valley, iced us up very badly.

Below: don't try to enter these bays except in calm weather with someone who knows the channel. It was so difficult to enter these rivers that a cannery in nearby Yakutat, **built a railroad** to Dry Bay rather than rely on boats to deliver the fish up the coast.

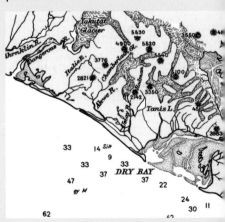

Tragedy at **Lituya Bay** - 21 men from French Explorer LaPerouse were lost when their longboats were overwhelmed by the tide rip at the entrance to Lituya Bay, June 1786.

Even today, mariners fear this bay. Not only does it have a very dangerous entrance, but has had a series of tidal waves, caused by landslides at the head of the bay.

Below: **LaPerouse Glacier** at Mile 1060 is a major landmark, easily visible from miles offshore.

Look for La Perouse Glacier at Mile 1060. With its almost perpendicular 200-300' face, it's an outstanding landmark along this section of coast. This is an active glacier! In some years, like 1997, advancing into the ocean, while just a year earlier receding enough to allow foot passage across the front at low tide.

The land to the east, from the coast up over the Fairweather Range, and into the Yukon Territories of Canada, almost to the Alaska Highway, is for the most part a vast wilderness. It does present, however, an opportunity for kayakers or rafters willing to travel for long distances far from any help or source of supplies.

Dry Bay, Mile 1100, is the mouth of the Alsek River, and the end of a popular kayak trip that starts when kayakers launch their kayaks where the Alaska Highway crosses the Alsek River.

For the truly brave hearted, the Upper Alsek includes the infamous **Turnback Canyon**. It was named after the 1898 gold prospectors who tried the Alsek as a route to the interior, had one look at the ten-mile chute of churning icy water and turned around.

This unforgiving canyon has become to kayakers what K2 or Everest is to climbers. A word of caution—sometimes high water and fast currents make this canyon truly impassable and kayakers are urged to have a contingency plan for a helicopter (at 132$ a minute) to shuttle them around the canyon. Also the chopper only takes 900 pounds, including kayaks, tents, food, etc.. Google

Turnback Canyon for some great Youtube videos of the helicopter trip! You can see for yourself why most kayakers opt for the chopper detour!

The shore from Yakutat down to Cape Spencer is nicknamed **Alaska's Lost Coast,** and a number of fit young individuals have traveled it with bikes and pack rafts (small inflatible rafts). You ride your bike when you can, push it through the woods and over rocks when you can't, and inflate and launch your raft to paddle (with bike) across the various rivers and wide creeks. Not for the weak-hearted!

Three bare, light colored bluffs distinguish Ocean Cape, the entrance to Yakutat Bay, at Mile 1162. This bay is the only really good anchorage for large vessels, in the 350 miles between Cape Spencer and Prince William Sound. Nevertheless, in very heavy weather, breakers or very high swells have been observed all the way across this 15 mile-wide entrance.

Yakutat, some five miles inside the bay from Ocean Cape, is the northernmost village of the Tlingit Indians, many of whom fish for salmon nearby. It is also a popular destination for sports fishermen who use it as a staging and jumping off place for remote fish camps.

The Roof of North America—East and north of Hubbard Glacier is an area that has been nicknamed 'The Roof of North America'—an immense rock, ice, and snow

The old *Island Princess* at Hubbard Glacier gives a clear sense of the size of this 400 foot high and 6 mile wide ice front! A bit isolated on the outside coast, Hubbard is usually only visited by ships traveling to either Seward or Whittier.

Below: Hubbard Glacier; note where it almost blocks off the entrance to Russell Fiord, lower right.

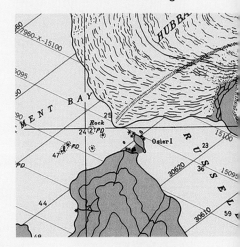

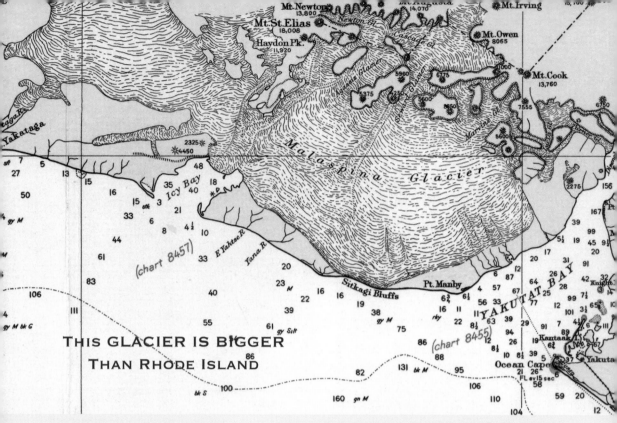

THIS GLACIER IS BIGGER
THAN RHODE ISLAND

Top: Icy Bay area, 1930s. Since then the glacier has receded back from the coast but it is still immense.

Above: bergs from Icy Bay occasionally still make it all the way out into the open ocean here.

world with many of the continent's highest peaks. Ten thousand-footers are common here, and there are at least four over 15,000'. Much of this area is the **Wrangell St. Elias National Park and Wilderness.** This mountain wall catches the eastward flowing moisture-laden air, which falls as heavy snow. The immense weight of the snow pack creates the largest glaciers on the entire Pacific coast. Hubbard Glacier is part of a vast ice mass that extends along a few miles behind the coast in an unbroken line (except for two places) almost to Anchorage, nearly 400 miles away. Today the glaciers have all receded substantially back from the shore, but a century ago, the ice reached the ocean in many places.

Just to the north of Yakutat Bay is **Malaspina Glacier,** a giant lobe glacier larger than the state of Rhode Island. Lobe glaciers are formed when glaciers emerge from their canyons and spread out onto the coastal lowlands. In the early part of last century, Malaspina reached all the way to the ocean, but today it has retreated substantially.

150 years or so ago, **Icy Bay,** like Glacier Bay in 1790, wasn't a bay at all, but a solid wall of ice, 10 miles wide, dumping big bergs into the open ocean.

Mariners have learned the hard way to be careful when anchorning here. One big steel crabber slipped in here to wait out a storm outside. But in the middle of the night a giant bang had the crew out on deck where an iceberg,

moving in the tide had slammed into them, dropping re-frigerator sized pieces onto their deck. Occasionall bergs escaping from Icy Bay will dot the ocean beaches north of the entrance!

The **Copper River** emerges from the mountains be-tween Miles and Childs Glaciers, and spreads out into a delta with many islands as it enters the Gulf of Alaska. The river delta and the myriad sand bars are the scene of considerable activity in the late spring and summer with shallow draft salmon gillnetters seeking the well-known Copper River Red Salmon. These are active glaciers! There is often much ice in the bay, and sometimes icebergs will drift out of the bay and form a regular line of stranded bergs along the outside shore, all the way northwest to Cape Yakataga.

"**Cape St. Elias**, the south end of Kayak Island, is an important and unmistakable landmark. It is a precipitous, sharp, rocky ridge, about one mile long and 1,665 feet high, with a low, wooded neck between it and the high parts of the island farther north. About 0.2 mile off the cape is the remarkable Pinnacle Rock, 494 feet high."
—U.S. Coast Pilot 9, 1964 ed.

Top: off **Cape St. Elias** at dawn, the 500' high pinnacle rock just off the lighthouse is clearly visible.

Lower: gillnetters picking fish in the Copper River Delta. The popular Copper River Reds, an intensely marketed seasonal salmon, comes from this area.

Tidal wave from landslide stripped hillside of trees down to bare rock, to a height of 1,800 feet above the water!

Around 10 on the evening of Aug 9,1958, anchored fisherman Howard Ulrich was awakened by his boat rolling suddenly in what had been a peaceful anchorage. He stepped up into the pilothouse and what he saw became etched into his mind forever:

"These great snow-capped giants [the mountains at the head of the bay] shook and twisted and heaved. They seemed to be suffering unbearable internal tortures. Have you ever see a 15,000- foot mountain twist and shake and dance?

At last, as if to rid themselves of their torment, the mountains spewed heavy clouds of snow and rocks into the air and threw huge avalanches down their groaning sides.

During all this I was literally petrified, rooted to the deck. It was not fright but a kind of stunned amazement. I do not believe I thought of it as something that was going to affect me.

This frozen immobility must have lasted for two minutes or longer. Then it came to a dramatic end. It so happened that I was looking over the shoulder of Cenotaph Island toward the head of the bay, when a mighty seismic disturbance exploded and there was a deafening crash.

I saw a gigantic wall of water, 1,800' high, erupt against the west mountain. I saw it lash against the island, which rises to a height of 320 feet above sea level, and cut a 50-foot-wide swath through the trees of its center. Then I saw it backlash against the eastern shore, sweeping away the timber to a height of more than 500 feet.

Finally, I saw a 50-foot wave come out of this churning turmoil and move along the eastern shore directly toward me."
— Courtesy of Alaska Magazine

This was an earthquake that knocked the needle off the seismograph at the University of Washington, 1000+ miles away. Ulrich and his son were lucky - their boat survived, barely. Another boat, the *Badger*, sank after being carried over the trees of the north spit, its crew survived in a dingy, while a third boat was lost with all aboard.

Ever since 1958, mariners anchoring in Lituya Bay do so uneasily. Wondering as they look up at the big glaciers behind the Bay: can it happen again?

THE EDGE OF THE KNOWN WORLD
(From a trip up the coast, March, 1971, in our 104' steel king crab boat)

Twenty miles north of Yakutat, one of the few harbors along that coast, a wind came up. After five minutes it was blowing seventy. The temperature was fifteen degrees. The first spray over the bow froze instantly on the wheelhouse windows; we turned around with hardly a discussion. Our vessel was the best that the finest Northwest shipyard could produce, built for winter in the North Pacific, but turn around we did.

In the outer part of Yakutat Bay, a sobering sight had us all up in the wheelhouse. The 140-foot trawler *Deep Sea*, pioneer of the whole king crab fishery, lay at anchor with a big covered barge in tow. She had iced up bad as had her barge, all the corners and sharp angles softened by the smooth and sinister contours of thick ice. But the really sobering part was the barge. The whole front of the structure built on it, sort of a long metal warehouse looking building, was crumpled in, the top and sides mangled for a third of the way back and in places the aluminum sheeting was ripped like paper. Our skipper got the story over the radio—the barge was a floating shrimp cannery, headed for Kodiak, four hundred miles to the west. They had gotten within 10 miles of the shelter of Cape Saint Elias, 130 miles north of Yakutat, when the wind came up. Two hours later, the seas had punched in the front of the barge, forcing them to turn around and run before the storm, icing all the way, as they went back to Yakutat.

We tied with frozen lines to a silent cannery wharf, and I walked up to the village with Johnny Nott and Misssouri Bob in the blowing, drifting snow. In the whole settlement we saw only two lighted windows, and nowhere a footprint or car track. We trudged back to the boat through the knee-deep snow with the trees only dark shapes on our left, and the cove on our right lit up by the brillant crab lights. Our boat, with the bark of her diesel generator filling the night, seemed almost like a visitor from another planet.

A blizzard swept in from the Canadian Yukon to the east after midnight. At the head of the harbor, in the lee of the great mountains, we lay sheltered from its force, but morning showed a grey and eerie world. Outside the windows of the pilothouse, a steady plume of snow settled down on us, drifting down from the wharf above. By noon, what little free deck we had was drifted rail to rail, almost waist deep with snow. It was as if barely 1200 miles north of Seattle, we'd come to the edge of the world as we knew it. And we still had some 1000 miles more to go.

Ah, I shouldn't have let Dad steer at night... that's how it all started—he was almost seventy then and his eyes were starting to go. We were headed up to fish Prince William, and I just laid down for a bit. There was a moon, and not much wind, so I thought he'd be OK. But then the next thing I knew we were in the breakers—he'd just gotten in too close to the beach. The boat started to break up and that was way before survival suits, so we just ended up on the beach in our woolies (long woolen underwear).

"It all happened so quick there really wasn't any time for a radio call. The snow was right down to the water's edge in places—it was late April—so I figured our only chance was to try and make it back to Cape Yakataga. I knew there was at least a lodge or something there...

"It was really tough going—seemed like every mile there was a stream that we either had to wade across, sometimes up to our chests, and all icy snowmelt.

"We slept just huddled together, and then on the afternoon of the second day, Dad told me to leave him—that he couldn't go on any longer... The worst part of it was that we'd lost our snoose (powdered or so called 'smokeless' tobacco) and our chew both with the boat.

"If we hadn't stumbled across an old trapper's cabin, and found some old moldy pipe tobacco that we could chew on, I don't think we would have made it. But we spent the night in there, and each of us got a good chew in our mouths so the next morning life seemed a little more bearable...

"Turns out BP had some sort of drilling operation at the Cape back then, and the first building we came to was the mess hall. It was noon, and we walked in the door, all scratched up, just in bloody ripped woolies and our rubber boots. Everyone turned as we came in the door, and for a long moment, you could have heard a pin drop in there..."

—Dick Kietel, fisherman

Top: If hypothermia doesn't get you, the bears might: tracks along the beach north of Dangerous River. Brenda Carney photo

Left: Some sort of weird Halloween? Actually this is my crew, practicing putting on their survival suits. Developed in the late 1970s the buoyant and insulating foam suits were quickly embraced by much of the Alaska fleet. Boats with no room to store them sometimes tied the suits to the mast.

Something woke me around midnight— the motion of our new steel king crabber that had seemed so big tied to the dock in Seattle: slow and loggy, hesitating at the end of each roll, as if it weren't sure it was going to roll back the other way. I dressed and took the steps up to pilothouse and immediately saw the problem.

Ice! A bitter wind had come up, ripping the spray off the ocean and freezing to our hull and rigging. Enough had accumulated to make us so top heavy that capsizing was a very real possibility. This was how vessels died, I suddenly realized.

We dressed quickly in warm clothes and rain gear, and, secured by a safety lines, inched out onto the bow, knocking the ice off with hammers and baseball bats and kicking the pieces over the side.

Once a large sea loomed suddenly out the night and the bow dipped into it and we were suddenly hip deep in the dark swirling water. Our skipper stared out in alarm from the pilothouse through the tiny circle of ice-free glass, and then the bow rose, and sea poured back over the side.

On the back deck, our double stacked pots were a hill of smooth ice and we struggled, hammering and shoveling until we were wet with sweat. Finally our boat seemed to ride a little safer, and we jogged slowly to the shelter of a tiny island, hammering and shoveling all the way.

We pulled the big steel hatch covers off, loaded as many of the heavily iced pots into the holds as would fit, laid the rest flat on the deck, lowered the boom and lashed it to the stern. The icy wind still clawed at us, but there was no sea. When we were finally done I looked around. We were probably the only humans within 50 miles and the vista— frozen islands, shore and mountains, now hidden, now revealed by moon and racing clouds, was unspeakably bleak.

"It's the Copper River wind, boy," the skipper's brother told me in the galley when we were done and warming up. "It just sucks down off the flats and ice after a little sou'west breeze. All that ocean air just gets frozen up there, and all of a sudden decides to roll back to the sea."

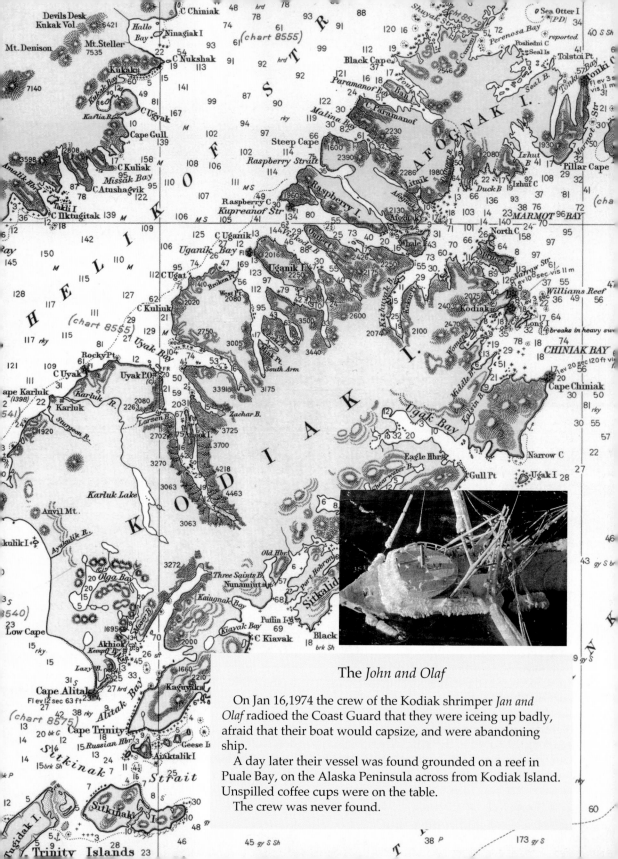

The *John and Olaf*

On Jan 16, 1974 the crew of the Kodiak shrimper *Jan and Olaf* radioed the Coast Guard that they were iceing up badly, afraid that their boat would capsize, and were abandoning ship.

A day later their vessel was found grounded on a reef in Puale Bay, on the Alaska Peninsula across from Kodiak Island. Unspilled coffee cups were on the table.

The crew was never found.

KODIAK ISLAND

Twice the size of Long Island, but with a population of just 14,000 souls, Kodiak Island is big and wild. With substantial salmon runs, commercial fishing was the first big industry and still is.

Home to the Sugpiaq tribe of Alaska natives, they were fishermen and hunters until the Russian's arrival around 1884. With an insatiable hunger for sea otter pelts, the Russians subjugated the natives in pretty brutal fashion, forcing them to hunt otters. After Russia sold Alaska to the United States in 1867, Kodiak was, due to its remoteness, only slowly settled by Americans, primarily coming to fish and raise foxes for their fur. Salmon canneries, each due to its remoteness, having to be a whole little town in itself, popped up in many bays around the island.

But the fishery that put Kodiak on the map, was king crab, now celebrated in the Discovery Channel series, Deadliest Catch. Today's boats are steel with impressive modern electronics and hydraulics; but in the early days it was wooden boats and tough, tough men. When the 200 mile limit was enacted in 1976 pushing the big foreign fleets out of the Bering Sea, Kodiak fishermen were among the first to get in on what was to become legendary fishing, with crew shares on top boats approaching 100,000$ in the late 70s and early 1980s.

Tourism, centered primarily on sportsfishing, is also a significant part of the Kodiak summer economy.

Top: where there's salmon, there are usually bears not too far away. At waterfalls, the alpha male gets the best spot, where he can actually catch jumping salmon with his teeth. When he's got one, he will walk over to the bank, put one hand on the fish's head, neatly strip off a fillet with his claw, flip the fish over to fillet the other side, and just flip the carcass to the gulls.

Above: king crab and happy crewman, 1971. This fellow, Walter Kuhr, started out as a deckhand in 1971, and within a decade was owner of several big crabbing and trawling boats. His story was not uncommon.

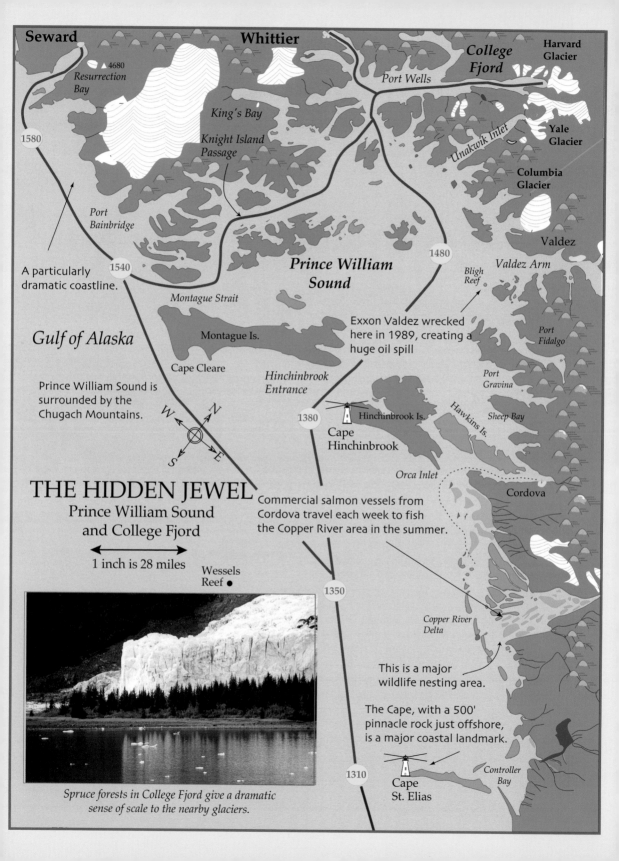

Seward

Whittier

College Fjord

Harvard Glacier

4680

Resurrection Bay

Port Wells

King's Bay

Knight Island Passage

Yale Glacier

Unakwik Inlet

1580

Columbia Glacier

Port Bainbridge

Valdez

A particularly dramatic coastline.

1540

Prince William Sound

1480

Bligh Reef

Valdez Arm

Gulf of Alaska

Montague Strait

Montague Is.

Exxon Valdez wrecked here in 1989, creating a huge oil spill

Port Fidalgo

Cape Cleare

Hinchinbrook Entrance

Port Gravina

Prince William Sound is surrounded by the Chugach Mountains.

W N S E

1380

Hinchinbrook Is.

Hawkins Is.

Sheep Bay

Cape Hinchinbrook

Orca Inlet

Cordova

THE HIDDEN JEWEL

Prince William Sound and College Fjord

Commercial salmon vessels from Cordova travel each week to fish the Copper River area in the summer.

◄─────►

1 inch is 28 miles

Wessels Reef ●

1350

Copper River Delta

This is a major wildlife nesting area.

The Cape, with a 500' pinnacle rock just offshore, is a major coastal landmark.

Controller Bay

1310

Cape St. Elias

Spruce forests in College Fjord give a dramatic sense of scale to the nearby glaciers.

CHAPTER 7
THE HIDDEN JEWEL:
PRINCE WILLIAM SOUND

Cape Hinchinbrook, Mile 1380, is the entrance to many-armed Prince William Sound, an area about the size of some small states. Except for three towns—Cordova, Valdez, and Whittier, and a few settlements, the area is mostly uninhabited, a dramatic island archipelago wilderness with many active glaciers.

If you are on a northbound ship, the early morning light here can be truly spectacular. First light comes real early in the summer, so as soon as you wake up, have a look out your window or if you have an inside cabin, dress warmly and step outside with your camera. The shining 12 and 13,000 footers of the Chugach mountains are sometimes clearly visible from 80 miles away.

Early Explorers: Captain James Cook briefly explored this area in 1778. Setting out from England in the spring of 1768, he made three voyages to become one of the most famous explorers in history. Much of his work was spent in filling in the vast blank space on the map that was the Pacific Ocean. Exploring this section of the coast was to be his last hurrah. Returning to Hawaii, he was tragically killed in a scuffle with natives in February of 1779.

The Sound teems with sea life such as sea lions, seal, and frequently, humpback whales. Sea otters in particular have made a remarkable comeback. After being hunted almost to extinction, their population has risen to over 100,000 statewide. A particularly good place to watch for them is on small floating ice pieces in College Fjord.

PASSENGER TIP
Have a look to the north when you enter Prince William Sound; you may get a glimpse of Columbia Glacier, the largest and also fastest receding tidewater glacier in Alaska. It was ice from this glacier that forced the Exxon Valdez to alter course and eventually hit Bligh Reef.

Below: this ice cave is probably 200' high - compare it to the full sized spruce trees on the left!

But it is salmon that has been the bread and butter for most fishermen here. During the summer season, tenders or fish-buying vessels spread out to the farthest reaches of the many fjords of the region, to buy fish from both purse seiners and gill-netters. These tenders acted like mother ships, often supplying groceries, water, and fuel for their boats, fishing too far from town to return at night. Many fishermen live in remote communities like Cordova where fishing was about the only game in town.

In the hierarchy of salmon fishermen in Alaska, (There are many salmon fishing districts in Alaska, each with its different style of vessel and gear.) the "Prince William Sound Boys" in the 1980s were doing well. Salmon prices were high, catches were good, and it was a scenic and reasonably calm place to fish. Life was good.

This comfortable world was shattered on March 23, 1989, when a long nightmare began—the oil spill.

The evening of March 23, 1989 was calm, with a little fog, when the *Exxon Valdez* carrying 211,000 tons of North Slope crude oil departed Valdez. A few hours later, Captain Josesph Hazelwood encountered some ice, not uncommon at that time of year. As the vessel was maneuvered around the ice, the tanker hit Bligh Reef, ripping her single skinned hull open.

Within 24 hours some 10 million gallons of crude oil had spread into a slick that covered about 18 square miles. Fortunately, the three days following the grounding were unusually calm—perfect weather for skimming and recovering oil from the surface of the water. Unfortunately, much of the oil spill response equipment promised to be always ready, wasn't available, and the spill

Top: where was the state of the art oil spill equipment that was promised to be always ready to respont to a spill? The barge that carried it was not available due to maintainance issues, and the booms, and other equipment to deal with a spill were buried deep in snow.

Below: closing the door after the horse has left the barn—a tug returning from tanker escort duty. After the spill the rules were changed to escort tankers all the way out of Prince William Sound. Would the availability of a tug have stopped the spill? Probably not as there was nothing wrong with the *Exxon Valdez*'s engines

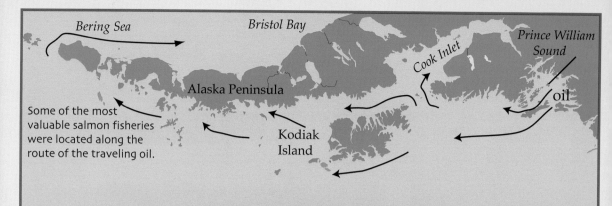

Route of Spilled Oil from *Exxon Valdez*

Despite promises that containment equipment would be available in case of a spill, several days passed before that equipment could be readied and brought to the scene of the great spill. By that time it was too late; the oil had congealed, becoming very hard to collect, and, traveling westward with the currents, closed commercial fishing areas along the way. In the fall of 2007, more than 18 years after the spill, many fishermen, including your mapmaker, were still waiting to be paid for the spill's damages.

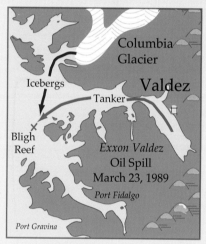

As the expression goes, "The only ones who win are the lawyers.." A settlement for punitive damages spent 20 years working its way up to the U.S. Supreme court, only to get slashed...

I had been hoping for enough for a little vacation - our fish prices took a big dip that year because of the spill - but the final was more like enough for a good night out on the town..

spread far and wide, closing many rich fishing grounds. For many fishermen it was their worst nightmare. Exxon organized and funded a huge cleanup effort that fortunately employed many fishermen and their boats.

The surprising recovery: in Prince William Sound, nature has shown itself to be remarkably resilient. Many affected sea life populations have returned to previous levels and the area appears to be as pristine as it always was. However neither herring nor salmon have returned to pre-oil spill levels.

The Columbia Glacier, 40 miles west of Valdez, is a big one, even by Alaska standards—some 450 square miles—and with its towering (over 200 feet high in places) six-mile-long face is as dramatic a sight as any in Alaska. It was ice from this glacier that the Exxon Valdez made its ill-fated turn to avoid.

All of Prince William Sound was hit hard by the 1964 Good Friday earthquake. In many areas the whole sea floor was lifted, destroying what had been a prosperous clam fishery. Valdez was particularly hard hit as, being built on less stable silt, it felt the violence of the quake more acutely than Whittier, just 75 miles west. Then after the shaking had essentially destroyed much of the town, four tidal waves or tsunamis demolished what was left. The damage was so bad that Valdez was rebuilt at a different, more earthquake resistant site, four miles west.

Valdez—This town of some 4,000 residents, backed by high mountains, has been called Alaska's Little Switzerland.Valdez' main feature, of course is the terminal for the Alaska pipeline. It takes roughly one supertanker a day to keep up with the flow through the insulated four-

foot diameter pipe that stretches 800 miles from Prudhoe Bay on the frozen Beaufort Sea.

The town has a truly spectacular setting, and is particularly popular with skiers and snowboarders seeking long runs and deep power snow. But with no ski lift to get the customers up to the snow, local entrepreneurs have invested in helicopters to take their clients up to the mountains, at around $100 a ride. The main base for heli skiing is at Thompson Pass, about 30 miles north of town. The location is far enough away from the salt water so that the coastal weather systems affect the flying much less than if it had been based in Valdez itself.

Cordova, in the far southeast corner of Prince William Sound, is only accessed by boat and plane. Originally settled to support the copper boom in the interior to the east, Cordova has become the main fishing port of Prince William Sound, and the population almost doubles in the summer when processing workers and commercial fishermen from the lower 48 come up to fish the Copper River and work in the canneries and freezer plants.

Faced with declining salmon runs in the 1970s for pink salmon, Prince William Sound fisherman invested in a substantial hatchery program to breed and release pink salmon. The program's success went a long ways to providing a stable base for the region's fishermen.

Before the tunnel into Whittier was modified in 2000 to allow cars to drive directly through (instead of being carried on rail cars,) Prince William Sound was fairly remote. But today, because of the easier access, more and more Anchorage and lower 48 residents are discovering the charms of this sheltered archipelago.

With so many islands and sheltered waterways, Prince William Sound has become very popular with kayakers. Many outfitters offer complete trips where they supply the kayaks, gear, tents, food, etc. Then you would be dropped by boat at a remote, sheltered bay and picked up at a later date. For those seeking a bit more of an upscale experience, some outfitters travel with you, set up the tents, cook up the food and provide the entertainment.

COLLEGE FJORD

Top: two glaciers merge on the west side of College Fjord. They are clearly shrinking as you can see from the bare rock along their sides.

Below: oiled sea otter in cleaning tank. A lot of these little guys perished when the *Exxon Valdez* hit Bligh Reef.

The hidden jewel of Prince William Sound is remote **College Fjord**. Within an eight-mile stretch at the upper end of this fjord five major tidewater glaciers reach the salt water. While Glacier Bay has emerged from the ice so recently that substantial trees have not gained foothold close to the ice, College Fjord is a place where the forests and glaciers have coexisted for centuries.

The result is a perspective on the great rivers of ice not seen in Glacier Bay. To see a glacier towering above the 100-foot-tall trees of a spruce forest, like Wellesley Glacier is really impressive.

Study the hillsides here. The upper slopes of these big glacial fjords, stripped of trees and covered with many berry bushes, are excellent bear watching territory. What you are looking for are brown or black dots that appear to be moving—these will be bears foraging for berries. Look also for white dots, often found in small groups—these will be mountain goats. You will see goats in places that an experienced rock climber would probably have trouble on.

Bears are also found down on the beach, especially if the tide is low. They are pretty good clammers, despite a crude technique. It goes like this: they look for the telltale water spurts of clams, dig them up with a big paw, smash them open with their other paw, and press the whole

mass, shells and all, up to their mouth.

So where are the really big icebergs? By the time most of this ice gets to the salt water, it has been fractured so much by those twisting mountain valleys, that most of the ice that breaks off is fairly small, say the size of a small apartment building at the most.

Remember that roughly 7/8 of an iceberg is below the surface of the water, so that something that looks small on top, like the size of a garage, still poses a significant danger to ships. Small icebergs and so-called "bergy bits" are notoriously difficult to see on radar.

Calving bergs: Before Alaska cruising got so popular, few big ships penetrated right up close to the glaciers here and in other places. The captains of those ships that did discovered that if the glacier wasn't actively calving when they were there, they could often dislodge some ice with a blow of the ship's steam whistle. Today such practices are prohibited, so it's just a waiting game. Often major calving is proceeded by small bits breaking off. I was here aboard the *Dawn Princess* in 1997, and the captain spied an apartment building-sized ice spire that seemed to be tipping toward the fjord. We circled slowly for more than an hour, watching and waiting, and were finally rewarded with a splash that must have been 280 feet high and a huge boom that echoed up and down the fjord.

College Fiord will be your best opportunity to see sea otters. Look particularly for what look like long dark spots on top of ice flows. Look with your binoculars—chances are they'll be sea otters, perhaps with their pups, which they often carry on their stomachs as they swim on their backs.

Below: this forest gives a good sense of the size of a College Fiord glacier.

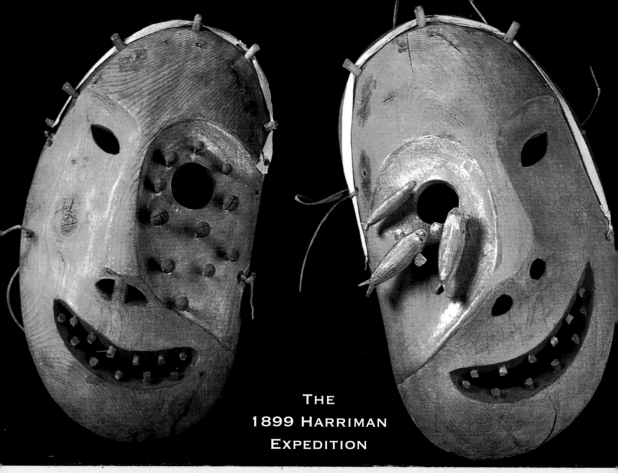

THE
1899 HARRIMAN
EXPEDITION

It's fortunate the Harriman Expedition came along when it did. For as Christian Missionaries came to Western Alaska, they viewed masks such like these as pagan and many were destroyed. ASM, IIA1451 & IIA1452.

Below: Tlingit visitors come alongside - notice the exremely graceful wooden canoes. UW NA2098

After suffering a nervous breakdown, railroad magnate (Union, Southern, and Northern Pacific) Edward H. Harriman was ordered by his doctors to have a "long vacation at sea." Prohibited from taking railroad men, he instead assembled one of the most remarkable literary, scientific, and artistic expeditions ever to come to Alaska. Chartering the steamer *George W. Elder*, Harriman arranged for a well-stocked library and some of the leading naturalists, artists, and scientists of the day including naturalist John Muir, photographer Edward Curtis, and many others.

Perhaps their biggest contribution was their extensive observations in Glacier Bay in June of 1899, just three months before a huge earthquake shattered many of the glaciers.

Entering Prince William Sound, they again found what some have called the two Alaskas—the spectacular beauty of the land in stark contrast to the grubbiness and even squalor of those who lived there, or like gold miners or cannery workers, exploited the resources.

Several days later, as their ship approached what is now known as College Fjord, they made a startling

discovery—while the chart showed Barry Arm ending at Barry Glacier, in fact, the glacier had receded enough for the ship to squeeze through, into the uncharted and unknown waters beyond. It was a genuine thrill for the group to discover and map this new territory that came to be named Harriman Fjord. A group including John Muir (naturally) spent two days camped in the new fjord while the ship returned to Orca for propeller repairs, after striking a rock.

Next was another unique opportunity—to name a fjord and its glaciers. Since many of his party were "Easterners," they surveyed many of the glaciers here, and named them for their New England colleges like Dartmouth, Harvard, Wellesley, and Vassar.

After leaving Prince William Sound, the George W. Elder proceeded "to the west'ard," touching at many places that are still extremely remote almost 100 years later, including King Island, Alaska, and Plover Bay, Siberia, on the Bering Strait. It was a remarkable expedition and they brought back a wealth of photographs, scientific data, and artifacts.

Top: Native seal hunters' camp with skins drying on stretchers. UW NA2103.

Below: Plover Bay, Siberia, also visited by the expedition. Note the whalebone framework of the strucure on the right. NA2113

Top:'downtown' Whittier is on the quiet side, but if you have the inclination the waterfront shops and cafes offer a pretty relaxed venue.

Below: Due to the deep, deep snow that buries town most winters, almost all the residents and business-es occupied these now abandoned buildings when town was basically an Army base.

220

Built originally as a World War II port alternative to Seward, 1940s and 50s era residents pretty much all lived in the ugly abandoned buildings east of the docks. With heavy deep snow on the ground for most of the long winter, it was convenient to have homes and services: stores, movie theatre, etc. all under a single roof!

When the military pulled out in 1960, Whittier became almost a ghost town, and the 1964 earthquake almost finished off the rest.

Finally rebuilt with a larger boat harbor that gave Anchorage residents a reason to come, Whittier began to grow again. Access was still a problem—you could drive your car onto a flatbed railcar and go through the tunnel with the rest of the train, but it was hardly convenient.

Finally, in 2000, a widened tunnel was opened that accommodated both cars (one way at a time) and trains. This better access was a boost for Whittier residents, and businesses have sprung up to serve the increased numbers of visitors.

Most passengers transit Whittier quickly to and from their ship. If you do have the time, there are some modest places to shop and eat along the shore just east of the cruise ship docks. A popular whale and glacier excursion operates here as well.

Be sure to take the train in or out of Whittier instead of the bus; it's a delightful ride.

Top: the Dawn Princess uses Whitter for its northern terminus and cruise turnaround point. Most other cruise lines during the itinerary across the Gulf of Alaska operate out of Seward.

Below: When you plan your cruise, be sure to take the train to or from Whitter; it's a great ride.

SEWARD

P&O

Top: Seward is also a major fishing port so have a look around if you have time.

Opposite top: the dramatic **Chiswell Islands,** a major bird rookery, is part of the Kenai Fjords National Park, centered in Seward.

Opposite bottom: mighty fat and sassy harbor seal at the Alaska Sealife Center, definately worth a visit.

Below: Several outfitters offer paddling excursions into the nearby Kenai Fjords N.P.

The Good Friday Earthquake - If this town looks fairly new, it's because it is—much of the port and downtown was destroyed in the violent events of March 27, 1964. When the ground started shaking, it essentially created sort of an underwater landslide that dropped most of the waterfront six feet and into the bay. Next the big oil tanks east of town ruptured, the oil ignited in a flaming sheet across the bay and set the stage for the next tragedy: the tidal wave.

As the shaken residents began to recover from the initial shocks, few noticed that the sea had receded substantially from the shore.

Then a 30 foot wall of water, carrying much of the flaming oil with it, blasted into what was left of downtown, basically destroying the entire waterfront, and it was more than a decade before the town had rebuilt and recovered.

Today, Seward's economy runs on commercial and sport fishing as well as tourism. Look just south of the boat harbor to the parking lot usually full of trailers and motor homes—mostly Anchorage residents combining a vacation away from the bright city lights with a salmon resource. It allows them to take enough to can or freeze as a significant food resource for the winter, especially if

several family members are all catching fish.

The **Alaska Sealife Center**, an aquarium, funded by Exxon after the oil spill, is a great place to see northern birds and mammal up close.

Seward is also the headquarters for the **Kenai Fjords National Park,** a dramatic area of narrow bays, steep islands and glaciated fjords, west of town. .

If you haven't gotten a chance to get up close to the ice yet, consider a tour or a taxi to **Exit Glacier**, about 8 miles west of town. As you'll see from the extensive glacial moraine that you will cross to get to the glacier, it is also receding at a good clip, melting away all along its front. However, be careful to give the face a respectful distance; a visitor was killed by falling ice and others have been injured.

If you're planning to spend some time in the area before heading home and have a hankering for a wilderness, but not too rough, experience, the National Park Service does maintain four remote cabins in Kenai Fjords. You'll need to bring in a sleeping bag, groceries, and maybe your fishing rod. These are fly-in; there is no road access but air taxi outfits in Seward can get you in and out. Contact the NPS at 907-224-3175 for information and availability.

Passengers that end or begin their cruise here may have a choice between train and bus to get to Anchorage. I reccomend the train; even though more expensive, it is a much more fun travel experience.

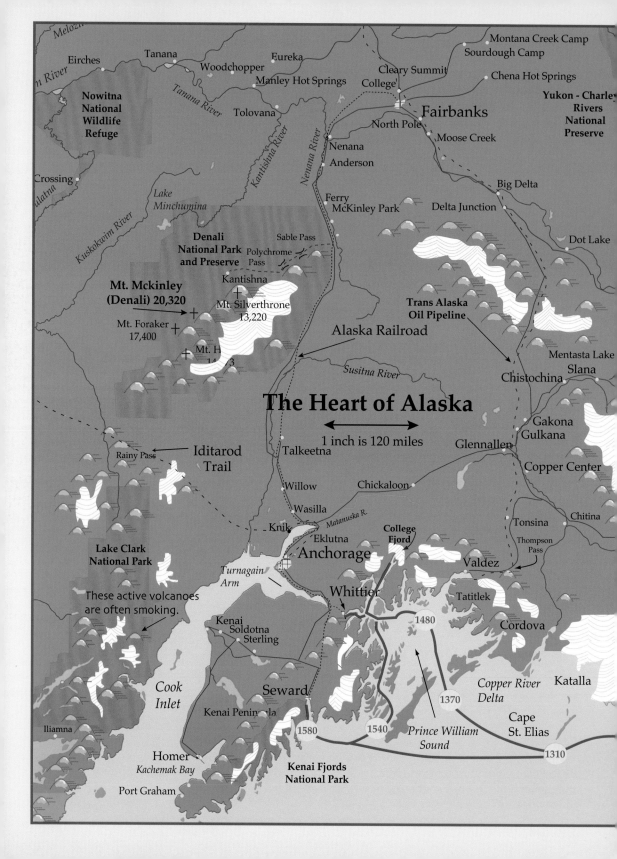

The Heart of Alaska

1 inch is 120 miles

"So off we went, the four dogs and I, to explore high mountains new to us.

"As the days went by, I wondered what the dogs got out of it. I had a supply of dried salmon on the sled, and they eagerly looked forward to their meal each evening. They loved to be in harness; as a matter of fact, as they were being hooked up in the morning, they were so happy that it was hard to handle them. The minute we were ready, off they would go in a great burst of speed."

— Olas J. Murie, *Journeys to the Far North*

When you plan your Alaska cruise, make time to explore a bit of the interior—at the minimum the Fairbanks-Anchorage corridor—for it is so dramatically different from the coast. Cruise lines encourage people to take the Alaska Railroad. Several lines have their own vistadome style rail cars and make at least an overnight stop at Denali, and then take the paddle-wheeler excursion out of Fairbanks. But if you have time, consider additional side trips.

If your cruise itinerary takes you to Seward or Whittier, consider renting a car (it may be much cheaper to travel to Anchorage first) and exploring the **Kenai Peninsula**, ending at Homer, about four and a half hours of driving. The peninsula was first settled by the Russians, and their influence is still felt, in churches, graveyards, and place names.

For generations, the rivers of interior Alaska were the only highways. Paddle-wheelers took freight and passengers to the most remote locations. But once the rivers froze up for the winter, travel was either by dog, horse-drawn sled, or by foot. The arrival of the first paddlewheeler in the spring with the first new food supplies and mail, was always a big event. This is the *Discovery III*, an excursion vessel out of Fairbanks, operated by a family that first started piloting paddle wheelers during the Yukon Gold Rush. It is a truly excellent excursion.

Ninilchik makes a great lunch stop on the way - you 'll find a small settlement overlooking Cook Inlet with an exquisite Russian Orthodox church and a number of places to eat. If you are there when the salmon are running in the Ninilchik River, you'll see what Alaskans have come to call "combat fishing," fishermen almost literally lined up bank to bank with their rods almost touching. If you haven't gotten your sportfishing fix on your cruise, this is a good place to go for salmon or halibut and there are several charter fishing operations.

Once a remote coal mining settlement, today **Homer** is a town of 5,000 set in a truly exquisite location, with a rich arts culture. Commercial fishing is the lifeblood here. Like Seward, Homer is at the very end of a road from Anchorage and is a gateway to many National and State Parks.

The Spit—Homer's most unique feature is a four-mile sand spit sticking out into Kachemak Bay. At the end of the spit is the harbor, marine support facilities, log dump, a growing number of eateries, gift shops, whale watching and kayak excursions, and other businesses catering to visitors. Locals call it the Las Vegas of Alaska, but it is an integral part of the Homer experience.

Sportfishing, as you may have guessed, is excellent here. One of the local hot spots is the lagoon just north of the boat harbor—hatchery-raised fish are moved to cages in the lagoon, causing them to imprint the lagoon's location and return there as adults to try to spawn. Naturally they are a little disappointed when they get there and don't find a stream or river, just a big crowd of fishermen! At times there are so many fish here that snagging - just using bare hooks pulled through the water - is allowed.

Halibut Cove, on the opposite shore of Kachemak Bay from Homer, is a roadless fishing settlement with a strong arts flavor, and a 12 block long boardwalk. A **foot ferry**, the Danny J, offers noon departures from Homer, a stop at Gull Island, two and a half hours for exploring Halibut Cove, and a 4 P.M. return. It is a totally great day trip. Save your appetite for the Saltry Restaurant, perched on pilings above Halibut Cove with great seafood and a wonderful view.

Top: A little second home construction on Homer Spit. Above: sports fishing is huge on the Kenai Peninsula.
Brenda Carney photo

227

Top: bowhead beluga mural.

Lower: Captain Cook's statue overlooks the inlet he named in 1778. Sadly after charting much of the Pacific basin, he was killed in a scuffle with Hawaiian natives less than a year later.

The old saying, "You can see Alaska from here," basically describes the relationship of Anchorage with the rest of the state. While some 40% of the entire state's population resides here, it's a good bet a lot of them blast out of town each weekend, judging from the number of planes, campers, snowmobiles, 4-wheelers, kayaks, etc., in the back yards all around town. Don't be surprised to see a moose meandering around town, and wandering bears are also regularly seen as well. Though Anchorage overlooks Cook Inlet and Knik Arm, it's hardly a waterfront town in the mold of Ketchikan or Juneau. There's no place for boats to tie up downtown—the rivers draining into the inlet bring a big silt load and there are extensive tide flats making it difficult to even get to the water in most places. Most marine activity is centered in Ship Creek, north of town. Anchorage boaters prefer to boat in Prince William Sound or the Pacific south of Seward, either trailering their boats, or keeping their boats there. Modifying the Whitter tunnel so that vehicles can just drive through—they used to have to ride on flatcars—was a big hit with Anchorage boaters.

The newest and shiniest high-rise office buildings usually belong to Big Oil in this town. The revenue from this industry basically redefined Alaska economics, and gave its citizens the unique distinction of getting the only state dividend checks in the country. Farsighted leadership in the early days of the oil boom established a large and so far untouched "Permanent Fund" which yields enough income for checks typically in the $1,000 range annually for each of Alaska's citizens.

In recent years, North Slope oil production has fallen

off, but state planners are hoping that a gas pipeline will be built to the Lower 48, creating yet another boom.

Take a few minutes and walk to the **Captain Cook Memorial**, overlooking the water at the end of 3rd Ave. You can get a clear sense of the very different shoreline below, but also it's an opportunity to reflect on the many unusual deeds of this English sailor, who charted much of the vast reaches of the Pacific Ocean.

Good Friday, 1964—Most folks were just settling down to supper when the most powerful earthquake to hit North America this century struck. Anchorage was mostly built on unstable clay, which is particularly susceptible to movement in an earthquake. So move it did—splitting apart, dropping whole blocks and tumbling expensive waterfront homes down steep bluffs. Within minutes, much of the downtown core was a ruin of fallen storefronts, crumpled streets, and shattered businesses.

Property damage was extremely heavy, but fortunately only nine people died.

Shopping—if your cruise is over and you haven't done all of your shopping, it's all here in downtown. Take an evening to explore these shops and especially the galleries of native arts and crafts. There are pieces here that would be hard to find anywhere outside Alaska.

Yup'ik style doll - face of sealskin and garment probably of seal intestines. Today a museum piece, but still occasionally found in gift shops.

Alaska honors its legendary salmon in many ways. This was one of numerous sculptures in a 2011 celebration!

Alutiiq style ceremonial hat, styled after those worn by natives in their hunting kayaks.

Galleries and other notable places—Alaska Center for the Performing Arts, 6th & F; Wolf Song of Alaska, inside J.C. Penny Mall, 6th & E; Reeve Aviation Picture Museum, 343 W. 6th; and Museum of History & Art, 121 W. 7th

SOME ANCHORAGE EXCURSIONS

Anchorage Flightseeing Safari
McKinley Flightseeing
Redoubt Bay Lodge Bear Viewing
Glaciers Catamaran Cruise
Glacier Discovery Train and Float Tour
Kenai Fjords National Park Cruise
Explore Anchorage City Tour

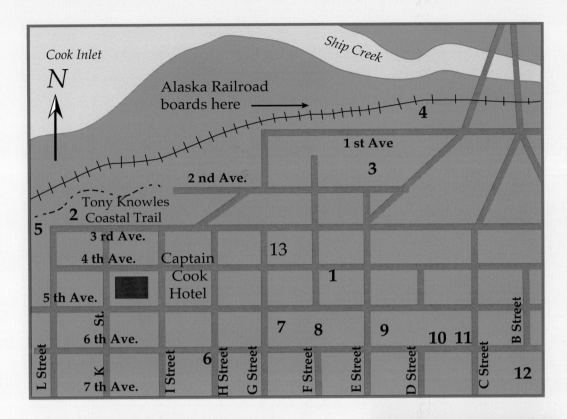

Cook Inlet

N

Ship Creek

Alaska Railroad
boards here →

4

1 st Ave

3

2 nd Ave.

Tony Knowles
Coastal Trail

2

5

3 rd Ave.

4 th Ave.

13

Captain
Cook
Hotel

1

5 th Ave.

J St.

7   8   9

10 11

B Street

6 th Ave.

L Street

K St.

I Street

6

H Street

G Street

F Street

E Street

D Street

C Street

12

7 th Ave.

DOWNTOWN ANCHORAGE

1. Log Cabin and Visitor Information Center
2. Tony Knowles Coastal Trail - ten mile trail
    that follows the shore with great views.
3. Alaska Statehood Monument
4. Alaska Railroad Depot
5. Resolution Park with Captain Cook
Monument
6. Oomingmak Musk-ox Producers Co-Op—
unique garments from strange creatures.
7. Alaska Center for the Performing Arts
8. Town Square Municipal Park
9. Reeve Aviation Picture Museum
10. Alaska State Trooper Museum
11. Wolf Song of Alaska - large wolf exhibit.
12. Anchorage Museum of History and Art—
    excellent collection; gift shop and cafe.
13. Alaska Public Lands Information Center

Old gold dredge bucket used for
flower display, downtown. Attached
together is sort of an endless chain,
they scooped gravel off river bot-
toms to be processed for gold dust
and nuggets. See P. 244

THE ALASKA RAILROAD

Anchorage, September 14, 1997, 7:45 a.m.: Our train sits waiting on a siding, near the water. The other passengers board quickly, their breath white in the chill morning air, but I stand aside, let the bus leave, to take in the surroundings. The days get shorter quickly in the fall this far north and the sun is still behind the Chugach Mountains to the east, yet just illuminating the volcanoes along the snowy wall of the Alaska Range, across Cook Inlet. The shiny sides of the coaches are yellow and pink, reflecting the sky, while all around is almost dark. Here and there along the waiting train, steamy air vents from beneath the coaches, cloak all in a mysterious other- world feeling. The last whistle finally blows, and I have to board. Yet I linger until the very last, unwilling to leave the drama of this moment."

Until 1972, when the **George Parks Highway** north to Fairbanks was completed, the train was the only transportation there was for the folks along much of the Anchorage - Fairbanks corridor.

Whistle stops were an everyday part of train life as the "local" trains dropped homesteaders off with their bags and boxes of groceries and supplies, often at trail heads where horses or four-wheel-drive vehicles waited to take them down some lonely dirt track to a remote home. Since the Highway was completed, winter passenger service is limited to weekends and Thursdays.

Every spring the passenger specials begin, with the domed cars that make it one of the most scenic rail rides in North America. Each day there is a northbound and a southbound passenger run. These trains generally have three different kinds of domed cars. Several cruise lines have had special railcars constructed for their passengers. These dome cars are usually a modification of dome cars used by railroads in the US western states. The domed section is usually made longer along with improving passenger amenities.

However you travel, these dome cars provide a wonderful chance to experience this dramatic country. Especially early and late in the season, you'll see some of the thousands, perhaps even millions, of birds and waterfowl that travel so far in their annual migrations.

Some of these birds, like the **Arctic Tern** make truly stunning migrations.

> "Fer Cris'sake, all it would take is for one of those Alaska Airlines jets to cream into Mt. Juneau and it'd take the the whole legislature with it..."
> — Heard around Alaska

Now that you've taken the cruise, seen Southeast Alaska and steamed up the wild and lonely coast to Seward, doesn't it seem a bit like there are two Alaskas? The drizzly, grey one down there with Ketchikan and

Top: The Anchorage to Fairbanks route along the canyon of the Susitna River.

Truly remarkable travelers, the Arctic Tern (black cap, red bill and feet, with a long, forked tail) summers in Alaska then takes off each fall for a 10,000 mile journey to winter in the Antarctic (it's summer there). Look for them in the Knik marshes.

Top: winter on their heels - one of the last excursion trains of the season arrives at the Denali National Park station in late September.

Below: with long daylight hours, vegetables grow to unusually large sizes like these big cabbages near Fairbanks.

Juneau, and the wide open one up here with Anchorage, Fairbanks and the whole really, really, big rest of the state? And doesn't it seem odd that the capital, Juneau, is so isolated down there? This same thought has occurred to many Alaskans. In the 1970s when the state was flush with oil revenues, "Move The Capital" was a popular bumper sticker

The only problem was where to move it. Anchorage and Fairbanks were such rivals that neither would accept the other as capital. So why not pick some centrally located spot in between, and make that the capital? Brilliant! So, in 1976, Alaskans voted to build a new capital near **Willow, mile 185.7**. So where is it, you say? Cooler heads prevailed when the first cost estimates came out...

Now and again, through the trees, you'll glimpse a road, the George Parks Highway, just to the west, or left of the train. Between this highway and the Bering Sea coast, 500 miles to the west, there are no roads. (Well, O.K., there are a few exceptions—the 20 miles of bumpy pavement between Naknek and King Salmon, on Bristol Bay, a few miles around Dillingham and a few more around Nome.)

The forest here is known as taiga, very different from that of Prince William Sound and Southeast Alaska. Gone are the tall hemlocks and cedars, replaced by low white and black spruce, poplar, birch, aspen and larch. Where the trees seem particularly stunted is a sign of either wet muskeg or frozen permafrost close to the surface.

Sometimes the train slows near mile 224, to let travelers get a good view of the Alaska range : Denali at 20,320', and her lower sisters, Mt. Hunter, 14,573', and Mt. Foraker, 17,400'.

The Susitna River is normally placid, but about 65 miles northeast of here it in turns violent in a five-mile rapids named Devil's Canyon.

In the summer of 1958 Talkeetna pilot Don Sheldon saw the wreckage of a U.S. Army survey boat in the canyon on a charter flight to a nearby lake, and upon returning, spotted survivors huddling on the rocky shore with almost no way out, unless he could somehow land in the river canyon. The rapids in the river created 6-foot waves—certain death to land on, but after a couple of passes through, Sheldon found a little strip of calmer water, where he thought it might just be possible to land. Sheldon made his approach, swallowed hard, and set his little Aeronica down. Once he was in the water, he had to let it carry him backwards, into the rapids, for him to get to the survivors were:

> "As the plane backed into the first of the combers, I felt it lurch heavily fore and aft. It was like a damned roller coaster. The water was rolling up higher than my wingtips, beating at the struts, and I could barely see because of the spray and water on the windows. All of a sudden the engine began to sputter and choke, and I knew it was getting wet down pretty good..."
> —Don Sheldon, in Wager With the Wind,

Somehow the engine kept going, and Sheldon managed to maneuver close enough to shore for one of the men to clamber aboard. Getting out was almost as hard—backing the plane down the rapids, until he came to another stretch just barely long enough to effect a take-off. Sheldon had to repeat this remarkable performance three more times to get all the survivors out.

Look for the little airstrip, through the trees to the east at Talkeetna. This village is the staging area for almost all expeditions to the top of Denali, and for most it begins with a flight to Kahiltna Glacier.

The construction of the Alaska Railroad, finished in 1923 was the first time Fairbanks had a reliable year round connection with the "outside" (via the port at Seward). Mile Zero for the railroad is at Seward, where construction was originally started.

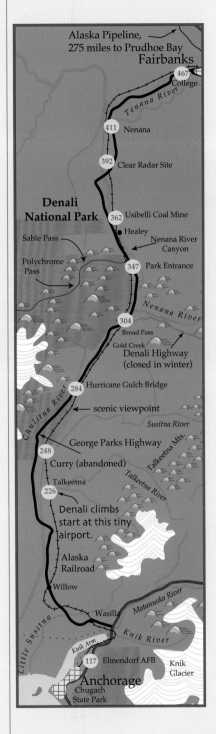

Consider yourself lucky if you get a view like this one from a hill above the Mt. McKinley Princess Wilderness Lodge. That's Denali in the center and 17,400' Mt. Foraker on the left. The Alaska Range essentially forms a barrier between two very different weather systems and climates. The result is that the mountain, unfortunately, is often covered by clouds. Early climbers had to struggle through the lowland forest and rugged lower slopes of the range before the hard part of their climb even began. Today ski-equipped small planes take climbing parties up to the new starting place at about 7,000 feet up.

Early explorers sometimes got a glimpse of a very high mountain to the north of Cook Inlet, a peak the natives of the region called Denali, which meant "The High One." An early prospector named it Mt. McKinley, but most Alaskans today refer to it as simply Denali.

At 20,320 feet, it is the tallest peak in North America. If this mountain were in California, or perhaps Peru, it would be a world class climb, but it wouldn't have the particular challenges that come with its high latitude.

The Alaska Range is a wall between Yukon - Arctic highs and North Pacific lows. The result is a highly volatile microclimate, and a mountain that can basically create its own weather very rapidly. Most climbing fatalities here are caused by rapid weather changes, combining wind, cold, and snow.

Many climbing parties have had the bitter experience of being turned back, sometimes just a few hundred yards short of the summit by wind and cold. Experienced Denali climbers know that they can only get near the top and hope that the mountain gods will allow them to tread on the top of the continent.

The Imposter's Claim—one of the oddest episodes in Denali's history was the 1906 claim by Dr. Frederick Cook, a very experienced Arctic explorer, that he and

a companion had made it to the top of the mountain, the first to do so, bringing down photographs for proof. Climbers familiar with the mountain doubted Cook's claims, but it wasn't until 1910 that a group, specifically climbing to dispute Cook, found the supposed summit photographed by Cook: 10,000 feet lower and 20 miles away from the actual summit.

Denali Today—The mountain has become a very popular climb, sought each summer by expeditions from all over the world.

However today's climbers face a much easier prospect than the early climbers. Instead of starting on the ground near Talkeetna, and struggling for several days before they even got to the top of the first glacier, they hop a plane from the Talkeetna airstrip and get dropped off at the base camp at Kahiltna Glacier at 7,000 feet. In a typical summer literally hundreds of climbers try to find a break in the weather and make it to the top so, this base camp is a busy place, with a ranger station, aircraft, and climbing parties coming and going. How very, very different from the rigors faced by the mountain's true pioneers!

But Denali should never be taken for granted. It remains an extremely challenging ascent, as witnessed by regular fatalities among those who attempt it.

Opposite: On Denali, 1932. When we look at all the high tech equipment today's climbers consider essential, our respect for the feats of the pioneer climbers grows. And especially since those climbers had to do without the services of pilots like Don Sheldon who with ski-equipped aircraft would drop them on Kahiltna Glacier, 7,000 feet up, saving today's climbers weeks of hiking with all their heavy gear! UAF Rasmuson Library 81-218-07n

"...The storm now became so severe that I was actually afraid to get new dry mittens out of my rucksack, for I knew my hands would be frozen in the process... The last period of our climb is like the memory of an evil dream. La Voy was completely lost in the ice mist, and Professor Parker's frosted form was an indistinct blur above me... The breath was driven from my body and I held to my axe with stooped shoulders to stand against the gale; I couldn't go ahead. As I brushed the frost from my glasses and squinted upward through the stinging snow, I saw a sight that will haunt me to my dying day. The slope above me was no longer steep! That was all I could see. What it meant I will never know for certain—all I can say is that we were close to the top."
— Belmore Browne, *The Conquest of Mt. McKinley*

"I was snowshoeing along about fifty feet back of the sled, with Harry (Liek) right behind me when, without warning, the snow fell away under my snowshoes. I plunged into sudden darkness.

I had time to let out a feeble shout. Then for a couple of long, long seconds I plummeted downward. I remember thinking, 'This is it, fellow!' Then my pack scraped against the slide of the crevasse, my head banged hard against the ice wall and I came to a jarring stop.

When my head cleared and I could look around in the blue darkness, I saw I was on a plug of snow wedged between the ice walls. On either side, this wedge of snow fell away into sheer blackness.

About forty feet above me I could see a ray of sunlight, slanting through the hole I had made in the surface crust. The crevasse was about twelve feet wide up there, it narrowed to two feet down where I was. Below was icy death."
— Grant Pearson, *My Life of High Adventure*

"But in half an hour, we stood on the narrow edge of the spur top, facing failure. Here, where the black ridge leading to the tops of the pink cliffs should have flattened, all was absolutely sheer, and a hanging glacier, bearded and dripping with bergschrunds, filled the angle in between... I heard Fred say, 'It ain't that we can't find a way that's possible, taking chances. There ain't no way.'

"We were checkmated with steepness, at 11,300 feet with eight days of mountain food on our hands. But remember this: also with scarce two weeks provisions below with which to reach the coast and winter coming. The foolishness of the situation, and the fascination, lies in the fact that except in this fair weather, unknown in Alaska at this season, we might have perished either night in those two exposed camps."
— Robert Dunn, *Shameless Diary of an Explorer*

"We tried to take some snaps, but had to give it up. For four minutes only did I leave my mittens off, and in that time, I froze five tips of my fingers to such a degree that after they had first been white, some weeks later, they turned black, and at last fell off, with the nails and all.."
— Erling Strom, *How We Climbed Mt. McKinley*

"There was no pride of conquest, no trace of that exultation of victory some enjoy over the first ascent of a lofty peak, no gloating over good fortune that had hoisted us a few hundred feet higher than others who had struggled and been discomfited. Rather... that a privileged communion with the high places of the earth had been granted... secret and solitary since the world began. All the way down, unconscious of weariness in the descent, my thoughts were occupied with the glorious scene my eyes gazed upon, and should gaze upon never again."
— Hudson Stuck, in *The Pioneer Climbs*

Above: Climber Belmore Brown made three Denali attempts, but was defeated each time. ASL PCA 01-3441

"... My mind was racing. I had to grab the rock near Dave with my left hand; it was bare, no mitten or sock. It would be frozen. I had to. Suddenly my bare hand shot out to grab the rock. Slicing cold.

I saw Dave's face, the end of his nose raw, frostbitten. His mouth, distorted into an agonized mixture of compassion and anger, swore at me to get a glove on. I looked at my hand. It was white, frozen absolutely white."
— Art Davidson, *Minus 148 Degrees, The Winter Ascent of Mt. McKinley*

RULES FOR BEAR COUNTRY

Brown, or grizzly (or just 'griz'), as well as black bear are common throughout this part of Alaska. While for the most part bears are content to mind their own business, visitors should remember a few rules.

First, let bears know you're around by talking, singing, wearing bells, etc. when you hike though the woods or wherever visibility is reduced. If a bear knows you're coming, he'll probably want to get out of your way. If, however, you surprise one on a narrow trail, it could get ugly, for you. Bears react badly to surprise...

Don't get between a mother and her cubs, or a bear and its food. Sometimes people have been mauled when they inadvertently got between a mother and cub, without knowing it, in thick bushes. If you see a bear, assume there are cubs nearby.

Don't run It could trigger an automatic, "chase food" reaction. Bears may look big and lumbering, but when they want to do so, they can accelerate faster than a man ever could.

Be careful where you put your food. Problems have sometimes arisen from campers carelessly leaving food out or stored near or in their tent or vehicle. Put your food in a container, away from your tent.

Bear encounter: the makings of a dangerous situation. In this case, we were walking down the road when there was a rustling in the bushes and two bear cubs appeared. At 300+ pounds, cuddly they were not. We were taken aback and essentially stopped in our tracks, the bears 50 feet or so ahead. Then the mom appeared, about the size of a Volkswagon, and definitely alarmed about seeing us so close to her cubs. Without turning around and actually running, which could have triggered the 'chase food' reaction, we walked backwards about as fast as we could. My 14-year old son, who was with us, forgot everything we had told him and just started running. When I finally caught up with him later, I told him he'd just flunked the bear test! Left: Alaskaphoto

241

DENALI NATIONAL PARK

Denali watching at the Eielson Visitors Center, about a three hour bus ride from the main visitors center by the park entrance. Alaskastock The weather isn't always just like this... Below: bear protective equipment is a growth industry here...

The park was originally established in 1917 as Mt. McKinley National Park, a wildlife preserve that didn't include the mountain for which it is named. Finally in 1980, the protected area was tripled in size, to include the entire mountain massif along with the caribou herd's winter range and calving grounds and renamed Denali National Park and Preserve.

The park has become sort of an icon for vistors, representing all that they have come to Alaska for. Yet, some, especially those who just have time for an overnight or two at Glitter Gulch–the nickname for the lodges/shops area just outside the park entrance–come away disappointed. Hours of bus riding on bumpy, dusty roads, a bear or moose sighting, maybe a glimpse of Denali through the clouds, didn't match up to the advertisements.

A bit of advice: the park's true grandeur lies in its being, as much as is possible with the limited visitor access, an intact subarctic ecosystem. For many, Denali Park is experienced in a bus with a naturalist/driver. For others, a visit might include camping at Wonder Lake, with backpacking through the wilderness. Don't expect a park with the visitor facilities of Yellowstone or the Grand Canyon.

Glimpsing Denali: If you get a view of the moun-

tain that looks anything like the photos in this chapter, consider yourself very lucky. Denali is so high that it acts as a mixing area for weather from the Gulf of Alaska and the great interior, meaning a lot of cloudy days. Generally in summer, expect two days out of three to be overcast. In reality your best views from the mountain are apt to be from the Georges Park Highway, from the Alaska Railroad, or from a place like the Mt. McKinley Princess Wilderness Lodge, near Talkeetna.

Take a walk: there are some good trails, like the Horseshoe Lake Trail, near the lodges at Glitter Gulch, so get out there! This is bear country, so while you don't need to be terrified, making noise is good. Remember, in almost all cases, if bears can hear you, they will move away.

Getting around: Private vehicles are only allowed as far as the Savage River checkpoint, about 14 miles in. Shuttle buses: The ARA Courtesy Shuttle, a beige bus loops between Glitter Gulch, the park visitor center, and Mckinley Village; schedules in hotels. The Sled Dog Demonstration Shuttle loops between the visitor center, Riley Creek campground and the Park Headquarters in time for the sled dog demonstrations at 10 a.m., 2 p.m., & 4 p.m. The Park Shuttle–green bus– is the main way of getting into the interior of the park, leaving the visitor center every hour for Wonder Lake (5.5 hr. one way $31 RT) and on the half hour to Eielson (4hr. one way $22.50 RT). Wildlife is often best viewed early, so consider getting up and onto one of the early buses. Wonder Lake is a spectacular place and the site for many of the photos of Denali, but 8 or 10 hours of bus riding is a lot. Your chances of seeing wildlife from a bus are high, and generally unless the animals are so close as to possibly pose a danger, buses will stop and allow passengers out for a photo opportunity.

PASSENGER TIP

There are no food, drinks, meals, film, insect repellent, etc. available in the park (except at Kantishna, 90 miles in...) even at the visitor's center, so bring what you need with you on the bus. This is not like the lower 48 National Parks

Alaskastock photos

243

Top: Gold dredge no. 3 along a Yukon River tributary around 1910. These giant machines chewed up the bottom, sifted the rocks and gravel for the heavier gold, and dumped the tailings out of the big boom. UW1945

Below: The business end of a big dredge.

The big weird thing near mile 362, as the train emerges from the Nenana River canyon is the Usibelli coal tipple. Inside is the equipment for filling the coal cars that run north to Fairbanks, or all the way south to Seward to be loaded aboard ships for the Orient.

The country changes substantially here as the trees seem to swallow us up until it seems we're traveling in a leafy canyon. This is all the northern tiaga—a taste of the vast, low, mixed black spruce and birch forests that cover much of the Yukon basin that drains interior Alaska. Plants and trees don't get very big here; the growing season is short and the ground has great frozen areas (permafrost) just below the surface.

The country is so flat here that the Nenana, barely thirty yards wide in places in the gorge, and rushing along faster than a man can run, breaks into many branches like Seventeenmile and Lost Slough, and almost seems to just disappear into the flats before finally rejoining to enter the Tanana River at Nenana. Early travelers on rafts often had to pole tediously through miles of shallows here.

Look for the big black and white wooden tripod (about 30' high), between the tracks and the river at **Nenana, mile 411**. Each winter this tower is dragged out onto the frozen river for the Nenana Ice Classic, a uniquely Alaskan lottery. What folks bet on is "Ice Out," the moment in spring when the frozen river breaks up.

It's entirely fitting that this be celebrated, for the rivers are the lifeblood for most of the towns in the immense drainage of the Yukon River.

Where there are no highways, the arrival of the first freight barge in the spring is always an exciting community event. This freight (usually in 40' containers or vans) usually begins its water journey from Seattle, stacked five and six high on a huge 400' oceangoing barge, towed by

a 5,000 horsepower tug. Somewhere near the mouth of the Yukon River, perhaps at **St. Michaels,** the containers would be hoisted onto a smaller barge, to be pushed upstream. Sometimes, for freight bound for communities on the smaller rivers, the container would be transferred a third time, onto a yet smaller barge, pushed by an even smaller tug.

Navigation is still tough! The river channels sometimes shift every few weeks; there are few buoys or navigational aids. Captains use hand drawn charts passed along from other captains and pilots. Sometimes the only way through is launching a skiff to sound out a particularly tricky channel before you entered it. Even with all these precautions, groundings are routine.

The river as highway. Despite what you may hear, not everyone who lives out in the bush has a floatplane in their backyard. But the majority of villages and settlements in the vast country between the Alaska Range and the Bering Sea and Arctic Ocean lie along one of the many rivers with native and Russian names like Kitchatna, Tonzona, Kantishna, Hoholitna, and Chilikadrotna, Ugashik, Nushagak, and Kinak. When the ice is out, watercraft ranging from big tugs and barges to outboard jet boats move people and supplies around. When the ice is in, it is usually hard and smooth enough for vehicles.

It was during those in-between months, the short spring and falls, that travel was difficult.

Suddenly, around **mile 466,** civilization appears—houses, streets, and people mowing lawns. After what seems like the endless tiaga forest stretching unbroken to the horizon, coming upon civilization so suddenly is almost a shock. First is College, and the University of Alaska at mile 467, and then a few miles later, Fairbanks.

Top: Oops, this paddlewheeler stayed on the upper Yukon a little too late, and is about to get frozen in for the winter. Its passengers might have a long hard hike ahead of them. Yukon archives.

Above: how the wealthy traveled to the Gold Rush - Paddlewheeler White Horse in Five Finger Rapids, Yukon River. UW 21255

FAIRBANKS

Top: the paddlewheeler *Discovery III* is a popular excursion.

Take the time to read the bronze plaques beneath the Pioneer's Memorial in downtown Fairbanks. It's a moving tribute to the courage and perseverance of the early settlers in bitter cold and dark winter condtions. Imagine what it must have been like before electricity, indoor plumbing and central heating!

The Wandering Trader—In the summer of 1901, E.T. Barnette was headed for the upper Tanana with a load of trading goods. Shallow water forced him to unload his goods right in front of what is now the Fairbanks Visitor's Bureau log cabin. He started to build an even shallower-draft vessel to keep going up the river, but when gold was discovered nearby, Barnette decided to build his trading post right where he was and Fairbanks was born.

Fairbanks today has a more stable economy, with a large military contingent from nearby Fort Wainwright and Eielson Air Force Base. For much of the century, however, it went through the many boom and busts that characterize so much of Alaskan economy.

"Thirty below zero this morning. Frost has crept through the walls and caused the bedclothes to stick to the wall on that side and it is mortal agony to crawl out of the warm nest in the center of the bed when daddy called."
— Margaret Murie, *Two in The Far North*

Winter in Fairbanks lasts from October to April, and before the modern conveniences like plumbing, electricity and oil heat, these months were an unrelenting challenge for residents, especially for women, perhaps raising families with their men away. Margaret Murie, who came to Fairbanks in 1911 when she was nine, grew up with a

keen memory of the routines and community activities that made life manageable for the women of Fairbanks.

The river was the highway, and the nearest town was ten days away by river boat. Between freeze-up in the fall and ice out in the spring, there was only the weekly horse-drawn mail sleigh that traveled a difficult trail through the mountains and over the frozen rivers to Valdez.

Ice out was a big event—notices were posted around town to keep residents informed: "Ice moved at Fort Gibbon this morning at 8 a.m.," for the first steamer of the season meant fresh vegetables, followed shortly thereafter by the "slaughterhouse boat" with its pens of cows, sheep, pigs, geese, and chickens, brought up from Seattle.

In a town of log homes that heated with wood, fire was always a worry. A big steam pump at the Northern Commercial Company power plant was always ready to pump river water from under the river ice to fight fires. On at least one occasion, when the wood-fired boilers couldn't keep up with the demands of a big fire, the cry went out to "Bring the bacon"—case after case of oily bacon was brought from the warehouse, thrown into the boilers, the steam pressure rose, the water flowed once more, and the fire was contained.

Today Fairbanks is the most northerly city in North America. There are many of the conveniences found elsewhere, but the long winters are still bitter, bitter cold, with all their unique problems like having your car go bumpity bump in the mornings because of the frozen flat place in the tires from sitting on the street all night long.

Top: The Trans Alaska Pipeline is a major visitor attraction and is included in some Fairbanks excursions. Above: float planes on the Chena River. A bush pilot demonstrating short field landings is often included in the *Discovery III* riverboat trip.

The most popular tour in Fairbanks is aboard this paddlewheeler, whose owners have been operating paddlewheelers on the rivers of Alaska for several generations. The *Discovery III* usually makes a stop in front of the riverfront homestead of the late Ididarod racer, Susan Butcher, where her busband, David Monson, or another dog handler will introduce their puppies. Another stop will be at an Athabascan village, where natives share their culture and crafts. A popular tour is a combination of the Riverboat *Discovery III*, a Gold Mine vist, and a stop at the Trans Alaska Oil Pipeline.

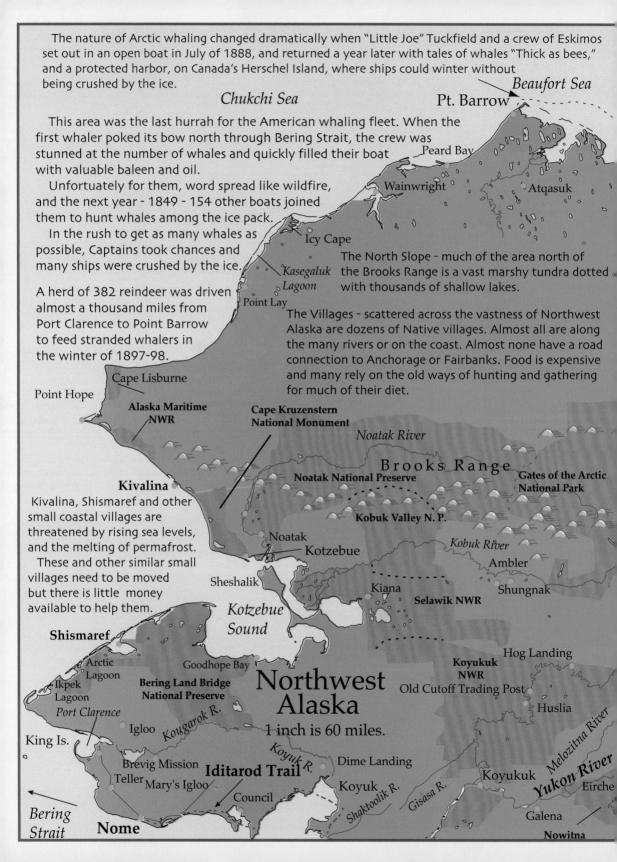

The nature of Arctic whaling changed dramatically when "Little Joe" Tuckfield and a crew of Eskimos set out in an open boat in July of 1888, and returned a year later with tales of whales "Thick as bees," and a protected harbor, on Canada's Herschel Island, where ships could winter without being crushed by the ice.

Chukchi Sea

Beaufort Sea

Pt. Barrow

This area was the last hurrah for the American whaling fleet. When the first whaler poked its bow north through Bering Strait, the crew was stunned at the number of whales and quickly filled their boat with valuable baleen and oil.

Peard Bay

Wainwright

Atqasuk

Unfortuately for them, word spread like wildfire, and the next year - 1849 - 154 other boats joined them to hunt whales among the ice pack.

In the rush to get as many whales as possible, Captains took chances and many ships were crushed by the ice.

Icy Cape

The North Slope - much of the area north of the Brooks Range is a vast marshy tundra dotted with thousands of shallow lakes.

Kasegaluk Lagoon

Point Lay

A herd of 382 reindeer was driven almost a thousand miles from Port Clarence to Point Barrow to feed stranded whalers in the winter of 1897-98.

The Villages - scattered across the vastness of Northwest Alaska are dozens of Native villages. Almost all are along the many rivers or on the coast. Almost none have a road connection to Anchorage or Fairbanks. Food is expensive and many rely on the old ways of hunting and gathering for much of their diet.

Cape Lisburne

Point Hope

Alaska Maritime NWR

Cape Kruzenstern National Monument

Noatak River

B r o o k s   R a n g e

Noatak National Preserve

Gates of the Arctic National Park

Kivalina

Kivalina, Shismaref and other small coastal villages are threatened by rising sea levels, and the melting of permafrost.

Kobuk Valley N. P.

Noatak

Kotzebue

Kobuk River

Ambler

Shungnak

These and other similar small villages need to be moved but there is little money available to help them.

Sheshalik

Kiana

Selawik NWR

Shismaref

Kotzebue Sound

Hog Landing

Arctic Lagoon

Goodhope Bay

Koyukuk NWR

Ikpek Lagoon

Bering Land Bridge National Preserve

Northwest Alaska

Old Cutoff Trading Post

Port Clarence

1 inch is 60 miles.

Huslia

King Is.

Igloo

Kougarok R.

Meloztina River

Koyuk R.

Dime Landing

Yukon River

Brevig Mission

Iditarod Trail

Koyukuk

Eirche

Teller Mary's Igloo

Koyuk

Gisasa R.

Council

Shaktoolik R.

Galena

Bering Strait

Nome

Nowitna

CHAPTER 9
TALES OF THE NORTHWEST COAST

Anvik, Newtok, Shismaref, Kotzebue, Kivalina, Shaktoolik, Arctic Village, Teller, Golovin, Nulato, Koyukuk, Huslia, Hughes, and Allakaket. Tiny dots on the vast landscape of Alaska, the remote native villages of Western Alaska are a world apart, little seen, for the most part, by visitors.

Of course, the 21st century is here as well as the old ways. Cell phone service is not uncommon. Snowmobiles have replaced dog teams, and bush planes offer service to the most remote villages.

The smallest have a few dozen inhabitants, the largest a few thousand. The young often can't wait to get out, the old often want to stay forever.

In the old days, winter was sometimes another word for starvation. Family survival might would depend on the success of the father as hunter.

When food was particularly scarce and the survival of the family was threatened, sometimes grandma or grandpa would take it upon themselves to wander out into the bitter wilderness, everyone knew, to starve.

The advent of modern transportation, and social support networks changed all that. Additionally the creation of regional Native corporations, funded by settling Native claims to land before construction could begin on the Alaska pipeline in the 1970s, gave many Natives access to the cash economy that they never had before. And so

Inupiat subsistence whalers with an umiak, or bearded seal skin boat, and wind blind, wait at the edge of an open lead in the pack ice and look for passing bowhead whales, during spring whaling season, Chukchi Sea, offshore from Barrow, Arctic coast of Alaska.

In the remote western villages, store bought food comes frequently by plane at high cost. For many villagers, hunting and gathering - the old ways - are still important and dependable food sources.

Alaskastock photo

Native woman showing her dried or smoked salmon. The fish runs up the rivers in the Kuskokwim - Yukon basin are key elements in Native diet. Many whole villages move each summer so as to be on the rivers when the fish run, and set up camp for the duration of the run.

today, life in the remote villages is a curious mixture of the old and the the new.

A new school with a white teacher might be the social center of the community. A pipe leading to a sewage lagoon might replace the old truck that lumbered around town to empty the honey buckets that were the household old sewage systems: take it out into the tundra and dump it. Cell service and wi-fi is creeping out toward almost even the most remote settlements. A child might chew on whale blubber while watching a cartoon on YouTube.

Many villagers might eat food flown in by bush planes that also brought whatever Amazon sold and natives had money for. But for others, their diet might not be too different from that of their grandparents.

Along the Yukon and Kuskokwim Rivers, salmon was a primary food source, both for Natives and for their dogs. **Fish Camp**, when a family, or sometimes an entire village, would move to a site where salmon were plentiful, was a tradition that went back thousands of years. Fish would be harvested by gillnets, weirs, or fish wheels, gutted, and hung to dry in the sun of the long days. The less desirable chum salmon would be dried to

feed the dogs (chum salmon are also called dog salmon) that provided transportation in the winter.

For tribes further north, along the Seward Peninsula, walruses were often a food source as well, one large animal providing many hundreds of pounds. Even further north, along the Bering Strait and the north coast facing the Arctic Ocean, whales and seals were on the menu.

Eskimos had long known that bowhead whales migrate north though Bering Strait and then east along the Arctic coast. Being mammals and needing to breath they would have to follow leads in the ice.

So it was here that the tradition of whaling in small skin boats or umiaqs (also umiak) evolved. The boat itself was constructed of a framework of either driftwood or whalebones (driftwood is scarce along the Arctic coast, whalebones not so much) with a thin hull of skins of bearded seals or walruses sewn togther by Eskimo women. The umiaqs were light enough to be carried over the ice by a whaling crew, and most importantly, much quieter in the water than aluminum boats.

Generally the whaling crews would travel to the edge of a lead in the ice, and with the umiaq ready, look for whales, often a process taking many days. Whaling

Top: Eskimos on the beach at Nome, around 1920, with fish drying on racks behind them. UW 17964

Above: Yup'ik style mask representing a walrus. Masks are used in dances that celabrate community history, honor the creatures that provide food, etc.

How times have changed - fifty years ago, a whale trapped away from open ocean would have been quickly dispatched by hungry Northwest Natives.

Here both natives and whites worked to save a grey whale that was trapped in a small open lead in the ice, too far from the open ocean for it to easily reach. By cutting a series of open pools where the whale could breath, it was led to the open ocean and freedom.

A few native villages still hunt a limited number of bowhead whales in traditional skin boats.
Alaskastock photo

crews would wear white parkas so as to blend in with the snowy landscape when whales surfaced to breathe. Once launched, the umiaq would be paddled as quietly as possible so as not to startle the whale. Finally the Captain of the whaling crew would spear the whale with a harpoon equipped with a detatchable tip, whose front would toggle open to secure itself to the whale. The other end would be attached to a float made of an inflated sealskin. Several lances and floats would be attached to the whale who would eventually tire.

Then came the hard part: pulling the heavy whale up onto the ice so that it could be cut up and shared among the village.

> "The bowhead is our brother. Our elders tell us that the whales present themselves to us so that we may continue to live. If we dishonor our brother or disturb his home, he will not come to us anymore.
>
> "The bowhead hunt is very dangerous. We must use our small boats in very rough and icy waters. In order to strike the whale you must be very close. You must be right on top of the whale because we use the hand-held harpoon with the darting gun attached."
>
> - Captain Burton "Atqann" Rexford

The eleven whaling communities of the Arctic Alaska coast are Gambell, Savoonga, Wales, Little Diomede, Kivalina, Point Hope, Point Lay, Wainwright, Barrow,

Nuiqsut, and Kaktovik. The whaling captains and crews from each village make up the Alaska Eskimo Whaling Commission. Barrow has the largest fleet with 52 whaling captains, and the tiny villages of Point Lay, Wales, and Little Diomede Island having just two crews each.

The Commission works with the International Whaling Commission (IWC) to develop levels of harvest that allow the Eskimos to continue their traditional harvests without negatively impacting the bowhead whale population. For 2018, the allowed take is 56 whales, less than half of one percent of the estimated population.

The natives hunted the whales for blubber which was used to both heat and light their homes, and meat, which was a vital part of their diet.

The first major appearance of white men in any numbers were the whalers who hunted from their ships, but also from shore-based stations both seeking the baleen, and to a lesser degree, whale oil from the bowheads. Bowhead are so-called filter feeders, straining large amounts of seawater through screens made of baleen, a hard plastic-like material. It was much in demand for making numerous items where flexibility and strength were required in the days before plastic, including back-scratchers, collar stiffeners, buggy whips, parasol ribs, crinoline petticoats, and corset stays.

The whalers also discovered that the Eskimos were eager to trade fox skins and carved ivory items for whiskey.

Whaler *Alexander* stuck in the ice. This was not uncommon: often the ice would move and free the ship. But in more difficult times the ship would be trapped, and eventually crushed. UW Nowell 31

Eskimo ivory carvers at Nome, around 1900. Shortly after gold prospectors began arriving in Alaska, Eskimos realized that the whites were eager customers for their carvings. These folks most likely were from King Island, about 90 miles Northwest of Nome. The islanders were well known for the intricasy of their carnvings and would lauch their skin canoes and paddle to Nome each spring after the ice broke up to set up their tents on Nome's beach and offer carved items for sale. UW 17963

Of course, this only led to problems as Alaska Natives frequently lack the gene that creates the enzyme that metabolizes alcohol into sugars. The result that Natives get drunk more quickly and remain that way for longer than whites.

They also brought something much worse than whiskey: diseases for which the Natives had little immunity. Flu, measles, chicken pox, and other maladies that were inconvenient for the whites were a terrible scourge when contracted by Natives, especially Eskimos.

Charlie Brower came to the Arctic as a young man seeking adventure and stayed 50 years, setting up a whaling station and trading post at what is now Point Barrow. He became both witness to and participant in most of the signifigant events in the next five decades of NW Arctic history. Once, after a particulary successful shore whaling season, around 50 umiaqs full of Natives arrived to celebrate, some of them from villages so remote they had never seen a white man. On the third day of the joyous celebration several whaling ships arrived, whose crews joined the festivities.

Unfortunately, along with whiskey, they also brought the flu. Knowing how fatal the white man's disease could

be among the Eskimos, Brower set out to see if he could help:

> "I shall never forget one camp we came to, with its three empty boats and a dozen bodies sprawled around on the bank. Men, women, children – all as cold as the ashes of the fires they'd tried hard to build...
>
> "From there we turned back, realizing that what we had seen was only a sample of what lay farther back along the remote inland waterways.
>
> All that fall and the next summer we kept getting reports from hunters of bodies discovered along far river banks, sometimes alone, sometimes with a few belongings scattered about.
>
> It is my opinion that of those two hundred or more husky inland Eskimos who so light-heartedly danced with us at Utkiavie, not one was left alive."

- Charles Brower, *Fifty Years Below Zero*

The first American whaler to take a bowhead in the Bering Strait area was Captain Thomas Welcome Roys, in the bark *Superior*, of Sag Harbor, Long Island, in 1848. Roys' discovery of so many whales electrified the whaling community; the following year **154 ships joined the hunt north of the Arctic Circle** for mostly bowheads.

One of my favorite photographs: six American whalers anchored at Port Clarence, AK, around 1900. The tent on the left has carved ivory figures on the pole. Behind the right hand tent is a bidarka, or kayak made out of skin stretched over a wooden frame.

Occasionally the whalers would travel far to the east in late summer, and let themselves get frozen into the ice at Herschel Island, in order to be in position to hunt whales in the spring. It made for a long cold winter.
UW NA2125

During the summer of 1890, Dr. Sheldon Jackson, General Agent for Education in Alaska, accompanied the revenue cutter Bear, Capt. Michael A. Healy, commanding, in its annual cruise in Bering Sea and the Arctic Ocean visiting all the important villages on both Alaskan and Siberian shores. The Alaskan Eskimos were found eking out a precarious existence upon the few whale, seal and walrus that they could catch. Yet across Bering Strait, in Siberia, but a few miles from Alaska, were thousands of tame reindeer supporting thousands of people.

Seeing the immediate need, Dr. Jackson began raising money and initiated the transfer of over 1,200 reindeer to Alaska, where they thrived.

These Eskimo ladies are proud of the reindeer they received after participating in an apprentice program.
UW Nowell 38

Two years later the fleet had grown to over 200 ships, and in 1852, the peak year for Arctic bowhead whaling, 2,862 of the big mammals were killed.

But the ice was always waiting to trap the unlucky or careless Captain. During most seasons a few ships were usually "nipped" by the ice, damaging their hulls, or in the worst cases, totally crushing a ship.

But the sudden movement of the ice pack south in September 1871 surprised the fleet: 32 of the 41 ships whaling in the Arctic Ocean were trapped by early ice, which began to crush their hulls. It quickly became apparent that winter had come early, and that the ice wasn't going to release the ships. Fortunately a handful of ships had been whaling further south, and still remained ice free.

So the 1,200 men (and even a few women and children) set out on a perilous journey in their wooden whaleboats to try to get to the ice-free ships before the ice got too thick to paddle through.

In a true miracle, all of the crews, pulling their whaleboats over pressure ridges in the ice when they had to, and rowing through water that was freezing even as they passed, made it to the ships that quickly sailed south to Hawaii!

But then came the hard winter of 1897-98. One by one eight ships, the *Rosario, Orca, Belvedere, Jessie Freeman, Newport, Fearless,* and *Jennie* were all trapped in the ice

Homes of the Eskimo Cliff Dwellers

in the vecinity of Point Barrow, and began to be crushed. The crews all made their way over the ice, some easily, some only after a harrowing adventure, to Charlie Brower's whaling station and store at Point Barrow, a total of almost 300 men.

Quickly getting whalers and Eskimos organized, Brower sent out sledding parties to rescue as much food as could be saved from the ships before they were crushed.

But even with what they were able to rescue from the ships, it was clear that they might run out of food before spring. Brower asked two men to try to get the word out. (there was no radio) Charles Walker trekked east to the McKenzie River in Canada and from there worked his way south from one trading post to another, and eventually to Edmonton. Brower then turned to the mate of the crushed *Belvedere* for another equally difficult trip:

"For Tilton I built a special sled and hired an Eskimo to take him as far south as Point Hope. Somehow he got from there to Kotzebue Sound; then working through the mountains by way of the Buckland River, to Norton Sound. After resting a while in the Army Post at St. Michaels he crossed to the Yukon, then the Kuskokwim and over the divide to Katmai. Here he found an old dory, and

Steep-sided and remote, King Island was once home to some 200 Eskimos living on the hillsides and eaking out a precarious living by hunting seal, walrus and other marine mammals. The King Islanders were reknown for their ivory carving skills. Many went to Nome in the summer to offer their carvings to tourists. Beginning after World War II, the population dwindled, and by 1960, it was essentially abandoned.
A wonderful book is **King Island Journal** by artist Rie Munoz, whow worked there as a schoolteacher in 1951-52. UW NA 2304

Pacific Whaling Company plant, Akutan Island, Alaska, circa 1915.
This plant, the only major shore whaling plant in the Bering Sea-Aleutians area rendering oil and drying baleen, closed in 1939.

in that frail craft crossed wide Shelikof Strait to Kodiak Island, where at last he caught a small steamer to Vancouver Island.

Both men reached civilization in April within a few days of each other.

Nowadays, such journeys in winter would be considered almost unbelievable sagas of The North. They were all in a day's work then.

- Charles Brower, *Fifty Years Below Zero*

The news galvanised then President McKinley to ask the Revenue Service (predecessor to the Coast Guard) to sent their cutter *Bear* back up to Alaska to try and help the whalers.

Stopped by the ice near the Arctic Circle, the *Bear* landed sleds and supplies at Cape Vancouver, over 1000 miles from the stranded whalers.

And so began a remarkable journey, even for Alaska. Working their way north. The party led by Lt. David Jarvis quickly realized that the best way to bring food to the stranded whalers was to let the food walk itself.

Fortunately the reindeer imported from Siberia beginning in 1892 for the express purpose of providing food to Alaskan Eskimos, had prospered, and the Coastguardsmen were able to lead 382 reindeer on a 14 week grueling journey along the Alaska coast, to the trapped whaling

crews, arriving at the end of March, 1898.

Undaunted even by the loss of so many ships, whalers kept coming to the Alaskan Arctic in search of bowheads.

A few years earlier, in the fall of 1888 whaler "Little Joe" Tuckfield and a crew of Eskimos set out to the east to prospect new territory for the whalers.

A year later they arrived back with exciting news: whales "thick as bees," but most importantly, a harbor protected from the crushing power of ice floes pushed by the wind, and with plenty of firewood.

So began a new era in Arctic whaling.

The key to this strategy was that the harbor was protected. Whalers already knew that bowhead whales migrated east in the spring along the Arctic coast long before the ice had broken up enough for them to follow. But the coast was all open, exposing any ship trapped in the ice for the winter to the crushing power of ice flows pushed by the wind. But at protected Pauline Cove on Herschel Island (actually in Canada), they could allow their ship to be frozen in for the winter, so as to be in position in the spring to harvest the bowheads. It is a measure of their hunger for bowheads that they would winter in the Arctic rather than their traditional winter berth: whaling out of Hawaii!

For the winter at Herschel was a very long one - ships would often be frozen in by the 15th of October, and by

The Revenue Cutter *Bear*, in the ice off Point Barrow, circa 1910. For many years, the Bear was the only presence of the U. S. Government throughout the vast reaches of Western Alaska. UW1782

Frozen in: the fleet at Herschel, Canada, circa 1905. Note the hockey and baseball "fields" on the ice. The island's unique location - with a protected cove that allowed ships to winter without being crushed by ice, and abundant driftwood from the Mackenzie River, allowed ships to winter over and thus be in position to hunt blowhead whales earlier in the spring. New Bedford Whaling Museum

mid November, the sun disappears for several months. (Though even in the middle of winter the midday sun is close enough below the horizon to create sort of a twilight.)

In preparation, the ships would rig tents over their decks, store firewood that had drifted down the Mackenzie River, and establish activities to keep the crews engaged and healthy.

Baseball and soccer were popular, though not without the hazards of the weather: at one game in 1897, a sudden blizzard swept through in the middle of a game and three baseball players died of exposure.

During the bowhead whaling glory years in the mid 1890s, there were around 1,500 men at Herschel Island, all whaling crews living aboard their ships. The peak was 1892, when after a winter at Herschel Island and a successful spring whaling season, the *Mary D. Hume*, at 90' a small whaler, docked at San Francisco with with a cargo of whale oil and baleen valued at $400,000, the most valuable cargo a whaler landed that century.

In the spring of 1912, the last whaling ship left the Alaskan Arctic, never to return, victim of the rise of petroleum as a fuel and the hardships of the Arctic.

With the distraction of the whalers gone, life for the Eskimos of the northwest coast settled into the traditional routines of subsistence hunting and trapping for furs to trade with the occasional white trader.

These were usually schooners with engines as well as sails that loaded up in Seattle with trade goods like

sewing machines, cloth, tins of kerosene, rifles, ammunition and the like that the natives could not catch or produce themselves. Anchoring off remote communties, the villagers would row out in their umiaqs with furs and carved ivory to trade. Often a single schooner visit would be a remote village's only opportunity to obtain such goods for a year or more.

The Missionaries

"They had been told (by missionaries) that it was wicked to strike a whale on Sunday, even if that were the one chance to secure their year's supply of vital whale meat and blubber. When our commercial whaling went by the board, the missionaries had tried every way to prevent families from moving farther out where fur-trapping was good. They wanted them nearer the church. They even urged the people of Nubook to abandon their homes at one of the best hunting and whaling spots on the coast and move to Utkiavie to be handier for church services.

"That was when I stepped in, going to the people of Nubook, and finally persuading them to stay where they were and let the preacher come to them. For this I was never quite forgiven."

- Charles Brower, *Fifty Years Below Zero*
Brower's experience was probably not uncommon. Numerous missionary groups came to the Alaskan Arctic

"Shoppers" - Eskimo ladies aboard a trading schooner, Bering Sea, circa 1920. Before the cash economy came to the remote villages, natives would trade furs and ivory carvings with the traders.
There were also numerous fox farms in the remote islands of western Alaska. Once when prices were depressed, Eleanor Roosevelt was seen wearing a fox fur, the market instantly rebounded making fur farmers happy. UWI7962

Yup'ik style doll - face of sealskin and garment probably of seal intestines. Today a museum piece, but still occasionally found in gift shops.

with the general goal of introducing their particuar brand of Christianity to the Inuits . They discouraged the use of native languages and rituals, particularly traditional dancing with masks.

The most notable and influential missionary was Reverend Sheldon Jackson, who frequently traveled with Captain Michael A. Healy commander of the cutter *Bear*, for many years the only government presence along the Alaska Arctic coast. Captain Healy, who was African American acted as a judge, doctor, and policeman to Alaskan Natives, merchant seamen and whaling crews. His ship also carried doctors and provided the only available trained medical care to many isolated communities. Natives throughout the vast regions of the north came to know and respect this skipper and called his ship "Healy's Fire Canoe".

However, Jackson also actively discouraged the use of indigenous languages, traditional cultures, and dancing and use of masks. To achieve this end, many natives were sent to schools where they were essentially stripped of their culture and occasionally beaten for using their own language. In some schools, physical, sexual, and emotional abuse of natives was a regular occurence.

Today most educators understand that deliberately separating anyone from their culture and language rarely has beneficial effects, and most Alaska natives attend school in their own communities.

Kivalina: On The Front Lines of Climate Change

Even with the spread of Alaska's social services and the barges and bush planes that brought in store bought food basically on demand, many natives retained an appetite for food caught, trapped, or shot in the traditional way. It was natural for these villagers, as had their ancestors, to live close to the water.

Unlike most of the rest of the state, the northwest coast is very low, with many villages being essentially a dozen feet or so above sea level, with the houses' foundations essentially being permafrost - the permanently frozen layer of ice and earth a foot or so beneath the surface.

Had this been a warmer climate the houses would have been washed away long ago by storm seas. However, this is the Arctic, with the ocean frozen right to the shore for most of the year, and only a narrow lane of open water between the shore and the ice in summer, so there was never a chance for seas to get large enough to threaten it.

That was then. Now is very different.

Kivalina, before the Bureau of Indian Affairs built a

school there, was simply a place that the Eskimos used to hunt at certain times of the year. But with the school, the Natives were informed that they had to settle there permanantly and enroll their children in school or face imprisonment.

So a year round comunity developed: a post office in 1940, an airstrip in 1960, new houses, a new school, and an electric system in the 1970s

But then came the fall storms of 2004. The fall ice hadn't settled in close to the shore that year as it traditionally had. The seas began washing away the land, covered the airstrip. A year later a worse storm hit; only by the community working through the night sandbagging, was the airstrip saved, but it was clear that only a larger effort would save the by then 27 acre island (decades earlier it had been over 50 acres.)

In the summer of 2006 a system of heavy mesh bags filled with sand and gravel was installed as a breakwater, despite locals warning that the fill would be quickly washed away. As it indeed was, by a storm on the day before a ceremony to celebrate its completion. Within a month the multi-million dollar project was completely destroyed.

Finally a substantial seawall of rock barged in was constructed. However, as the engineer supervising the project put it, "Oh, it will buy the people 10-15 years, but it's not a permanent solution."

So, by 2010 or so, it was obvious that the site that these villagers were forced to move to by the Bureau of Indian Affairs, would be uninhabitable by 2025 because of the lack of sea ice and rising sea levels caused by global warming.

The village goverment began a search for a solution: selecting alternative village sites and working to find the funding to proceed.

It became an excercise in frustration. They discovered that there was money available to mitigate the damage that floods produced, but none to relocate an entire town, even one of less than 400 inhabitants. They could not even find a Federal agency that would take the project on.

In desperation, they even sued the major oil companies but again to no avail.

The irony is this: Alaska is the state with the smallest population and the largest percentage of its income from oil royalties. And yet it seems to be unable to help Kivlina, whose impending destruction was being caused by the effects of burning that very oil.

And Kivalina is not alone - almost all Native villages built on the shoreline of NW Alaska will suffer in greater or lesser degree from sea level rise and permafrost melting.

Top: Kivalina, after the rock seawall was installed at great expense. Unfortunately, winter storms still ravage the village, and it will either have to move or eventually be destroyed by higher waves brought on by rising sea levels. Alaskastock photo.

Top: salmon mask from author's collection. It was purchased from Dennis Corrington's Ivory Gallery and Museum in Skagway. Corrington became friend and marketer for many Eskimo carvers.

Right: Shaman or medicine man trying to exorcise evil spirts causing the young Eskimo to become sick.
UW Thwaites 0134-493

Opposite top: Eskimo masked cancers circa 1920. Such dances were discouraged across Northern Alaska after the arrival of Christian missionaries, but have been revived recently and today are once again, a regular and important part of Native culture.

Agayuliyararput:

Our Way of Making Prayer*

Before the arrival of the white missionaries, the Yu'pik, Inuit, and other northern tribes had a belief set today called Animism.

It's key principle is that all living and non-living things had a spirit. That included people, animals, inanimate objects, and forces of nature. And that all things happen though the involvement of some spirit. That spirits can affect people's lives and can be controlled by magical charms and talismans.

The local Shaman (healer or Medicine Man) was believed to have powers to communicate with and influence these spirits. The Shaman would often dance with a carved mask in a ceremony to inflluence the spirits. For these northern tribes, celebrations with masked dancers are also way to celebrate important events, such as a successful whale hunt. Or sometimes the masks are the user (or dancer's) way of communicating some personal feelings.

The missionaries changed much of that, converting much of the native population to Christianity.

Unfortunately, upon arriving in the remote villages and encountering native dancing, the missionaries assumed the masks were pagan idols and discouraged their use, resulting in the destruction of many exquisite masks.

In the early 1950s a Disney film crew came to northern Alaska to film The Alaska Eskimo. The popularity and wide distribution of the film gave outsiders a deeper appreciation of the culture of western and northern Alaska. Some say that it was this film that led to a new interest in traditional native culture such as dancing.

In any case, missionaries or not, masks and dancing with masks are today an integral part of western Alaska culture. Mask making has grown to a small cottage industry, with the masks both sold to the public and used in dances.

* Agayuliyararput: Our Way of Making Prayer is the name of both an unusual book about Yup'ik culture and masks, and a Smithsonian exhibition.

THE LEGENDARY KING CRAB FISHERY

Top: The Bering Sea is always probing, always trying to find a vessel's weak spot. Here the almost brand new *Key West* sinks after a crab pot broke loose from its lashings during a storm, and broke off a 12" diameter vent pipe, flooding the lazarette and sinking the boat. As you can see, another boat was nearby and saved the crew. Bart Eaton photo.

Above: my shipmate, Walter Kuhr, Bering Sea, 1971.

In the early 1960s Alaskan fishermen began to expand fishing for a remarkable spider-like creature—the king crab. Unlike most crab, king crab traveled in herds across the bottom of the Bering Sea. When fishing was hot the big pots would come up with up to 2,000 pounds of crab after less than 24 hours in the water. Boats would get a 200,000-pound load in a few days! It was legendary money, but legendary work as well—when you were on the crab, 18 - 20 hours on deck a day were routine.

The heaviest concentration of crab was found in the Alaska Peninsula - Bering Sea - Aleutian Islands area. In the winter, this area has some of the stormiest weather in the world, and many able vessels and crews were lost to violent winds, big seas, and low temperatures. Perhaps the biggest threat was the buildup of heavy ice on a vessel's superstructure and any crab pots on deck when below freezing temperatures combined with strong winds, a fairly regular event.

After almost two decades of spectacular growth both in catch and fleet size, the crab population crashed in the early 1980's. For a while the joke in Alaska banks was that when you started a new account, you got a crab boat free as a premium.

Today the crab fishery continues, but at a much lower harvest level than in the boom days of the '70s and early '80s. In recent years the TV show, "The Deadliest Catch" celebrates the fishery and its risks.

In the 1950s, the only outside contact for 19 isolated native villages on the Alaska Peninsula and Aleutian Islands was the 114-foot mailboat *Expansion*, which made regular round trips from Seward, skippered by owner Niels "Cap" Thomsen, one of those entrepreneurs that Alaska seems to attract. About the first thing "Cap" noticed on his stops was how some native villages seemed to have a lot of single young men, and another village, maybe a hundred miles away, single women, but neither group of singles was aware of the others:

"So I bought a Polaroid camera and took pictures of the unmarried natives. I'd write their names and towns on them: 'Nona Popalook from Gambrel Bay,' etc. I put the pictures up on two bulletin boards, one for single women and another for single men. Pretty soon after that the word was out, and any time we'd round a point to come into a harbor where a native village was, the singles would be jumping into their boats and rowing out as fast as they could to meet us even before we got the anchor down! They'd come aboard and head right for the singles bulletin boards. Also back in those days, to be legally married, the natives had to go to Cold Bay, a long way away. So I got a Justice of the Peace license, so I could marry them right aboard the boat!"

— "Cap" Niels Peter Thomsen

"Cap" Thomsen aboard the iced-up *Expansion* after a difficult trip up She-likof Strait to Seward in wintertime. Top: Is this a boat? The *Expansion* iced up at Seward. Icing up was a constant problem for vessels traveling the western Alaska coast in winter. Photos courtesy Niels Thomsen

"Cap," also advertised his summer mailboat trips for birdwatchers, but his brochure might have added in the section describing the visit to Dutch Harbor, "And help your captain paint his other boat,:" For "Cap" had purchased a tired processor ship, and tried to work on it for a few days whenever he was in Dutch.

TROUBLE IN THE OIL PATCH

The discovery of **North Slope oil** in 1967 was a transformative event for Alaska. The impact of so much money on the budget of an extremely thinly settled state almost a third of the size of the rest of the US was huge. All kinds of services were funded: libraries, schools, roads, medical facitilies and much more without taxing residents.

And, immensely popular with Alaskans, and unique among American states, was the **Alaska Permanent Fund and dividend program.** As soon as oil started flowing through the Alaska Pipeline in 1976, the legislature, spurred in by forward looking Governor Jay Hammond, established the permanent fund by an ammendment to the Alaska constitution to put 25% of oil revenues into a fund whose initial goal was to preserve some of that windfall for further generations. As part of that, each resident receives a dividend check once a year, often averaging around fifteen hundred bucks. For a family with three children living in a rural area, 7,500$ was huge. Currently the balance in the Permanent Fund is around 55 billion dollars.

For the first 35 years or so after oil started flowing, life was good in Alaska: good services, no taxes, regular dividend payments, etc.

Additionally, oil brought a lot more people to the state, both from folks coming with their families to work in the oil and support indus-

tries, and those just wanting to see the state that was suddenly in the news.

The collapse of oil prices after 2010 also had a transformative effect on Alaska a state where over 50% of total income and 90% of discretionary spending comes from oil revenue. At the same time oil prices were dropping, the main Prudhoe Bay oil field was in decline. In the late 70s and 80s, Prudhoe Bay was producing at the full capacity of the Alaska Pipeline: 1.5 million barrels per day. Most recently, average production was around 270,000 BPD, or around 1/6 of what had been produced a few decades earlier, and at a lower price.

Difficult decisions ahead are taxes (a new experience for most Alaskans), substantial cuts in services residents have become used to, and even some discussion at least of touching the third rail of Alaska politics: reducing the Permanent Fund dividend.

This will be hard. Modern Alaska is deeply entwined with services provided by the remarkable abundance of North Slope oil.

Top: a section of the Trans Alaska Pipeline carrying oil from the north coast of Alaska to the tanker terminal in Valdez. Note the moose passing underneath! UW 16854 The fins on top of the posts are part of a system to cool the post foundations so they don't melt the permafrost.

THE WRECK OF THE KULLUK
A CAUTIONARY TALE

On Dec 21, 2012, the giant oil rig *Kulluk*, left the Aleutian Islands for the 2,000 mile trip to Seattle, towed by the mighty *Aiviq*, an immense tug, specially built to operate in the rough waters of the Arctic and North Pacific.

But instead of taking the shorter and deepwater passage across the North Pacific to Cape Flattery in Washington State, the *Aiviq* and *Kulluk* followed the coast so as not to be out of helicopter range. (It would have been shorter and safer to go direct, but the *Kulluk*, being registered in the Marshall Islands, had to follow the Mashall's rules on having a crew aboard while they were being towed.)

The trouble started at 11:32 a.m. on Dec. 27th, when the towline parted. Seas were running high, and in the process of doing a u-turn to try to pick up the towline, the big *Aiviq* rolled sharply enough to cause minor damage and well as putting the fuel vents briefly underwater. It took 3 hours to get reconnected in the heavy seas, and by dark at 4 p.m., they were towing, although slower, to ease the strain on the towline.

But after midnight, another problem came up: one by one all four of the main propulsion engines of the mighty *Aiviq* died due to the salt water that had gotten into the fuel. Luckily a big Coast Guard cutter arrived on scene with the idea of towing the *Aiviq*, which was still connected to the *Kulluk*, but wrapped a towline around her propellor in the rough seas and was lucky to even be able to limp back into the Coast Guard base at Kodiak.

To make a long story short (and a great one: The Wreck of the Kulluk, New York Times, Dec 30, 2014) another tug showed up, towlines parted again, choppers lifted the crew off the drifting oil rig, which ended up on a remote rocky beach. It was eventually refloated with minor damage, but Shell decided to send the rig, reputed to cost over 500 million dollars, to China to be broken up for scrap. Later it developed that one of the reasons the *Kulluk* was towed out a protected harbor with a big storm brewing, was to avoid paying Alaska property taxes.

Luckily, no oil was spilled, no one was hurt, but the incident was a sobering reminder of the challenges and dangers of Arctic drilling. Shell tried again in 2015 with 23 support ships and 2 giant floating oil rigs, but didn't find enough oil to make the project worthwhile, and abandoned further drilling. The Arctic was probaby relieved at the decision!

It's completely beyond what any of our models had predicted." "I never expected it to melt this fast." Such were the comments among scientists at a recent symposium on the Arctic. There still may be debate in a few quarters about global warming, but not in Arctic Alaska: it's here.

The tidewater glaciers up and down the Alaska coast had been receding slowly for years even before global warming was a household word. But recent events in the Arctic and implications for the future, especially for species dependent on wide areas of sea ice like the polar bear, are sobering.

Up until a decade or so ago, the sea ice covered most of the Arctic in winter, melting and receding a bit in the summer and then refreezing again in the winter. But in recent years the sea ice has receded dramatically in the summer. From 1979-2000, the average area of ice in the Arctic was around three million square miles. In August of 2007, that number had shrunk by half, a truly staggering reduction. One scientist predicted that the Arctic would be totally ice free in summer by 2030!

It may even happen sooner, for as the ice melts, the darker ocean absorbs much more heat than the white ice which reflects the sun's rays, further increasing the melting.

In the changes this brings there would be los-ers and winners. The Northwest Passage ship route from Atlantic to Pacific would become reality. Vast new areas would be open for mineral and oil exploration. Valuable fish species like salmon and pollock might thrive and move their range further north.

The polar bear would probably be a loser. They depend on the ice pack for habitat and if it disappeared in the summer, the only polar bears would be in zoos.

Many native villages in the Arctic are built close to the shore, but had been protected from storm seas by the ice. As the ice recedes, the seas become larger, and villages must either relocate or eventually be swept away. Permafrost—frozen earth close to the surface of the ground—is another huge issue. Most small buildings and houses in the Arctic essentially have permafrost foundations. As the ice in soil melts, the buildings slowly settle into the soggy ground.

Can global warming be stopped? In theory, yes. But the realities of a rapidly developing Asia and a global economy built on high energy use make it unlikely.

So–if you want to see Alaska in its present state, go soon!

Alaskastock photo

A Few Notable Places:

I'm a fan of old charts and maps so I was excited to find https://historicalcharts.noaa.gov where I could browse among thousands of old and new maps and charts. Here are a few of places of particular interest.

This one is a US Postal Service map from 1916, showing the many routes across rural Alaska in 1916. In winter these would often be by dogsled, in summer, on horseback or by steamer along the many rivers. It also shows the many, many small native villages scattered across the vast Alaska interior.

INNOKO COUNTRY

165

Mt. Hurst

K.C.

Takot

Por

t. Joseph

Store

Dominie
300 Vill

Langley

Crater
Mt.

Two Slough
Vill

Deminti

Dikeman

Discovery
Cabin

Richmond

Iditarod

Holikachek

Flat

Disco

IDITAROD
COUNTRY

Otter City

Dome Discove

Shageluk Sept. 30.

Swingen

Road Hou

Vill

June 1 to

May 20 to

400 Dome

Vill

Once from May 20

Conglomerate
Dome

Route
From Holy Cross,
or Kaltag

Oct. 1 to Apr. 30

George R.

MOUNT

78156

78131

KUSKOKWIM

Portage
Vill

Georgetown

Noonach

Portage Vill

Park

ymute

Aniahwagamut

Route 780

100

Oskwalit

eoknugluk

Island Vill
Home Vill

Barometer
Mt.

Tuluganak
Crow Vill

Chukhak

Cinnabar Ingrichagamut

Forks Vill

Aniak

Russian
Mission

Ledge Napaimut

Vill

tshak

Kolmakof

Unimak Pass

This wide passage between the western end of the Alaska Peninsula and the Aleutian Islands is often the roughest part of the great circle route from the US west coast to Asia. Here the big tides flowing back and forth between the Bering Sea and the North Pacific can create immense seas that can sweep containers or log bundles off 800 foot freighters.

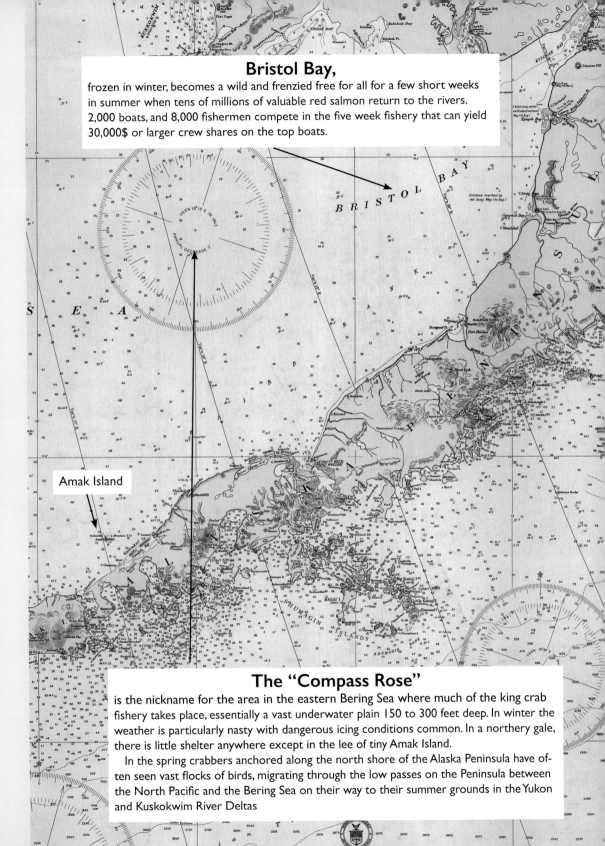

Bristol Bay,

frozen in winter, becomes a wild and frenzied free for all for a few short weeks in summer when tens of millions of valuable red salmon return to the rivers. 2,000 boats, and 8,000 fishermen compete in the five week fishery that can yield 30,000$ or larger crew shares on the top boats.

Amak Island

The "Compass Rose"

is the nickname for the area in the eastern Bering Sea where much of the king crab fishery takes place, essentially a vast underwater plain 150 to 300 feet deep. In winter the weather is particularly nasty with dangerous icing conditions common. In a northery gale, there is little shelter anywhere except in the lee of tiny Amak Island.

In the spring crabbers anchored along the north shore of the Alaska Peninsula have often seen vast flocks of birds, migrating through the low passes on the Peninsula between the North Pacific and the Bering Sea on their way to their summer grounds in the Yukon and Kuskokwim River Deltas

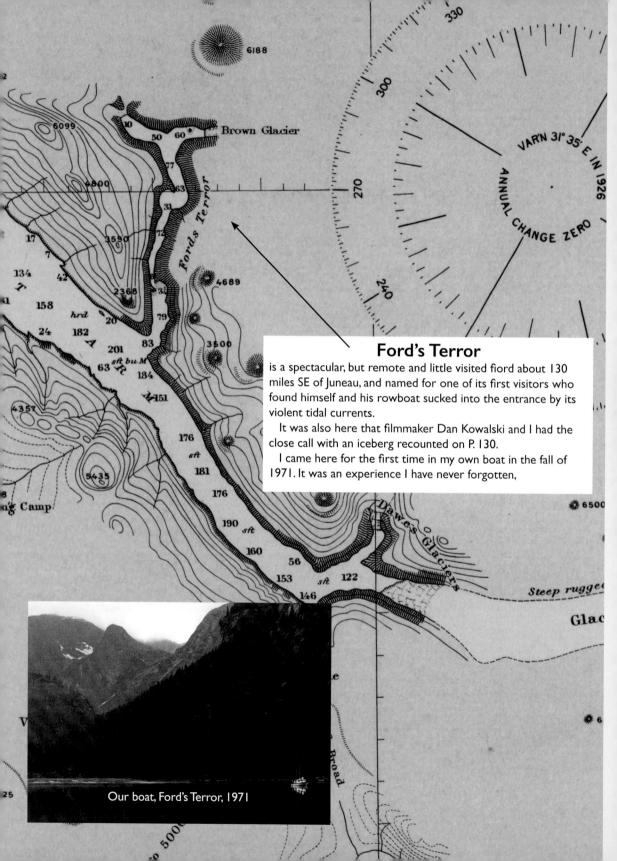

6188

6099

Brown Glacier

10

50 60

77

4800

63

31

17

7

42

72

134

3590

2368

158

hrd

24

182

201

63 sft bu M

184

83

4357

151

176

sft

181

176

190

sft

160

56

153 sft 122

146

g Camp

5435

4689

3500

Fords Terror

79

20

32

VAR'N 31° 35' E IN 1926

ANNUAL CHANGE ZERO

330

300

270

240

Dawes Glaciers

6500

Steep rugge

Glac

6

Ford's Terror

is a spectacular, but remote and little visited fiord about 130 miles SE of Juneau, and named for one of its first visitors who found himself and his rowboat sucked into the entrance by its violent tidal currents.

It was also here that filmmaker Dan Kowalski and I had the close call with an iceberg recounted on P. 130.

I came here for the first time in my own boat in the fall of 1971. It was an experience I have never forgotten,

Our boat, Ford's Terror, 1971

25

5000

Broad

V

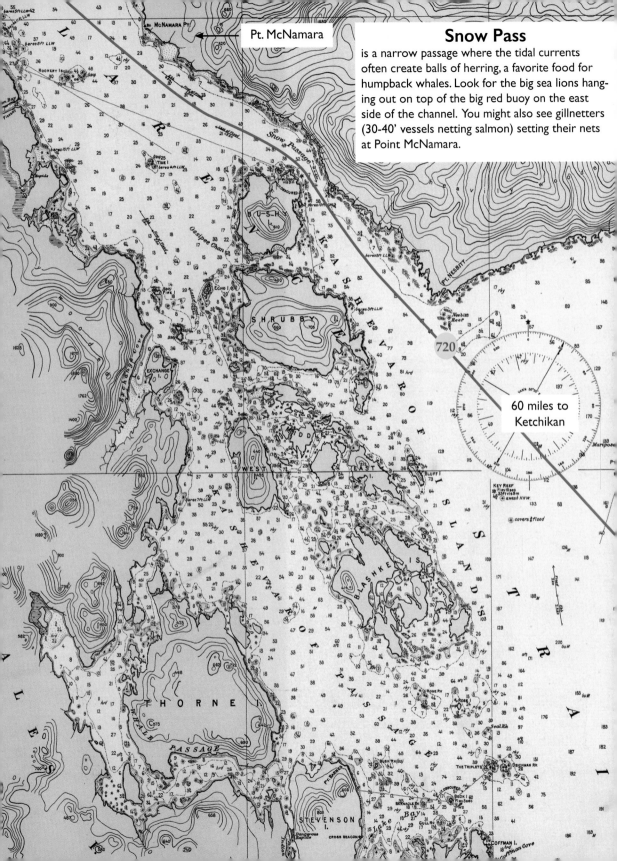

Pt. McNamara

Snow Pass

is a narrow passage where the tidal currents often create balls of herring, a favorite food for humpback whales. Look for the big sea lions hanging out on top of the big red buoy on the east side of the channel. You might also see gillnetters (30-40' vessels netting salmon) setting their nets at Point McNamara.

60 miles to Ketchikan

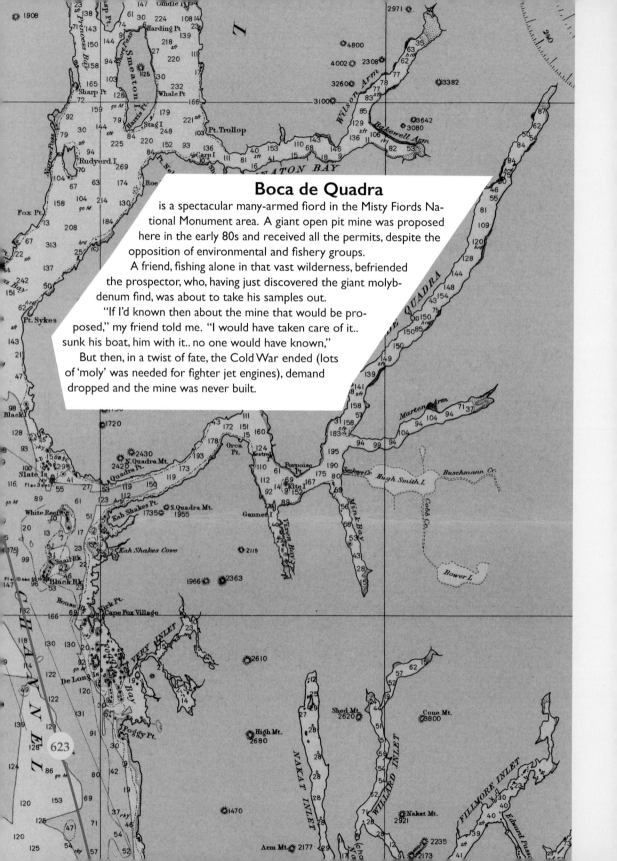

Boca de Quadra

is a spectacular many-armed fiord in the Misty Fiords National Monument area. A giant open pit mine was proposed here in the early 80s and received all the permits, despite the opposition of environmental and fishery groups.

A friend, fishing alone in that vast wilderness, befriended the prospector, who, having just discovered the giant molybdenum find, was about to take his samples out.

"If I'd known then about the mine that would be proposed," my friend told me. "I would have taken care of it.. sunk his boat, him with it.. no one would have known,"

But then, in a twist of fate, the Cold War ended (lots of 'moly' was needed for fighter jet engines), demand dropped and the mine was never built.

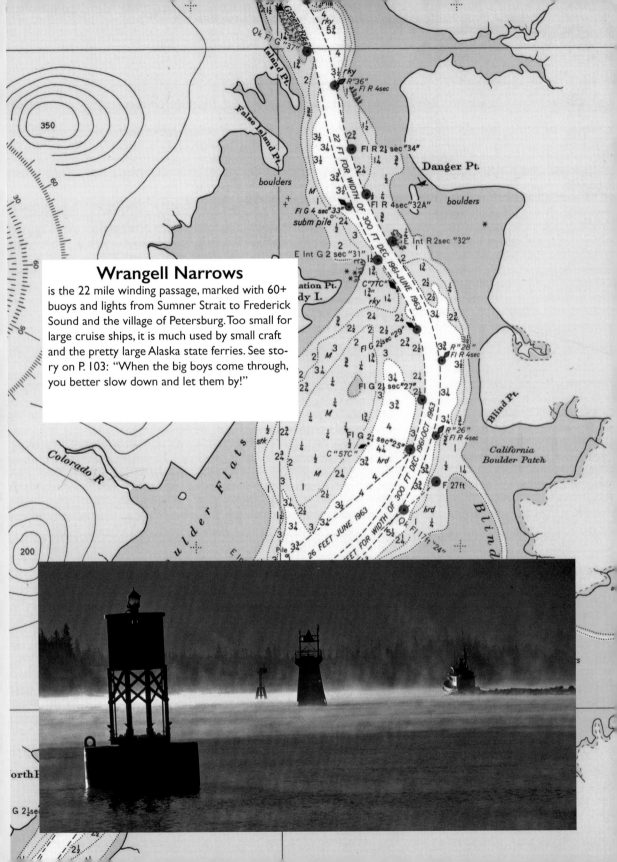

Wrangell Narrows

is the 22 mile winding passage, marked with 60+ buoys and lights from Sumner Strait to Frederick Sound and the village of Petersburg. Too small for large cruise ships, it is much used by small craft and the pretty large Alaska state ferries. See story on P. 103: "When the big boys come through, you better slow down and let them by!"

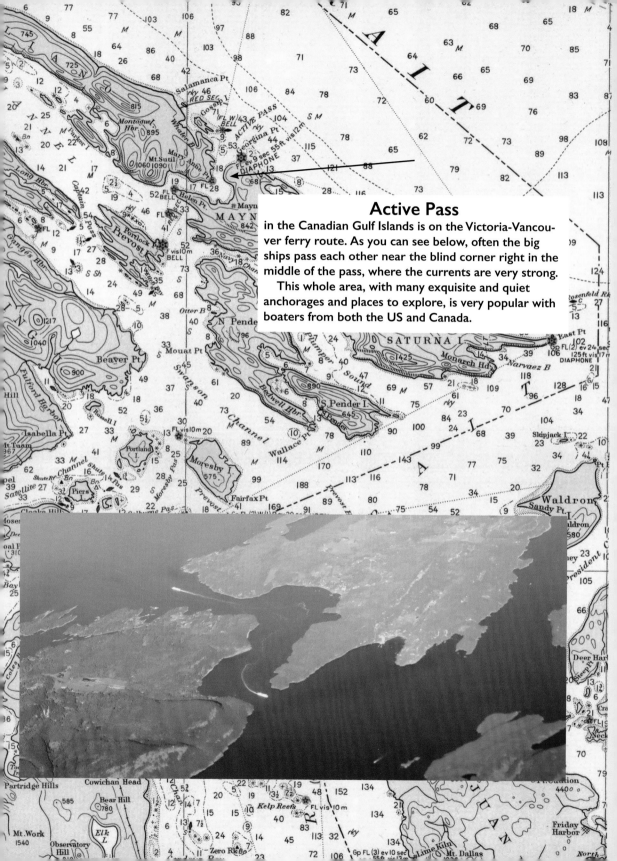

Active Pass

in the Canadian Gulf Islands is on the Victoria-Vancouver ferry route. As you can see below, often the big ships pass each other near the blind corner right in the middle of the pass, where the currents are very strong.

This whole area, with many exquisite and quiet anchorages and places to explore, is very popular with boaters from both the US and Canada.

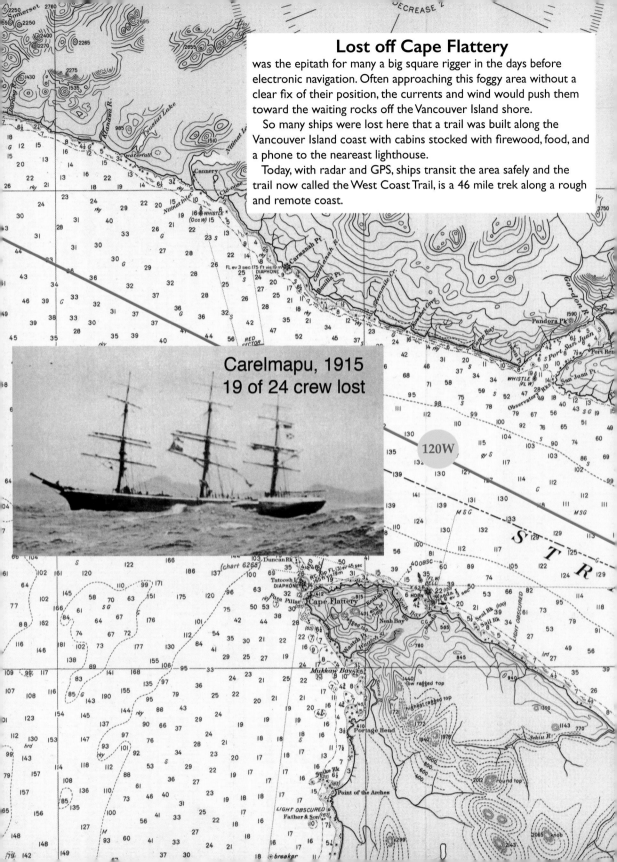

Lost off Cape Flattery

was the epitath for many a big square rigger in the days before electronic navigation. Often approaching this foggy area without a clear fix of their position, the currents and wind would push them toward the waiting rocks off the Vancouver Island shore.

So many ships were lost here that a trail was built along the Vancouver Island coast with cabins stocked with firewood, food, and a phone to the neareast lighthouse.

Today, with radar and GPS, ships transit the area safely and the trail now called the West Coast Trail, is a 46 mile trek along a rough and remote coast.

Carelmapu, 1915
19 of 24 crew lost

Troller, Big Port Walter.

Rhapsody of the Seas, Gastineau Channel

Wilderness Adventurer, Endicott Arm.

Bibliography

Allen, Arthur, *A Whaler & Trader in the Arctic*. Anchorage: Alaska Northwest Books,1978.

Armstrong, Robert H. *A Guide to the Birds of Alaska*, Seattle: Alaska NW Books, 1971.

Blanchet, M. Wylie. *The Curve of Time*, N. Vancouver: Whitecap Books Ltd., 1990.

Bohn, Dave. *Glacier Bay: The Land and the Silence*. New York: Ballantine Books, 1967.

Bolotin, Norm. *Klondike Lost*. Anchorage: Alaska Northwest Publishing, 1980.

Caldwell, Francis, *Land of the Ocean Mists*, Seattle: Alaska Northwest Books, 1986.

Canadian Hydrographic Service: *British Columbia Pilot, Vol I & II* . Ottowa, 1965

Craven, Margaret. *I Heard the Owl Call My Name*. New York: Doubleday,1972

Farwell, Captain R.F. *Captain Farwell's Hansen Handbook*. Seattle: L&H Printing, 1951.

Gibbs, Jim. *Disaster Log of Ships*. Seattle: Superior Publishing, 1971.

Goetzmann, William & Sloan, Kay, *Looking Far North, The Harriman Expedition to Alaska, 1899*, Princeton: Princeton Univ. Press, 1982.

Hill, Beth. *Upcoast Summers*. Ganges, British Columbia: Horsdal & Schubart, 1985.

Hoyt, Erich. *Orca: the Whale Named Killer*. Buffalo: Firefly Press, 1990.

Huntington, Sydney, *Shadows on the Koyukuk*, Seattle: Alaska Northwesst Books, 1993.

Iglauer, Edith. *Fishing With John*. New York: Farrar, Straus & Giroux, 1988.

Jackson, W.H. *Handloggers*. Anchorage: Alaska Northwest Publishing, 1974.

Janson, Lone, *The Copper Spike*, Anchorage: Alaska Northwest Books, 1973.

Jonaitis, Aldona, editor. *Chiefly Feasts*. Seattle: University of Washington Press, 1991.

Jonaitis, Aldona. *From the Land of the Totem Poles*. Seattle: U.. of Washington Press, 1988.

Kent, Rockwell, *Wilderness*, New Haven: Leete's Island Books, 1975.

MacDonald, George, *Chiefs of the Land and Sky*, Vancouver: UBC Press, 1993.

Mckeown, Martha. *The Trail Led North: Mont Hawthorne's Story*. Portland, Oregon: Binfords & Mort, 1960.

Moore, Terris, *Mt. McKinley, The Pioneer Climbs*, Seattle: The Mountaineers, 1981.

Muir, John. *Travels in Alaska*. Boston: Houghton, Mifflin Co., 1915.

Murie, Margaret, *Two in the Far North*, Portland: Alaska Northwest Books, 1975.

Murie, Olaus, *Journeys to the Far North*, Palo Alto: The Wilderness Society, 1973.

Newell, Gordon and Joe Williamson. *Pacific Tugboats*. Seattle: Superior Publishing, 1957.

Nicholson, George. *Vancouver Island's West Coast*. Victoria, B. C.: Moriss Printing, 1965.

Ritter, Harry. *Alaska's History*. Portland: Alaska Northwest Books, 1993.

Rushton, Gerald. *Echoes of the Whistle*. Vancouver: Douglas & McIntyre, 1980.

Ryan, John J. *The Maggie Murphy*. New York: W.W. Norton & Co., 1951.

Sherwonit, Bill, *To The Top of Denali,* Seattle: Alaska Northwest Books, 1997.

U. S. Dept. of Commerce. *United States Coastal Pilot, Vol 8 & 9*. Washington, D.C. 1969.

Upton, Joe, *Alaska Blues*. Anchorage: Alaska Northwest Publishing, 1977.

Upton, Joe, *The Coastal Companion*, Bainbridge Island, WA: Coastal Publishing, 1995

Upton, Joe, *Journeys Through the Inside Passage*. Portland: Alaska Northwest Books, 1992.

Vancouver, George. *A Voyage of Discovery to the North Pacific Ocean and Round the World*, London, 1798.

Walbran, Captain John T. *British Columbia Coast Names*.

White, Howard, editor. *Raincoast Chronicles: Forgotten Villages of the B.C. Coast*. Madeira Park: Harbour Publishing, 1987.

Index

British Columbia and Yukon Territory place names:

Other

Traveling northwest waters as a commercial fisherman since 1965 in small craft and large, Joe Upton gained intimate knowledge of the coast from Puget Sound almost to the Arctic Circle.

In the 1970s Upton lived and fished out of a tiny island community in the roadless wilderness of Southeast Alaska. His first book, *Alaska Blues*, based on those years, was hailed as "One of those books you want to proclaim a classic" by the *Seattle Post Intelligencer*.

In 1995, Upton established Coastal Publishing to produce illustrated maps and guidebooks for Alaska visitors.

Upton teamed up with filmmaker Dan Kowalski in 2009 to start making videos to accompany his books and maps.

Joe and Mary Lou Upton live on Bainbridge Island, WA, and Vinalhaven Island, Maine.